The EVERYTHING®
Destination Wedding Book

Dear Reader,

I love the recent trend toward destination weddings. Couples are now starting to focus on what's most important to them where their weddings are concerned, and the answers they're coming up with have nothing to do with a $3,000 wedding cake or the biggest stretch limo they can find. Their thoughts are centered on bringing people together to celebrate this special occasion for a week or more. And that's really what a wedding should be about: Reconnecting with loved ones; feeling at peace in the days before the wedding; focusing not on the size or grandeur of the church, but on the important elements of the ceremony itself.

If you're considering a destination wedding, I hope that this book will be a big help to you. You'll find that you can choose to go in many, many different directions, both literally and figuratively. Just remember: In the end, you need to plan the wedding that will make you and your groom happiest, not a wedding that fits someone else's idea of perfection. If you can meet that simple goal, your day will be perfect, no matter where you are!

Best Wishes,

Shelly Hagen

The EVERYTHING® Series

Editorial

Publishing Director	Gary M. Krebs
Director of Product Development	Paula Munier
Associate Managing Editor	Laura M. Daly
Associate Copy Chief	Brett Palana-Shanahan
Acquisitions Editor	Kate Burgo
Development Editor	Katie McDonough
Associate Production Editor	Casey Ebert

Production

Director of Manufacturing	Susan Beale
Associate Director of Production	Michelle Roy Kelly
Cover Design	Paul Beatrice
	Matt LeBlanc
	Erick DaCosta
Design and Layout	Heather Barrett
	Brewster Brownville
	Colleen Cunningham
	Jennifer Oliveira
Series Cover Artist	Barry Littmann

Visit the entire Everything® Series at *www.everything.com*

THE
EVERYTHING®
DESTINATION WEDDING BOOK

A complete guide to planning your
wedding away from home

Shelly Hagen

Adams Media
Avon, Massachusetts

For my sister Kathy, who taught me to love words.

An Everything® Series Book.
Everything® and everything.com® are registered trademarks of F+W Publications, Inc.

Published by Adams Media, an F+W Publications Company
57 Littlefield Street, Avon, MA 02322 U.S.A.
www.adamsmedia.com

ISBN 10: 1-59337-720-7
ISBN 13: 978-1-59337-720-5

Printed in the United States of America.

J   I   H   G   F   E   D   C   B   A

Library of Congress Cataloging-in-Publication Data
Hagen, Shelly.
The everything destination wedding book / Shelly Hagen.
p.   cm. — (An everything series book)
Includes index.
ISBN-13: 978-1-59337-720-5
ISBN-10: 1-59337-720-7
1. Destination weddings—Planning. 2. Weddings—Planning. 3. Wedding etiquette. I. Title.
HQ745.H17 2007
395.2'2—dc22
2006028139

This book is available at quantity discounts for bulk purchases.
For information, please call 1-800-289-0963.

Contents

Acknowledgments

I'd like to extend my thanks to Jacky Sach at
Bookends Literary Agency for the help and advice
she always has for me at a moment's notice.

∾

Thank you to the Meissners from Brooklyn, New York,
for letting me in on the particulars of putting together a
beautiful destination wedding without the help of a planner.

∾

And last but not least, thanks to Kate Burgo at Adams for
allowing me the opportunity to work on such a fun project.

Top Ten Considerations When Choosing the Perfect Destination Wedding Spot

1. *The destination or resort itself.* It is classy enough for a wedding? Is it somewhere you'd love to spend two weeks?

2. *Cost.* Can you comfortably afford a wedding in this particular place?

3. *Accommodations.* Will all of your guests be able to attend a reception in this place, or will you have to cut your guest list?

4. *Season.* A wedding in Jamaica might be a better choice in January than in July (during the height of hurricane season)!

5. *Deals.* Does your ideal spot also offer several free nights' lodging if you book a ceremony? Sounds like a done deal.

6. *Adventure.* Is there enough going on around your preferred location to prevent you and your guests from becoming bored over the course of a week or two?

7. *Length of travel/vacation time.* Elderly relatives are unlikely to travel halfway around the world for a wedding.

8. *Your nerves.* Can you handle planning a wedding without being able to pop into the reception site once a week (just to make sure it's there, ready and waiting for you)?

9. *Surroundings.* Is the resort located in an interesting area of the state or country you've chosen? Guests are more likely to come if they can plan a side trip or two.

10. *Assistance.* If your ideal resort also has a wedding coordinator to take most of the planning work out of your hands . . . what are you waiting for?

Introduction

A *beautiful wedding without all the work. Sound perfect to you?*
Well, you aren't alone. Brides-to-be are flocking to destination
wedding resorts for many reasons, not the least of which is that many of
these resorts offer the services of an on-site wedding coordinator to make
your life (and wedding) easier!

What's another reason brides are taking their wedding shows on the
road? Cost. Some engaged couples are deciding that diving into significant debt to pay for a big wedding just isn't worth it in the long run.
Depending on where you live, the final tally for the average in-town wedding (which is a term you'll see over and over again, referring to traditional weddings held in the bride's hometown) is somewhere between
$20,000 and $30,000—for a one-day event! A bride can pack up her
dress, plan a week in the sun with her family and her fiancé, and end up
shelling out *way* less money.

That may leave you thinking that destination weddings are always
small events. Not so. You absolutely can plan a large wedding in some
far-off paradise and include a couple hundred of your closest friends and
family. Obviously, this is a costlier option, but some couples don't care.
To them, the destination wedding is about giving everyone the opportunity to get away and have some fun. Wedding guests seem to love that
philosophy, much more so than the idea of spending time in a (perhaps
rather dull) little town where a traditional wedding might be held. If
you're the least bit worried about people not showing up at your destination wedding, think again. Give them someplace good to go, and just
watch who shows up!

Ease of planning is one reason why brides are embracing destination weddings these days. So many resorts have wedding planners on their payrolls that all you have to do is sign on the dotted line and all of your choices will be presented to you (as opposed to your having to go out and find them). Still, some brides prefer to plan destination weddings in locations that don't offer the services of a wedding consultant. Are these women setting themselves up for a big-time fall? Not at all. Planning a beautiful, meaningful destination wedding on your own is hardly an impossible task. All you need is some inspiration and great organizational skills!

Although this book is geared toward brides, don't forget to let the groom in on the planning, too! When you're talking about arranging a week of activities for yourselves and your guests, you're going to need all of the ideas you can get. It's his wedding (and his vacation) too, so make sure you're both going to be happy with the end result.

No matter where your destination wedding may take you, this book will help. It contains all the advice you need to see you safely (and sanely) from Point A (your engagement) to Point B (the ceremony). You'll find the answer for every question you may have, from how to pack your dress (eek!) to interviewing vendors yourself to writing your thank-you notes. So what are you waiting for? Start reading, start thinking outside the box, and start planning the wedding of your dreams in a land far, far away!

Chapter 1
Why Fly the Traditional Wedding Coop?

Once the engagement ring hits your finger, you're immediately faced with decisions. Where, when, and how will you take your vows, and how much is it going to cost you and your fiancé? Many brides and grooms are choosing to take the show on the road these days by planning destination weddings. There are a couple of reasons behind this trend: Some couples are looking for a unique wedding atmosphere, while others want to choose a central location for their guests.

Save Your Sanity

Here's the bottom line on destination weddings: Many resorts, hotels, and other popular wedding spots take the hassle of planning a wedding out of your hands. They narrow down the choices for you and offer them up in neat, easy-to-read-and-comprehend packages. In other words, you won't decide which florist to use or which band to audition, but which bouquets are prettiest and how many hours of music you'd like to have at your reception.

Hometown weddings are being edged out these days for a simple reason: Brides are busy. Sure, there are still engaged women who are thrilled by the prospect of investigating every chapel, reception hall, and baker in a sixty-mile radius, and for them, an in-town ceremony and reception is a welcome project. For plenty of other brides-to-be, though, the thought of holding down a full-time job, planning a wedding, and finding time to nurture the relationship that's on its way to the altar is just too much to bear. These women realize that it's really hard to focus on everything—life, work, and wedding planning—all at once. They're realistic enough to know that their wedding day will be happiest if they're totally relaxed—and how better to achieve that goal than to plan a vacation *around* the ceremony?

 E~ssential

Even though we've made great strides in gender equality over the last few decades, most of the wedding planning still typically falls to the woman. Along with this responsibility comes a certain amount of stress. When you book a destination wedding, you willingly give up some of that responsibility and the resulting worry, and focus instead on enjoying yourself! ✿

Some brides willingly admit that they need to be in control of their wedding at all times. Should a woman who fits this description think twice about planning a destination wedding? After all, if you're leaving the details to someone else and you're *very* particular, isn't this just a recipe for disaster? Not at all! Though you won't be able to fly down to your wedding spot every weekend to check on the details, you can prevent most problems by choosing the right spot in the first place. We'll discuss this more in Chapters 8 and 9.

Very Vogue

If you have a sister, cousin, or friend from an older generation, ask her how she planned her wedding. Chances are, she went traditional (even if she was a hippie) by planning an in-town wedding and reception site. Destination weddings were unusual events until relatively recently—and then they started with a whisper, not a bang. Engaged women started hearing tales of brides who had said, "The heck with this one-day business! I'm planning an entire week of pre-wedding fun for my guests and myself!"

Depending on where you're going and what your plans are once you arrive, planning an out-of-town wedding *could* be every bit as stressful as preparing for a ceremony and reception in your own city. The big difference is that destination weddings are usually focused on fun. Sure, you're still concerned about having a beautiful exchange of "I do's," and you still want a beautiful reception—but, unlike the traditional in-town wedding, you'll combine your wedding with a vacation *and* a honeymoon, and you'll be able to spend days with your guests, rather than a few short hours.

Another reason destination weddings are so in nowadays is cost. In-town weddings can be insanely expensive, and now that it's becoming commonplace for the bride and groom to pay for their own wedding, a lot of couples are starting to look at each other and ask, "Wouldn't it make more sense to put this money toward a wedding *and* a vacation?" When couples start thinking along these lines, there's usually no turning back. They're already gone, at least in their minds—to the Caribbean, or to Rome, or to Hawaii.

Follow Your Instincts

Of course, just because something is trendy doesn't make it the right choice for everyone. If the only reason you're considering a destination wedding is because it's what all the cool brides are doing, stop in your tracks and ask yourself these questions:

* What is your idea of an absolutely perfect wedding?
* Is it important for you to spend lots of time with your guests?
* Is vacation time a precious commodity in your life?

There is a lot of meaning behind your answers. If you've always dreamed of having a traditional wedding in the church where you were baptized or in the synagogue where you celebrated your bat mitzvah, think long and hard about how you'll feel about a change of scenery. You *can* plan a destination ceremony that's very traditional and religious, of course, but if you have a hard time imagining yourself walking down a foreign aisle, you may be better off keeping your wedding local.

E~Question

Will I really have to spend every moment of this trip with these people?

Pretty much. When you invite people along on a trip honoring you and your fiancé, you're obligated to spend a lot of time with them. There's no escaping that. So, think long and hard about this before making the decision to have a destination wedding.

Spending time with your guests is one of the big perks of planning a destination wedding. Families are flung far and wide these days; college friends, once inseparable, end up going where the jobs are—which means that you may only see your loved ones and friends over an occasional holiday. If, however, you feel that you already spend way *too* much time with your family and friends, planning a week's worth of activities with them just prior to your wedding might be too much to handle. It's not as though you're going to get rid of them if you stay home to get married, but at least you have your own place and an established routine there (in other words, you can escape from them without feeling terribly guilty).

A destination wedding is perfect for couples who really need a vacation—but it's also great for couples who love to travel. Try not to shortchange yourself on time. The whole point of a destination wedding is to lighten up a little bit, to take a break from everyday stress, to try new things, to spend time relaxing and laughing—and, yes, to come home married. If your workload is so heavy that you know you won't be able to leave it behind, or if you're just one of those people who despises travel, then buck the trend and stay home. You'll be happier (and ironically, less stressed) when the big day arrives. You can always plan a honeymoon for a later date, when work lightens up. If you're not the travelin' type, you can plan a special weekend at a four-star resort in town.

Location, Location, Location

Obviously, this is the biggie. By definition, a destination wedding takes place out of town. But even though there are many popular destination wedding sites, a destination wedding can take place anywhere, even in a little town no one's ever heard of (well, almost no one). The location doesn't have to be extravagant or chic or posh; it just has to be somewhere other than your hometown and other than where you currently live.

How Do You Choose?

If you can choose from the entire planet, how do you finally settle on one spot? Well, some brides fall in love with a resort they've spent some time at already, while others may attend a friend's destination wedding and be inspired by something they've seen there. Many brides sit down at their computers and start scouting out locations by doing some research.

They let price or availability lead the way, and then narrow down their options from there.

Choosing a spot isn't always easy, but it's not nearly as difficult as it may seem if you don't already have a site in mind. Let your intuition—about location, season, climate, the amount of travel involved, price—jump-start your thought process, and go from there.

Make It What You Want

Some brides hear the words "destination wedding" and conjure up images of a drunken cruise ship ceremony presided over by a showgirl and a steward. Other brides crinkle their noses thinking that saying "I do" on a beach is somehow less of a commitment than reciting those words in a cathedral (or in a country club, for that matter). The truth is, a destination wedding can take any form, from lighthearted to serious, just as an in-town wedding can. Furthermore, as long as you have taken care of the marriage license requirements (something we'll talk more about in Chapter 16), your marriage will be 100 percent till-death-do-you-part legal.

❀ **E~ssential**

Can't decide between a formal, religious ceremony and a breezy "I do" on the beach? You don't have to! Your wedding doesn't have to be all serious or all fun. It can be both, and this is what a destination wedding does beautifully. By simply taking your wedding out of a traditional setting, you're opening up all sorts of unexpected possibilities—for yourself and for your guests. ❧

No matter what the crux of your ideal wedding ceremony, whether it's religious or not, you'll be able to plan a destination wedding around it. Now, this isn't to say that you should try to plan a solemn wedding in a casino. You need to have realistic expectations about what your chosen destination can deliver—or you need to be willing to change the locale.

Delving into Details

How would you compare an in-town wedding to its destination sister? Are they complete opposites? Not really. There are significant differences, but there also can be startling similarities. It depends on what you and your fiancé want and what you're willing to do to make it so.

The Guest List

You've been to local weddings where 400 guests gathered under a tent and danced the night away. Although the idea of a destination wedding appeals to you, you know you can't invite all of your friends and family—or can you?

E~Alert

Traditional wedding etiquette says that as long as someone is invited to the wedding, she can also be invited to the bridal shower. Now turn that around: *Don't* invite someone to your shower if you know her name is not on the guest list for the wedding.

A destination wedding can be as big or as small as you want it to be. In order to be able to invite hundreds of guests, however, you'll have to find a location that can accommodate your party, and you'll have to take the cost of entertaining so many people into consideration. For now, though, just know that at least theoretically, you *can* have a destination wedding on the grandest scale—which also means that you won't necessarily have to lose out on your bridal showers!

The Bride Wore a Bikini

For many brides-to-be, the dress is the thing they've dreamed about since childhood, and finally having the chance to wear it is worth any hassle involved with planning a wedding. But you can't very well sashay your way down the beach in a heavy satin beaded gown, and you have no intention of wearing flip-flops to your wedding. Hence, you say, the destination wedding is off!

Hold on there, Sister. Very few brides actually show up at their ocean-side weddings wearing a bathing suit (but for those who do, more power to them). While heavy gowns are not exactly the best choice for tropical weddings, bridal dress manufacturers have seized upon this very concern of brides who are planning destination weddings. You'll find no shortage of light, beautiful, almost indestructible (read: very packable) dresses. And if you're really set on planning a wedding around a heavily beaded dress, consider a Valentine's Day wedding somewhere in the Rocky Mountains.

Dinner, Dancing, Tossing the Bouquet

All right, so tradition is fairly important to you and your groom. You have an image of the two of you reciting your vows on the beach, and you're wearing a lovely, lightweight wedding dress (score one for tradition!). The image starts to fall apart, though, when you imagine your reception as a bonfire on the sand with a keg of beer and a bucket of clams for refreshments. Might you have to make these types of serious concessions in order to have a destination wedding?

No concessions are necessary. Your destination wedding reception can include the most traditional elements. Consider whether you'd be sorry if the following things were excluded from your wedding day:

* Being escorted down the aisle by your dad and/or mom
* Gathering with your bridesmaids before the wedding
* Religious elements (vows, a canopy, exchange of blessed rings)
* A reception, whether cocktails only or a full meal
* Cutting the cake
* Toasts from members of the wedding party and/or families

* Dancing with your father and your new husband
* Throwing your bouquet

Yes, you really can have an otherwise traditional wedding somewhere in paradise. The two ideas are not mutually exclusive, and in fact are combined every day by brides and grooms in this country (and many others).

Will You Miss Out on the Honeymoon?

Here's another nice thing about the destination wedding: You're essentially honeymooning the entire time you're there. In fact, a lot of couples refer to their destination weddings as a "weddingmoon," because it so successfully blends the two events.

E~Alert

The wedding and the honeymoon often blend together at destination weddings. Unless you pick up and move to another hotel (which you probably won't do, as your room will likely be included in any wedding package), you may run into friends and family at the pool and in the dining room, even after you think you're officially on your honeymoon. ✍

Of course, even though one benefit of this trip is that you get to spend loads of time with your guests, you may expect a far different level of privacy after the ceremony. This preference may vary from couple to couple. Some brides and grooms opt to spend all of their time—before and after the ceremony—with their friends and family, reasoning that it's kind of weird to be on a faraway island or in a hopping city and not have anything to do with their loved ones just because they're now officially man and wife (and especially if they've been living together for quite some time, anyway). Other couples part ways with their guests right after the ceremony and move their belongings to a honeymoon hut or suite, where they will be (mostly) out of view—but probably not completely.

In these ways, the honeymoon may differ for couples who opt to have a destination wedding. If you are dead-set on having a private, separate honeymoon, you can either plan one for later, or hop a flight to somewhere else after the wedding.

Do Something Nice for Your Guests

Inviting someone to attend a wedding seems like a small enough favor to ask. After all, you don't get married every day. Plus, *you've* been to countless ceremonies and receptions over the years, many of them in the middle of nowhere, where you spent the hours before and after the wedding watching the paint dry. Now it's time for those people to return the favor.

However, if you've ever been to an out-of-town wedding where you were bored out of your mind, you know that even though guests attend a wedding so they may wish the couple well, and they would not want to miss it for the world (no matter where the bride and groom choose to say "I do"), they aren't always thrilled about making the trip. And since we're such a mobile society today, you'll probably have at least a few people traveling a great distance just to watch you walk down the aisle. Why not make it worth their while by choosing a spot they might otherwise never get to see?

✿ E~ssential

When planning a wedding in a tourist hot spot, it's helpful to send a travel guide along with the save-the-date cards. This may persuade friends or relatives who are unsure about making the trip that it is going to be great fun! ✿

Think of it: So many people dream of touring the countryside of France, or visiting the volcanoes in Hawaii. Having your wedding in a really interesting place will probably ensure that most of your guests will at least try to make the trip. In fact, more of them may show up than would have for an in-town ceremony, because they'll be intrigued by the whole thing. This isn't just another typical wedding! It's an opportunity for them to say to themselves, "Well, we've always talked about going there, so let's do it."

Here's what's expected of guests (and what guests may expect), whether you choose to have an in-town ceremony or a destination wedding. Guests will:

* Pay for their travel
* Pay for their hotel
* Pay for their meals, with the exception of the reception
* Look for ways to fill their time before and after the wedding
* Want to have time to talk with you

For these reasons alone, destination weddings make so much sense these days, and even more so if a huge percentage of your guests will be traveling a great distance for the wedding. Let's say you're originally from Boston, you went to college in Houston, and you live in San Diego now. Your San Diego–based fiancé, meanwhile, is from Chicago, went to school in Ohio, and spent time traveling and working in Europe after college. You've got wedding guests coming from literally around the globe, so you might as well pick a place that's going to delight everyone, make them feel as though their time and money have been well-spent, and give them a chance to catch up with the two of you over the course of several days.

 E~Fact

You needn't have global jet setters as friends in order to consider a destination wedding as a perk for your guests. Having families from different regions of the country is a great way to get everyone together for a week and get to know each other before the wedding. 🕊

Heck, your whole family can be from the same hometown and still never see each other, so a destination wedding is a great way for everyone to get together for a family vacation. They'll be able to relax, have some fun, and let their hair down in a way that they wouldn't be able to during a one-day traditional wedding.

Consider, too, the chance to have some in-law bonding time. Does your mother realize how much fun the groom's mom is? Is one afternoon of fishing all it will take to make your dad and your future father-in-law realize that they really are "partners in crime"? Your wedding could be a uniting experience for the whole family, something that in-town weddings, with their heightened pace and heightened tensions, usually aren't.

Chapter 2
Destination Wedding Versus Elopement

One common belief among people who haven't yet done a whole lot of research on destination weddings is that they're just fancy elopements. Nothing could be further from the truth. For one thing, elopements are often spur-of-the-moment, whirlwind affairs, whereas a destination wedding can take a year or more of planning. This chapter tells you about this and other significant differences between eloping and planning a destination wedding.

What Makes a Destination Wedding Different?

Talk to someone you know who has eloped. Chances are she didn't mail out invitations to the event. She probably didn't announce her intentions before the fact, and she sure as heck didn't have 100 guests waiting in the wings. Elopements are usually very small and at least somewhat secretive. They're a great way to save some serious cash on the whole wedding deal, because they seldom involve anyone aside from the bride and the groom.

Small Destination Weddings

"Hold on!" you say. "I want to have a very small destination ceremony, with just myself, my groom, and our parents. Won't people think we've eloped? And won't they wonder why?" The answer is no, on both counts. First of all, if you're truly interested in having a destination wedding, you're going to have to do a lot of research. You're going to make many phone calls, visit plenty of Web sites, and compare your findings to determine the best location for your wedding. You're not running to the first justice of the peace that you can find because you just have to get married *right now*. You're not choosing a place based on its easy marriage-license requirements. And you're not keeping this a secret. Even if you're planning on having a very small ceremony, you can tell anyone you want about it. (Just don't promise to invite them!)

Large Destination Weddings

Destination weddings don't have to be small events! As long as you can find a place to accommodate all of your guests, you can invite as many people as you want—and because destination weddings are gaining in popularity, the list of options for large ceremonies and receptions is growing. A cruise ship might be perfect for you and your friends and family, or maybe a resort on the California coast is your style.

This is a chicken-or-the-egg issue: Do you draw up the guest list first, or do you find a location first? It really comes down to which is more important to you: Getting married in a particular spot or having lots and lots of people at your wedding.

Once you determine which of these issues takes top ranking, the other one will fall into place.

✿ E~ssential

No matter where you have your heart set on getting married, chances are you can make it a reality. Be ready to do a lot of research and/or talk to a travel agent to get her recommendations for traveling in the area. Don't give up until you're happy with your choice! 🐦

It's All in the Planning

When you elope, there are almost no vendors to speak of. You might pick up a corsage or a bouquet at a flower shop, but you don't spend months comparing and contrasting floral styles with a florist. Certainly, for an elopement, you'd dress your best, but you probably wouldn't drop thousands of dollars on a custom-fitted gown. And while you and your groom might dance the night away in a nightclub or a romantic restaurant if you eloped, you wouldn't be paying the musicians by the hour.

When you plan a destination wedding—even if you choose a resort that takes most of the work out of the planning for you—you will have to make decisions about:

- ✳ Flowers
- ✳ Music
- ✳ Pictures
- ✳ Ceremony readings and vows
- ✳ Reception food and drink
- ✳ Music for the ceremony and reception
- ✳ Wedding cake
- ✳ The wedding dress

Many—though not all—of these elements are usually eliminated during an elopement. You can see just by looking at the list that destination weddings have an element of work attached to them, whereas an elopement can be a fly-by-the-seat-of-your-pants kind of thing.

There are two ways to plan a destination wedding: You can choose a resort where most of the wedding services are already in place, or a place that may not specialize in destination weddings, but certainly has some wedding vendors nearby, ready and willing to help you plan your event. (Wedding vendors aren't hard to find, once you know where to look. Chapter 9 walks you through the process.)

❁ E~Fact

When planning a destination wedding, you'll be looking for a ceremony and reception site; possibly a caterer (if the reception site does not serve food); a florist; musicians; a photographer; a baker; and a hotel, resort, or bed-and-breakfast for you and your loved ones to relax in! ❧

Planning a destination wedding takes more effort than planning an elopement. You'll need more time, more money, and more ideas. Elopements are very short-lived events; destination weddings usually have their guests coming together a week or so before the wedding. That means you'd better have some fun things planned for your grandma and your future in-laws to do!

Choosing to hold your wedding at a resort that specializes in destination events is unarguably easier than trying to put a wedding together piece-by-piece. When all of the vendors have already been corralled by someone else, all of the activities have been arranged, and all of the resort's services have been put together in a nice, neat, easy-to-manage pamphlet, you can check off the things you want and be done with it. This is a major, major perk of a destination wedding: Aside from your having to come up with a way to pay for the affair, it's largely stress-free.

Planning a destination wedding without the benefit of a resort to guide you through it is a little more difficult, but not exactly impossible. In fact, it's done every day—and it's being done with more and more regularity as destination weddings become more common. This is great news for brides everywhere, because as more and more wedding vendors in Middle America become accustomed to working with out-of-town couples, their processes for doing so become more streamlined, and the chances of major mixups drop considerably.

Money Matters

You've just read that destination weddings usually take place over a week or more. Then there's the cost of the ceremony itself, and the honeymoon. Destination weddings are usually quite a bit more expensive than elopements (depending on the length of the trip and the formality of the ceremony and reception), and can actually be every bit as expensive as regular in-town affairs—but that doesn't mean they have to be. There is a destination wedding out there for every budget.

Big Bucks

Working with a bottomless bank account? There's no limit to what you can do, where you can go, or who you can bring along. You might be interested in cruising the Greek Isles, or perhaps you'd like to rent a European castle. Your destination wedding will be a once-in-a-lifetime event with unique floral arrangements, the best local cuisine, extraordinary musicians, and, no doubt, some interesting entrances (in a helicopter, perhaps), exits (by speedboat, maybe), and entertainment (ethnic dancers, circus performers, and fireworks at midnight).

Consider the possibilities of being able to host your wedding anywhere in the world! You can fly off to Thailand and get married on a beach, or you can invite everyone to Egypt for a ceremony in the shadows of the Great Pyramids. You might rent out a ski resort in the Canadian

Rockies for a week of winter fun before your wedding, or charter a yacht on the French Riviera.

Unless you are ultra-organized and have loads of time to do your own research, you'll be better off not planning this type of destination wedding on your own! Find a travel agent who specializes in destination weddings and let her do what the wedding-themed resorts do for their clients: narrow down the options significantly.

Small Budget

What if you can't quite afford the yacht or the dancers? Does that mean that eloping is the better idea after all? Only if eloping is what you have your heart set on. You can plan a very interesting destination wedding in Las Vegas for right around a thousand dollars. You might not stay a week in the nicest resort, and you might not have anyone twirling plates at the reception, but . . . so what? You'll bring a couple of friends along for the fun, and you'll come home married. You can also plan a small wedding in Maui (yes, Maui!) for about the same amount of money. In fact, no matter where you're headed, you can find a way to plan a wedding with a relatively small amount of money.

What's the secret to planning a destination wedding on the cheap? You have to be willing to give up *something*, whether it's the exotic location, the huge guest list, or the weeklong stay.

E~Alert

Overspending on any type of wedding—whether it's an elopement, a destination ceremony, or a traditional, in-town event—is never a good idea! Draw up a budget before you start planning and stick to it! Also think of clever ways to save a buck here and there. If you have a short guest list, perhaps you can make your own invitations. Do you have a seamstress in the family? Ask her to alter your gown.

Generally speaking, if you want to keep your budget in the low- to mid-thousands, you should plan on having a fairly small wedding. The great news about this, though, is that small doesn't equate to boring or dull. Several thousand dollars can go a long, long way, particularly at some of the resorts in the Caribbean. Many of the popular destination wedding resorts offer a free ceremony if you book your honeymoon there also, or several nights of free lodging if you book the ceremony. So decide where you want to be *first*, and then start looking for your best deal.

Get Your Act Together

Eloping and planning a destination wedding both require a certain level of organization. Jumping into *any* wedding without organizational skills can turn your planning into a nightmare. There are just so many things that you're going to need to refer to (itineraries, contracts, etc.), or give to someone (marriage license, rings) that if you don't get your head on straight, you just might come home as single as when you left!

Legal Issues

Any marriage that takes place *anywhere* requires some sort of state-sanctioned legitimization. In this country, that tool is the marriage license. Did you know, though, that license requirements differ from state to state, and that some states even have a waiting period between the time you apply for the license and the day you can get married?

It gets even more interesting if you're planning to get married overseas! Some foreign countries forbid the marriage of noncitizens, and others have strict requirements regarding the marriage of non-nationals. So you'd better know what you need before you board your flight, and then make sure you have those documents in your carry-on luggage! Chapter 16 explains everything you need to know to make sure that your ceremony is legal as well as beautiful.

Calling All Vendors

When you plan a destination wedding without the help of a resort, *you're* responsible for keeping in touch with all of your vendors. You can't do that, obviously, if you can't find their phone numbers (or even remember their names).

In this way, destination weddings require far more work than elopements and every bit the amount of organization needed for in-town ceremonies and receptions. While it may seem that leaving town will make things a whole lot easier, it doesn't always. And if a problem rears its ugly head, it'll be much easier to take care of if you have the number right in front of you. In Chapter 4 you'll learn the best ways to keep all of your wedding details organized so that you can arrive at your destination relaxed and happy.

Dressing the Part

As mentioned earlier in this chapter, eloping tends to involve a much faster planning process than does a traditional or destination wedding, and it also tends to be much less expensive. Here's one reason why: When brides elope, they often forgo the whole bridalwear ensemble. Translation: no traditional wedding dress or headpiece. This is not the case for destination brides, who spend just as much time looking for the perfect dress as do brides who are planning in-town ceremonies. The difference, though, is that the destination bride has to find a dress that's not only appropriate for the climate she's headed to, but is also easy (relatively speaking) to ship or pack. Fortunately, as you'll learn in Chapter 10, the wedding-dress industry offers plenty of options for the bride who chooses to wed far from home.

The Ceremony

Many elopements are performed by a justice of the peace. The reason for this is that it's usually easy to find a civil servant to perform a quick ceremony on short notice, whereas clerics are often booked months in advance, and at the very least will want to sit down and speak with you and your fiancé before the wedding. Destination weddings can go either way: You might choose to plan a traditional, religious service, or you may prefer a civil ceremony.

 E~ssential

Most destination wedding sites are prepared to deal with either a civil or a religious ceremony, so you shouldn't have any trouble planning your ideal exchange of vows. However, if you're planning a destination wedding without the benefit of a tried-and-true wedding resort, you'll have to find your own officiant. ﾟﾟ

Time Is on Your Side

Without a doubt, one of the biggest reasons that couples choose destination weddings is because it gives them something that other weddings (particularly elopements) lack: enough time to do everything, talk to everyone, and take in all of the emotion of the event. Couples who plan a one-day event might have the loveliest ceremony in the history of weddings, but it's still over in a matter of hours.

You know how people say that there just aren't enough hours in the day? Time seems to just evaporate on the typical wedding day. Everyone has anticipated the moment for so long, and there are so many details to contend with that before you know it: Poof! The day is *gone*. Destination weddings slow down everything, which may be just what you have in mind.

Catching Up

If you elope, who are you going to see on your wedding trip? Your new husband, your officiant, maybe a couple of random witnesses in the wedding chapel, and perhaps countless strangers (depending on whether you've eloped to a big city or a remote island). If this sounds like the perfect wedding to you, elopement may be your best choice. If you'd rather see and spend time with your family and friends, however, you definitely should consider a destination wedding, which typically is all about enjoying the company of your loved ones!

A destination wedding lets you take the time to really talk to people. You can reconnect with family members and catch up with your college pals. You still have to be able to budget your time among your guests so that you aren't spending every minute with your friends from high school and ignoring your relatives; but this is *so* much easier to do over the course of a week rather than over the span of just a few hours—especially in a place with built-in entertainment.

Reveling in the Wedding

When you arrive in town for your destination wedding, you've left the office behind. You've left your leaky sink behind. You've left your nutty neighbors behind. You've left real life behind, and you're there to focus on your wedding.

✿ E~Alert

The bride who is planning a secret elopement is still readily available—and expected—to take her boss's "emergency" phone calls in the days leading up to her marriage. She's also completely at the mercy of people who don't realize that she's getting married in just a few short days! ✍

By leaving town and surrounding yourself with loved ones for *days* before the ceremony, you're entering into a relaxing atmosphere where you can sit back and just let yourself soak in the joy and fun of the occasion. If you enlist the help of a wedding coordinator (or if one is provided for you by the site), you'll have very little to even concern yourself with in the week leading up to the ceremony, other than getting on a plane and arriving at your destination.

Choosing Attendants

What else makes a destination wedding different from an elopement? Well, how about the fact that when you plan a wedding, you also get to include your friends and relatives as attendants? Surrounding yourself with the people closest to you can go a long way toward making your wedding a truly memorable experience. It also tightens the bonds that already exist between you and your friends, and strengthens budding relationships, like those with your future sister(s)-in-law.

Lightening the Burden

If you've ever served as a bridesmaid for a rotten (translation: highly demanding) bride, you may be thinking twice about having any bridesmaids in your wedding. You wouldn't want anyone to go through the same horrible experience, after all.

However, you have the ability to make this a pleasant experience for your bridesmaids simply by treating them well. They should be willing to help you in any way during the course of the wedding planning, but you shouldn't hit them with bizarre requests ("Change your hair color so that it matches mine!" or "Lose ten pounds so you'll look nice in my wedding pictures!").

Bottom line: Treat the bridesmaids well, and they'll treat you well in return. Just make sure that they know up front what you expect of them, and don't be shy about spelling out the seemingly little things (for instance, that you expect them to arrive at the destination on the same day you do, and that you expect them *not* to be blind drunk at the reception). You must also make sure that bridesmaids understand that they will incur wedding-related expenses. You'll read about this in more detail in Chapter 7.

Feel the Love

Including other members of your family in the wedding is also a huge difference between a destination wedding and an elopement. If you planned on eloping, for example, you couldn't ask your mother to do a reading at the ceremony, nor would she be able to shop for the perfect dress. Most important, she would miss out on watching her baby walk down the aisle, and although it may not seem like that should be a devastating blow to her (or other members of the family), it very well could be.

E-Fact

Weddings tend to bring families together, and this is the biggest difference between an elopement and a destination wedding. You're including other people in your plans, and in the end, it may end up bringing you closer than you've been in years.

Having your family around you on your wedding day—even if they're the only people at the ceremony—usually turns out to be the one thing brides appreciate most about their wedding experience, whether it's a destination wedding or a traditional, in-town affair. Until the actual day of the wedding arrives, you may not realize how much it means to you to have your parents looking on as you recite your vows. Your wedding could be the beginning of a great new phase of your relationship with your whole family, which it should be (and which elopements often are *not*).

Chapter 3
Money Talk

If there's one thing that every engaged couple will hear over and over again from the time they decide to get married until they actually say "I do," it's this: Weddings are expensive. In fact, let's add a truthful little qualifier in there: Weddings are wildly expensive. Or at least they can be. This chapter will give you an overview of the expenses of a traditional wedding, what a destination wedding could end up costing you, and where to find some happy compromises where spending is concerned.

Breaking with the Past

It's funny, but weddings bring out the traditional side in some of the least traditional people. Suddenly, a bride who long ago declared her independence from her parents is hinting to Mom and Dad that it might be nice if they were to contribute to the wedding fund—because, after all, it's traditional for the bride's family to pay the lion's share of the final bill. The opposite also holds true, in that traditionalists start looking for the newest trends; for instance, Mom and Dad may start voicing their approval of the groom's family chipping in an equal amount. Yes, that's progress, and they'll be darned if they're going to be behind the times.

The bride's family has traditionally been held responsible for providing just about everything for the bride and the guests, including:

* Bride's wedding ensemble (dress, shoes, veil, and so on)
* Invitations, announcements, save-the-date cards
* Transportation for the bridal party
* Ceremony fee
* Flowers for the ceremony and reception (including the bridesmaids' flowers)
* Pictures and video
* Reception hall
* Food and beverages at the reception
* Entertainment at the reception
* Wedding cake
* Engagement party
* The groom's ring and wedding gift

The groom's family has gotten off relatively easy, at least in the big financial picture. Traditional expenses pinned on the groom's family include:

* The bride's engagement and wedding rings
* Officiant's fee

* Marriage license fee
* The bride's bouquet
* Corsages for the mothers and grandmothers of the bride and groom; boutonnieres for groomsmen
* Wedding gift for the bride
* Rehearsal dinner
* Honeymoon expenses

Keep in mind that when these guidelines were established, weddings weren't the mega-industry that they are in this day and age. Nowadays, each and every bride wants to outdo all of the others, and that mindset is usually too expensive for one family to support. (Sure, you can have an appetizer at your reception that no one has ever heard of, but boy, are you going to pay for it!)

Also, when these traditions were in full swing, brides and grooms were younger and less established in the world. In other words, today's bridal couples are often in their late twenties or early thirties and have been working for several years before deciding to settle down. These men and women are able to pay for their own weddings, or at least contribute mightily toward them. And let's not forget that Mom and Dad may have already made a substantial financial contribution to the bride's or groom's college education (another cost that has skyrocketed in recent years). You know they really love you, but you can only expect so much from your parents.

In light of these recent developments, it often makes the most sense for the bride and groom to throw tradition out the window and work out a financial strategy that best suits their own needs.

Ask for Help or Do It Yourself?

Should you depend on a contribution from both sets of parents in order to finance your wedding? Should you even ask? This varies from family to family. Some parents are more than happy to pitch in; some are more concerned with their retirement nest eggs than with making sure their daughter has the perfect wedding dress (and perhaps in the long run, when they're not dependent on you in their old age, you'll be happy they had this mindset).

If your mom and dad helped pay for both of your sisters' weddings, then chances are they're probably planning on tossing you some cash for your jaunt down the aisle. Same thing goes for your future in-laws: If they pitched in on a wedding for their other son, then they'll probably be willing to help with this wedding, too. Just keep in mind that you aren't really entitled to anyone else's money, so resist the urge to compare and contrast how much your sisters' weddings cost to how much your parents are willing to give you.

This is easier said than done, of course. But if you're ready to officially enter adult life, this is the ultimate test: Being grateful for what you're given, instead of wishing it were more.

❀ E~Alert

When preparing to grease the parental money wheels, remember that money is a very touchy subject for some people. For example, if you know your father is uncomfortable discussing money with anyone who isn't immediate family, think twice before you drag your fiancé along when you ask for the wedding cash. ❧

You know your parents best. You know how and when to bring up the subject of money, how to ask for it, how to negotiate the terms. Let your fiancé decide the best way to approach his parents for a contribution. The bottom line: It's not worth a fight. If parents can't or won't contribute, move on and do the best you can with the resources you have. You don't want hard feelings about your wedding following you around for the rest of your life.

There are definitely some benefits to paying for your own wedding, especially if you and your mother regularly butt heads over such trivial issues as which dish soap works best or whether it's day or night at any given moment. Some engaged women have the notion that planning a wedding with Mother will bring the two of them closer together than they've ever been. Usually, though, the reality is that wedding planning can be stressful under the best of circumstances (when a bride and her mother just love, love, *love* being together). Put a mother and daughter who constantly bicker together in a bridal salon and watch the sparks fly!

It seems that there are very few shades of gray when brides plan a wedding with a mom who's paying. Either the bride goes on an ultimate kid-in-the-candy-store shopping spree (which results either in the bride being blissfully happy or the bride spiraling wildly out of control) or the mother of the bride takes charge and plans the wedding she would have had thirty years earlier if she (or her parents) had had the money. In the first scenario, Mom often ends up jittery and unhappy; in the second scenario, the bride is the one taking the emotional hit. So, you see, a little financial independence on your part can make planning the wedding easier on everyone.

Staying on Top of Expenses

The cost of the average wedding is rising by the day. And this isn't even in reference to the largest weddings, or the most elaborate ceremonies. The average wedding can *easily* run into the tens of thousands of dollars. Of course, just how many tens of thousands of dollars is largely dependent on where you live. A wedding in midtown Manhattan is going to be a bit pricier than one in Muncie. That's doesn't mean that the Muncie wedding won't be as beautiful—it's just a reflection of the high cost of living in certain areas of the country.

Some couples don't mind emptying their piggy banks to finance a large in-town affair. It's their dream wedding, and they wouldn't have it any other way. Other couples price reception halls and limousines and wonder if it wouldn't be less expensive to go another route—specifically, the destination wedding route.

Benefits of a Budget

The word *budget* conjures up images of a 1950s housewife diligently pinching pennies (and enjoying it). Truth is, many men and women of marrying age these days have never even considered creating a budget—and wouldn't know how to if they were forced.

E~Alert

If you and your future husband are of average means and paying for a large portion of your wedding, there's no time like the present to figure out what you can truly afford. A grand wedding may seem worth the exorbitant price tag now, but post-wedding life includes big-time expenses such as saving for a house and paying off car and/or college loans.

Why would anyone want to budget for a wedding, you ask? Between the two of you, you have two paychecks and twelve credit cards and since you're such excellent consumers, your credit limits are, shall we say, substantial. Why establish credit in the first place if you shouldn't use it for big expenses—like, say, a wedding?

It's not a matter of whether you should use it, because, as you'll read in the following section, it's actually advisable to use your credit card for some of your wedding expenses. It's more a matter of knowing the bottom line: How much can you spend on a wedding without putting yourself into debt for years to come?

One very easy way to budget for your wedding is to create a separate wedding account to be used for wedding expenses only. If you and/or your fiancé have been saving for this event, put that money into the account.

Maybe you want to deposit part of every paycheck into the account. Set up a direct deposit with your bank for that purpose. If your parents are giving you money for the wedding, stash it away in this account. You'll end up with a very solid idea of where you stand and how much you can comfortably afford. You also will know right away if and when things start getting too expensive.

Credit Card Caution

For many couples, a wedding is one of the biggest expenses they'll incur until they set out to buy a house. Unless you have some experience with long-term, high-cost purchases, you may not realize that you'll be faced with option after option, and pretty soon, money can almost become meaningless. ("What? $400 for these hand-beaded shoes? Oh, who cares? I just spent $200 on a purse, and $5,000 on my gown. I'll take them!") You're unlikely to make too many overspending errors if the money is coming directly from your wedding account. You'll feel the bite—and the resulting panic and guilt—almost immediately.

E~Fact

Credit card companies will usually enter into a dispute only after you have made a good-faith effort to settle the matter on your own. If a problem arises with a store owner (or a caterer, or a baker, or any other wedding professional), do your best to state your case calmly and clearly. If you find you're getting nowhere, let the big guns step in and try to clear things up.

However, the flip side of the coin is that your credit card offers you a measure of protection, something you need when you're paying big bucks for a wedding. Let's say that your wedding dress arrives tattered and torn at the bridal shop. If you've paid by check, your money is *gone*. Good luck trying to get the shop's owner to order another dress at her expense. You can call your credit card company, however, and ask them to help you fight that charge. At the very least, the store owner won't get paid until the issue is resolved, and that could take several weeks. Businesses are more willing to work out a happy compromise when faced with a loss of revenue.

Realistically, when planning any sort of wedding, you're going to have to flash your plastic for the larger expenses. Here's how to keep your spending in check:

* *Have a wedding expenses log.* Use Microsoft Excel if you're really good with the computer; use Word if you aren't. Heck, use a notebook if you hate the computer, but keep track of your spending. At the end of each day, you and your fiancé should note the planning/expenses you've tackled that day.
* *Use your credit card for larger expenses.* You'll have to book your hotel and airline tickets with your card, and it's always good protection in the event of some sort of monetary dispute with any wedding vendor.
* *Pay for smaller purchases with cash or check.* It's not so hard, actually, to remember that you charged your resort package on your card. It's those smaller expenses (such as shoes, undergarments, clothes, and other provisions for your wedding week in the sun) that add up quickly. Keep your receipts and cancelled checks in one neat folder or file at home.

Credit is not necessarily synonymous with *bad spending habits*. It's an old piece of advice, but it holds true: Use your credit wisely and sparingly. You'll thank yourself later.

The Dangers of Debt

Your goal is to get married and live happily ever after, right? Just remember that starting off the marriage in the red is not usually conducive to a lot of happy conversations at home. It's a good idea to have some money socked away, not just for a rainy day, but for real-life, after-the-wedding expenses, including:

* ✳ Rent
* ✳ Utilities
* ✳ Transportation
* ✳ Food
* ✳ Clothing
* ✳ Entertainment
* ✳ Emergencies (the car breaks down, medical emergencies, and so on)

Although many men and women are already paying these expenses long before they walk down the aisle, some are living off the good graces of Mom and Dad up until the day of the ceremony and are shocked to find that living day-to-day is expensive. Other couples upgrade their living quarters after the wedding and find that their earnings don't stretch quite as far anymore. If you didn't overspend on the wedding and you have some savings to get you through these tough times, you're likely to be happier—in your marriage, in your job, in general—than those who end up living paycheck to paycheck.

One brutally honest piece of advice before we move on: Newlywed life really starts to lose its innocence and charm when you're married, broke, and wishing you hadn't paid $8,000 for your wedding dress. Don't set yourself up for a big financial fall.

Comparison Shopping

So what's the monetary difference between paying for an in-town wedding and paying for a ceremony in a far-off land? There is no hard-and-fast answer to that question, because just like a regular wedding, destination weddings can be as grand or as small as you'd prefer.

The Breakdown: What You Will Pay For

Some couples are frightened away from planning a destination wedding because they assume that they'll end up paying not only for a ceremony and reception, but also for their guests' expenses. Not true. Here's a list of what you will pay for:

* Your own travel
* Your lodging
* All wedding-related expenses

You are *not* responsible for paying for your guests' travel, food, or lodging. If they can't afford it or they don't want to spend the money, they won't come. It's as simple as that.

As for picking up the tab for your attendants' travel and lodging, there are two schools of thought on that. Most traditional wedding etiquette states that the bride's family should pay for attendants' travel and lodging. It's easy to see the logic in extending that kind of generosity by offering to pay for your attendants' travel-related expenses for a destination wedding. However, in reality, most attendants end up footing the bill for their flights and hotels.

Here's the deal: If you really want to do something nice and/or you're saving a lot of money by having a destination wedding, it never hurts to contribute to someone else's travel expenses, especially if you know that your best friend will have to sell her CD collection just to pay for her plane ticket. If you're doing this for one member of the bridal party, though, you have to do it for all of them (or risk a mutiny on the altar when word of your selective generosity starts spreading).

Family is a different matter. You can help out a close relative with travel expenses without paying for everyone else, but you might put yourself in a spot. It's best to give this kind of assistance confidentially, so it won't seem as though you're playing favorites.

When you ask someone to be in your bridal party, or when you're discussing the wedding with a guest before the invitations have been mailed, be forthright about what they'll be paying for—namely, their entire trip. You don't need to blurt out, "You'll have to spend $150 a night on a hotel room!" You can simply mention that you are going to book a block of rooms and that you'll let them know what kind of discount the resort is giving to the members and guests of your wedding party. That message comes through loud and clear.

 E~ssential

If a sibling just can't afford the travel expenses and you can help her out, go ahead. But do it quietly and with the condition that if she tells anyone else, you'll dunk her in the ocean once you arrive. Weddings often unearth long-buried familial tensions, something you do not want to deal with during your wedding week. ✿

When you mail the invitations, enclose the travel information, including the name of the hotel and the rate under which you have reserved your block of rooms; names of other nearby hotels; and airline information. (More on this in Chapter 6.)

Good Things Come in Packages

Resorts that regularly play host to destination weddings have the planning down to a science, which is one reason so many brides and grooms are flying off to tropical weddings: Planning is a snap.

What you'll typically encounter when planning a destination wedding at a resort is that you'll have options for each area of the wedding. For example, you'll choose a site for the ceremony: Will it be on the beach or in the resort's chapel? Do you want your reception on the patio or inside the restaurant? Would you like to have a harpist, flutist, or pianist during the ceremony? What about a vocalist? Do you want a photographer for six hours or eight? Black-and-white pictures or color?

You'll choose food and music for the reception, and you may have an option of choosing transportation for a grand entrance. Basically, you'll make decisions about everything you would for an in-town wedding; the difference is that your choices will be limited to what's offered. Most popular destinations have an array of choices; you won't have only two types of flowers to choose from, for example, and your choices of ceremony and reception sites may be quite extensive also. For many brides, this is just fine—it's part of the reason they've chosen the site. For other brides, this just won't do. They have definite, creative ideas, which rules out choosing their wedding elements from an à la carte list.

E~Fact

If you're finding yourself feeling walled in rather than relieved by the choices, you may be better off planning a wedding in a less popular spot, where you'll most likely have to find your own florist, musicians, and other professionals. It's more legwork, sure, but you'll be happier in the end.

If you've fallen in love with a certain resort but not necessarily with the choices you've been given for your ceremony and reception, you may be able to find some wiggle room. It never hurts to ask if the florist might do something really different with your bouquet, or if you can do something unique with the table settings. You may not get what you want, but it never hurts to ask.

The Upside of Keeping Expenses Low

There's nothing wrong with booking your wedding in a popular place, but the hotter the spot, the bigger the bill for you—and for your guests, some of whom may not be able or willing to fork over a whole lot of money to stay at a luxury resort. One way to get around feeling as though you should help friends and family members with travel expenses is to choose a location that isn't insanely pricey. It's well within the realm of reality to find a beautiful spot that will fit (mostly) everyone's budget.

Take Brian and Jeanne's wedding, for example. When this Manhattan-based couple decided to get hitched, they knew they wanted something out of the ordinary. Brian's family spends its summers on the Finger Lakes in upstate New York, which are breathtakingly beautiful in the summer months. Deciding on this general location was the couple's starting point.

Although the Finger Lakes region was somewhat out of the way for Jeanne's family members (who are scattered all across the country), it was a decently centralized location for the couple's New York City–based friends and for Brian's family, most of whom are from Buffalo. The majority of the guests were able to drive to the wedding and find very reasonably priced lodging in the area. Brian and Jeanne feel that their choice of location brought more family to the wedding than might have attended otherwise, and definitely more than would have attended if they had booked a cruise ship or resort wedding. Because upstate New York is fairly inexpensive (especially when compared with paying for food and lodging at a resort in the Caribbean), travel costs weren't a huge deterrent. In fact, several of their guests decided to explore the state, popping over to Niagara Falls and/or the Adirondack region for a couple of days.

 E~ssential

If your family is frugal and you want them to witness your wedding vows, don't choose an expensive location. Although some guests will simply decline the invitation if it is beyond their means, other family members will feel obligated to attend. You don't want anyone to view your wedding as a hardship, so do your best to accommodate those you hold nearest and dearest. ❧

The moral of the story? If you really want people to show up for your destination wedding, be realistic not only about your own budget, but also what your guests are willing and able to spend in order to attend.

Accommodating Any Budget

Destination weddings encompass such a broad spectrum of possibilities that they're really affordable for just about everyone. If you were planning to have an in-town wedding of any significant size, you can reshape it into a destination affair. You just have to know where to spend your money wisely.

Where Your Money Is Best Spent

Start by prioritizing your wants, and weighing them against your needs. Do you *want* to have 150 guests attend your cruise ship wedding, or do you *need* to have a more intimate ceremony? Do you have to have your wedding at a castle in Scotland, or will you be just as happy reciting your vows in a lodge in Montana? Needless to say, when making a list of "must-haves," it helps to have an open mind about some things. Unless you're printing money in your basement (or you have a job where you do the basic equivalent), or you've been saving for a long, long time, or you want to go deeply into debt (not advisable), you and your fiancé may want to splurge on certain areas of the wedding and cut back on other, less important (to you) areas.

Costs to prioritize include:

* Location (including lodging and travel expenses to and from your destination)
* Food
* Drink
* Flowers
* Music (ceremony and reception)
* Wedding attire for you and your fiancé
* Transportation (to and from the ceremony)
* Pictures and video
* Rings

The interesting thing about this list is that it contains exactly the same items that an in-town wedding list would. The bride who is marrying in her hometown has to consider where she wants to spend the bulk of her wedding fund; so do you.

That said, most couples who are planning a destination wedding focus on the location. These brides and grooms reason that even if the food at the reception is fair-to-middlin', the guests are going to be so entranced with the beauty of the location and with the entire travel event that a few subpar appetizers aren't going to be viewed as critically as they would be back home at the country club. And they're probably right. If your guests are willing to make the trip, make it worth their while and pick an interesting place. (Note use of the word *interesting* instead of *popular* or *extravagant*.)

Anything's Possible!

If money is not an issue as far as your wedding is concerned, lucky you! You have the entire globe to scout out and choose a location from. If you decide that's just too much work, though, you can find a fairly nearby destination wedding resort that offers unique add-ons. Take Walt Disney World, for example. If you plan your destination wedding there, you can choose to arrive in Cinderella's carriage (for an extra fee of $2,500); you can hire two Disney characters to hang out with your guests at the reception ($1,070); you can even hire actors to play obnoxious tourists who have crashed your wedding ($1,200). One of the coolest things that Disney offers is a private fireworks display ($2,500) after the ceremony and/or reception.

E~Fact

You actually have your work cut out for you if you have a huge budget, because the possibilities are endless! Grab your fiancé as soon as possible and start brainstorming about what you'd like to make happen.

If money is tight, you can still find a spot with unique wedding "extras." In the Viva Las Vegas Wedding Chapel, for example, you can have an Elvis-themed wedding for under $1,000. The price includes an Elvis-impersonator officiant, flowers, and a photo package. For just $150 more, you can actually roll into your wedding in the back seat of a pink Cadillac driven by your "Elvis" minister; for an additional $150, a fake Priscilla will sit up front with him. That deal is hard to beat.

Truly, no matter what kind of budget you're working with, you can find a way to make your destination wedding unique!

Chapter 4
Organization Is Key

After receiving the ring, the first thing many brides do is to purchase some sort of planner in order to keep their thoughts, research, and receipts organized. In fact. this isn't a bad idea. The brides who aren't convinced of the necessity of keeping each little piece of pertinent information handy often end up frazzled, or they wind up paying too much for flowers or cake or airline tickets. This chapter will show you how to best get organized, including how to organize your registry.

The Perils of Disorganization

Your phone bill is under the sink. Your address book is filled with blank pages, and your desk looks like a paper storm just came by. None of this really bothers you; you know that you can pay your phone bill online, you can look up phone numbers as needed, and you work best with a messy desk.

Some people really do thrive (or at least survive) in the midst of massive disorganization. However, when you're planning an event as significant and as expensive as your wedding, you've got to pull things together and find some way to keep all of the information in the same vicinity—even if this is only a temporary revision of your normal routine.

Even in this day of advanced technology, the best way to keep yourself organized is to buy a binder and put (or enter) all of your pertinent wedding information into it as soon as you receive it, or at least as soon as possible. Why go so low-tech, you ask? You'll be generating a paper trail of contracts and receipts, most of which will not be electronic. But let's say that some of them are. Suppose that you purchase your wedding shoes online. Print out the purchase order and shipping confirmation (and receipt, if necessary) and file them in case the shoes arrived damaged—or don't arrive at all! Also print out any e-mails you receive from potential wedding sites; don't let them just sit in your inbox (which is filled with 300 other messages that you haven't bothered to delete). Write down phone numbers so that you can easily access them. Place contracts and other mailings into your binder/folder/organizer and keep it in the same place all the time!

How a Destination Wedding Can Help

The truly sweet thing about dealing with a destination wedding site is that most of the details are taken care of already. Your choices are whittled down for you, and you're not hunting down vendors. Pretty easy stuff—once you get to that point. If you don't already have a solid idea of where you want your wedding to take place, though, you're still in the early stages of research. As you review possible sites for your wedding, you will compare several features:

- ❊ *Location.* Caribbean or Hawaii? Which one is right for you?
- ❊ *Package deals.* What do they include? How do the prices compare to one another?
- ❊ *Accommodations.* Are these places large enough to accommodate your guests?
- ❊ *References.* What do other brides have to say about their experiences at this site?
- ❊ *Travel expenses.* This includes both you and your guests. You want the best deal for everyone, so if one place is significantly less expensive, it may be the better option.

You can blindly choose a spot based on its beauty or even based on a previous vacation you spent there, but it's much more advisable to take an investigative look at your intended wedding spot. Many times, a couple will have their hearts set on one site and then learn through their research that the place is far too small to hold their guests, or that the prices are outrageous, or that other couples have had horrible experiences there.

If you're considering a wedding site based on a vacation you've spent at the place, do some extra research to make sure the facility's weddings are up to snuff. There's a huge difference between having room service delivered and ordering fifty grilled mahi mahi dinners. Always ask for references—and check them!

As you can see, organization and research are bosom buddies when it comes to planning your wedding. They go together like wedding cake and frosting. Can't have one without the other.

Where to Begin

Research has its role when you're planning a wedding, obviously. But it's also important to trust your judgment from the beginning, or you could drive yourself crazy hopping all over the globe via the Internet, looking for the perfect wedding spot. Since destination weddings are all the rage these days, you'll find no shortage of beaches, castles, and amusement parks willing to roll out the red carpet for you and your groom.

❊ E~ssential

The bonus to getting yourself organized during your wedding planning is that your new habits might just carry over into everyday life. Yes, filing papers and keeping track of important information can be a huge pain in the rear, but it does make life infinitely easier in the long run. The wedding planning process may help you realize that it's not all that difficult to maintain a minimum level of structure.

You already know what types of settings you like and don't like. You know what will feel right for your wedding, and what will feel cheesy—and this differs from couple to couple. Let's say your best friend got married at a mountaintop resort. The wedding was cozy and comfortable, and for that reason, you're afraid to plan your wedding in a castle in Ireland—afraid it will seem too formal, too overblown.

Hey, it's your wedding, and besides, brides usually love to break the wedding mold. Although there can also be a sense of, "Am I doing the right thing here, or am I completely out of control?"—especially when you're shooting for a really unique event. Destination weddings already have this angle covered. Your guests are expecting something out of the ordinary.

Organization begins with your own narrowing of choices, then. It's all right to waver between a couple of very different choices at first. For instance, would you prefer a wedding in summerlike weather, or one with a wintry backdrop? You love both seasons so much, you may need to do further research on different locations before you can make a final decision. After a short while, though, you have to trust your own preferences and then move along the planning stages—or you'll be going nowhere, fast. (Then some other bride will be getting married at your location on your wedding day. How will you feel about *that*?)

First Things First

Deciding where you're going is obviously the first thing to do, 'cause you can't very well book the reception hall (or lanai) in an apparition of a place. Here are some factors that might help you reach a decision:

- ✳ *Cost.* If price is a consideration, plan to do comparison shopping.
- ✳ *Season.* You want to get married in August in Miami? Keep in mind that late summer is the height of hurricane season in the Atlantic!
- ✳ *Travel.* If you know that the farther away the wedding, the less likely it is that your family will show, that should narrow down your choices a bit.
- ✳ *Accessibility.* Is it easy to find out about this place? If you've called and e-mailed for information to no avail, that's not a good sign.

After you've taken care of these issues, you can move on to the more specific decisions, including choosing an exact date, looking through the various packages, and personalizing your ceremony. These decisions will be made infinitely easier when you speak to the site's wedding coordinator.

❁ E~Question

Do I have to hire a wedding coordinator at a destination wedding site?

The coordinator is almost always included in a destination wedding package and is a vital source of information. He or she is your primary contact and can offer recommendations when you're unsure at any given point during the wedding planning. This person will also fill in the blanks (by answering your many questions) during the wedding planning process. ❧

Planning with Help

Planning a destination wedding at a resort follows a fairly standard regimen. For the purpose of this discussion, we'll assume that you're beginning your planning a year in advance. If you're thinking about a significantly sized wedding in a popular spot, you'll need at least that much time. If your wedding is going to be at a little-known place, or is going to be a small gathering, you may be able to pull things together on shorter notice. Follow this timeline for planning a destination wedding with help:

* *One year prior to the wedding (or as soon as possible).* Choose a site and book it. You'll need to know how many guests you're going to invite and what kind of budget you'll be working with in order to do this. Also, start looking for a dress. Although destination weddings often call for less formal gowns, you still may have a hard time finding the perfect look, and once you do order a dress, it often takes several months to receive it.

* *Eight months prior.* Pick your attendants and start looking for bridesmaids' gowns.

* *Six months prior.* Make your honeymoon plans and start looking for the best travel deals before everything gets booked. Make sure passports are up-to-date, and start checking out the legal requirements for marriage in the area you're headed to. Send out save-the-date cards, and think about where you're going to register.

* *Four months prior.* Make sure the groom and ushers have chosen their attire. Start looking for your invitations. Pick out your wedding bands. Your registry should be complete by now.

* *Three months prior.* Make the plans for the rehearsal dinner. Most of the wedding should be finalized by now, or at least close to it: flowers, musicians, baker, transportation. Touch base with your wedding coordinator to tie up any loose ends.

* *Two months prior.* Send out invitations. Make appointments for hair and makeup for yourself and the bridesmaids on the day of the wedding. Pick out gifts for your attendants. Bridal showers are

usually planned for this time period (bridesmaids are traditionally held responsible for planning and paying for these parties).

* *One month prior.* Make sure announcements to your local newspapers have been sent. Time to give everything the once-over: What has absolutely, positively been done, and what hasn't? There's no more time to play with, so get going on any last-minute tasks!

* *Two weeks prior.* Pick up your dress and ship it, if need be. Start packing. Make sure you have your marriage license, passport, and airline tickets. Speak to your wedding coordinator to confirm *everything.* You may need to give a final head count at this point, or you might be able to wait until one week prior to the wedding.

* *One week prior.* Leave this last week for emergency errands. Scheduling any planning for this week will only lead to an overwhelming feeling that you've forgotten something.

You've left quite a bit of planning to the wedding coordinator, but you'll note there's still plenty for you to do. Don't put off anything until the last minute—just do it!

Planning on Your Own

Making the calls to vendors all by yourself and otherwise fitting the pieces of your wedding puzzle together is a big, big job, especially when you're doing it from out of town. So–when will you start planning? Who do you need to talk to, and when? Again, start as early as possible. It's not a bad idea to start making calls a year and a half before your planned wedding date; in fact, in many regions, it's necessary. Here's a typical timeline for planning the out-of-town wedding by yourself:

* *Twelve months prior (or as soon as possible).* Choose the spot, and make sure your intended date is open. Look for a reception site, and ask for references from former clients. When you're satisfied with these two big bookings, ask your reception site coordinator

for the names of other reputable vendors, such as a baker and caterer. Call these vendors as soon as possible to see how far in advance they're booking weddings. Start looking for your dress.

  ❋ *Eight to ten months prior.* Hunt down your florist, musicians, limo service, photographer, and officiant. Finalize the wedding party and start searching for the bridesmaids' dresses. Now is the time to order your dress, since many dresses take months to deliver and require alterations once they arrive.

  ❋ *Six months prior.* Send out save-the-date cards with travel info for your guests. Make your honeymoon plans now in order to get the best deals. If you're getting married out of the country, update your passports if necessary, and check on the legal requirements for marriage wherever you're headed. Start thinking about your registry (where you'd like to register and what you really need).

  ❋ *Four months prior.* Order your invitations. Your registry should be finalized by now. If they're renting tuxes, the groom and ushers should have their wedding attire reserved, especially if you're getting married during May or June (which are big prom months).

  ❋ *Three months prior.* Call vendors to confirm that everything is on track. Start planning the rehearsal dinner.

  ❋ *Two months prior.* Send out the invitations. Book hair and makeup appointments for the wedding day for yourself and the bridesmaids. Order presents for attendants.

  ❋ *One month prior.* Finalize plans with vendors. Send announcements to the newspaper.

  ❋ *Two weeks prior.* Pick up your dress; pack. If your dress is being shipped, send it now. Make sure travel arrangements are in order.

  ❋ *One week prior.* Leave this last week for emergency errands. Scheduling any planning for this week will only lead to an overwhelming feeling that you've forgotten something.

As you can see, there's some overlap in these two planning schedules. What's different in the second list is that you'll be doing a lot more legwork than you would if you were working with a resort. But for the organized bride, it's not difficult. Just remember to keep those phone numbers handy, save your paperwork, and file, file, file that information away!

❋ E~Alert

When making your airline reservations, make sure to reserve your own seat in your maiden name. You'll have to show a valid form of ID when you check in at the airport, and with security as tight as it is these days, no one at the ticket counter is going to accept any excuses. So, although you're almost a Mrs., book yourself as a Ms. on these flights. ✍

Are you mad, trying to plan an out-of-town wedding by yourself? No. It's done all the time. The difference between a challenging experience and one that spirals down into nightmare territory is your level of organization. If you can't find the one phone number you need, or you can't even remember the name of the baker you've chosen, you're going to have a very hard time with the details. Resolve to make your wedding an experience you *want* to look back on, and don't get buried in disorganization.

Timesaving Tips

There is no rule that says the bride has to do all of the planning by herself. Get your groom-to-be or your mother involved. Enlist the help of your maid of honor or best man. Have them do Internet research, make phone calls, or talk through potential plans with you. It can start to seem that everything is the best option (carrot cake is great, but so is chocolate— and white cake!), and once in a while, you'll just need a second opinion.

Planning the out-of-town wedding requires a bit more attention to details and a little more research than the typical in-town wedding does, so if you can cut down your workload by pulling in other people, *do it*. Just make sure you're only asking for help from people you trust;

otherwise, you might just make things even more difficult, when, for example, your sister is supposed to find a florist and she puts it off . . . and off . . . and off . . . until you have to go with whomever is available instead of the florist you really would have preferred.

Once you find reputable vendors, the planning process gets easier. You'll still have choices to make, but the vendors—a good caterer, for instance—will be able to give you solid recommendations. In that way, your wedding could proceed like a resort-style wedding, where the choices are narrowed down for you. The difficult part of planning an out-of-town wedding is finding the names of decent vendors and checking references (all in a timely manner). Fortunately, one good vendor can usually recommend another, so even though your planning process may start out as a seemingly insurmountable wall, that wall will fall like a stack of blocks once you find your first trustworthy business owner.

The Registry

Part of planning for the wedding is planning for your lives together after the marriage ceremony. Since many couples live together before the wedding, and since many brides and grooms are waiting until they're older before they take the leap into marriage, many people feel that registries might be a thing of the past. Who needs dishes and silverware these days? Of course, you know very well that there's always something missing from any house, and that every house eventually needs repair.

Where to Register

This is a highly personal choice. The big-box stores have everything you need under one roof, which is really convenient for you. However, if your tastes tend to be more unique, you might want to go with a local, smaller shop instead. There are pros and cons to each decision.

Before you commit to any store, check its policies for returning damaged items. If you receive three slow cookers, for example, will you be given a cash refund, or will you receive a store credit instead? If an item is shipped to your doorstep and arrives broken, will the store pay for the item to be picked up, shipped back, replaced, and reshipped, or will you have to do all the legwork yourself?

It's best to have a feel for the store you're working with. A pleasant return-or-replace policy should be in place for engaged couples for two big reasons: First, by registering with a store, you're bringing in a decent amount of business, so the store should try to be as accommodating as possible. Second, every registry runs the risk of repeat gifts, even in this age of computerized gift-giving. If you sense that replacing an item is going to be beyond frustrating, move on to another shop.

When you register, the store will give you registry cards to include in shower invitations. (They don't go in the wedding invitations as a rule of etiquette.) Bigger stores will also put your registry on their Web sites, which makes giving—and receiving—*so* much easier on everyone!

E~Alert

Some registry Web sites are not automatically updated, which makes it look as though you haven't received a gift when you already have. Also, gift buyers don't always use registries correctly. They may check your list to see what you've chosen, but if they don't let the salesperson know that they've purchased an item for you, the item will remain on your registry.

Because more stores of all types are adding registries, it's worth your while to check out all of the options before committing to any one of them. If you honestly don't need a thing for the house, then get creative. For instance, your travel agent may be able to set up a honeymoon fund registry, or perhaps a car dealer would be willing to work with you to set up a car fund for your wedding. Couples who don't need anything at all often choose a favorite charity in order for donations to be made in their name.

It can't ever hurt to be inquisitive about unique registries; you may not get what you want, but you'll know you gave it your best shot.

The Basics

What if you do want and need the standard stuff for your new home? What, exactly, is this stuff, how much will you need, and what will people realistically be willing to purchase for you?

First things first: Take a good, honest look at your lifestyle. Do you love to throw big parties, or do you have just a few close friends? Do you already have the basic countertop appliances, or is there something you really, truly need? Your registry is not so much a free-for-all wish list as it is a plea for the housewares you're lacking. Now, this isn't to say that a few big-ticket fancy items can't make the list, but for the most part, you shouldn't be going way, way overboard choosing things you'll never use. That's a waste of money. (And if you're like a lot of newlyweds, without tons of money to throw around, you might come to regret your choice of $200 candlesticks when you really could have used a food processor.)

 E~ssential

Even if you'd really prefer to receive money for your shower and wedding gifts, there's no polite way to say this, so don't even think about slipping this request into any invitations. Your mother can attempt to pass the word among relatives, but that's about the most you can (politely) do.

In keeping with the theme of organization, here's a breakdown to help you organize your thoughts. Your registry may include items such as:

* *Dishware.* You need everyday dishes for sure. Choose something neutral if you're renting right now. (You don't want to move into a new home only to find that your dishes clash horribly with the new countertops.) Fine china is something you'll never buy for yourself, so register for it now. Ten place settings should suffice.

* *Tableware.* In addition to dishes, you'll need to decide on platters, a soup tureen, candlesticks, a butter dish, chafing dishes—anything you'll need to set the table completely. Choose wisely here and imagine your cooking style and what you could really use. If you never serve soup, for example, skip the tureen.

* *Flatware.* Everyday silverware is a must (no more using plastic utensils). Good silver is another one of those things you'll never want to spend the money on, so choose it now. A good set of kitchen knives is a must if you cook a lot. They aren't cheap, but the better brands are worth every penny.

* *Glassware.* You'll need glasses for your soda and iced tea (long and tall), and for your gin-and-tonics (rocks glasses—short and stout). You may want pilsner glasses for beer, or mugs to serve that purpose. If you entertain a lot, you'll need a substantial set of glasses for this purpose. Crystal wineglasses, water goblets, and champagne flutes are for setting your formal table; the number of these should match the number of china settings you've chosen.

* *Bakeware/cookware.* Casserole dishes and pots and pans. Bakeware that is dishwasher-, microwave-, and oven-safe is very practical for the average cook. Standard, nonstick pots, pans, and cookie sheets are fine, but do your research on brands before you make a final decision. Cheaper pots sometimes lose their nonstick surface more quickly. You also want something that heats evenly.

* *Linens.* Towels, sheets, tablecloths, napkins. Choose a color scheme for each room and stick with it! If you're renting, your best bet is to stick with neutral colors for your linens. (You just never know where you're going to end up next—or what color the bathroom walls may be!) Monogramming linens personalizes your choices and gives everything a more formal feel.

* *Canisters.* For coffee, sugar, tea, pasta.

* *Small appliances.* Toaster. Coffeemaker. Sandwich grill. Electric can opener. Toaster oven. Electric griddle. Iron. Blender. Vacuum. Carpet cleaner. It's these little things that make life in the kitchen (and the rest of the house) so much easier, so choose wisely.

* *Décor.* Vases, framed artwork, mirrors, lamps, or whatever will dress up your home and make it feel inviting.

These are really the basics; there are many other things you can add. Again, the most important thing about the registry is to *avoid* filling it with items that will end up sitting in a closet, unused, for the rest of time. And remember, every guest wants to feel as though he or she has given you something you need and will put to good use. A little practicality goes a long way!

Chapter 5
Announcing the Big Event

Once you're engaged, your first instinct might be to play the part of the town crier, announcing your good fortune to acquaintances and mere passersby alike. There are a few common rules of etiquette both for destination brides and in-town brides; however, there are also some slight variations in these rules for each subset of bride. In this chapter, you'll read about who gets to know your good news—and when and how.

5

Who to Tell First

No matter what kind of wedding you're dreaming of, there are certain rules you need to follow when announcing your engagement. First of all, make sure you've made the most important calls before you start spreading the good news all over town. If your mother hears about your engagement by eavesdropping at the grocery store, she'll probably be a bit upset. Of course, if your beau declared his intentions to your parents before he proposed, you don't have to worry about this so much.

Asking for Your Hand

It seems like a tradition whose time has long passed us by, but a lot of men still take the time to ask their best girl's father for her hand in marriage. Although it's hardly necessary in this day and age (chances are pretty good that you'll end up marrying your guy even if your dad disapproves), it's still a nice gesture—and one that might just win over a father who is less than thrilled at the prospect of seeing his little girl walk down the aisle toward a life with another man.

E~ssential

If your boyfriend is up to the task and he wants to have a man-to-man chat with your father before the big proposal, encourage him to do so. It's a good way for your dad to start viewing your boyfriend as a real, honest-to-goodness man, brave enough to ask for your hand. Your dad will probably admire his courage and his sense of tradition. Dad will also start to view you as a woman, and he'll be happy for your good fortune instead of sadly wondering where all the years have gone.

Although this conversation has traditionally been between the two men in a woman's life, there's no reason that your mother should be excluded, especially if she's the one who raised you! It's always thoughtful of your fiancé to want to reach out to your father, but if Dad has always lived 3,000 miles away from you and didn't have all that much to do with your upbringing, it just makes more sense for your fiancé to touch base with the parent(s)-in-residence first. That includes stepparents, too!

Mom and Dad

If your fiancé didn't schedule a meeting with your parents to let them know of his intentions, then you need to let them know about your engagement *very* soon after it happens. When you make the list of people you need to call, your parents should be at the very top of that list, even above your best friend. It's just the right thing to do.

 E~ssential

Maybe you know that your mother is going to react badly to this news because she's just not a very happy person. Call her anyway. She may surprise you. Plus, you'll be letting yourself off the hook, because she won't be able to hold it over your head that you didn't let her know about your engagement.

Now, what if you haven't spoken to your parents in years? Do they still have to rank at the very top of that list? Well, families become estranged for all sorts of reasons, and this book won't even attempt to delve into the most painful family circumstances. However, as long as contacting your parents isn't going to cause you any physical harm, then yes, you should give them a call and let them know that you're getting married.

Getting down to logistics: Ideally, you and your fiancé should tell both sets of parents at roughly the same time (a difference of one day between telling your parents and calling his parents isn't a big deal unless you know they're going to run into each other), and you should *both* tell them the big news. No, you don't need to be on separate phone extensions when you call your parents, but your mom and dad will most likely want to speak to their future son-in-law, so make sure he's available and up to the task.

One Big Happy Family

If you or the groom have children from a previous marriage or relationship, they should be among the first to know about your engagement. Even if your relationship with your fiancé's kids is just barely cordial, they should still know before you start telling everyone else.

There is no doubt that this is a familial make-or-break issue. Letting the kids in on the news before everyone else knows makes them feel important and as though they're in on something really major and special (which they are, after all). On the other hand, if they find out that you've been engaged for a month and you're just now getting around to telling them about it, you can bet that they're going to feel left out. No matter how your fiancé's kids feel about their dad (and no matter whose idea it was to wait to tell them), they're probably going to place a good part of the blame on you.

E~Alert

Even if you know that the kids' reactions are going to be neutral at best (and negative at worst), tell them as soon as possible. This is another one of those things that makes you look like a solid, mature person who's ready to tackle marriage (and mothering, by the way) if you handle it properly—and makes you look like a selfish, immature woman if you handle it incorrectly.

Now, what about the mother of your boyfriend's children? Your fiancé should tell her the news *before* you tell the children. Ideally, she is mature enough to handle the introduction of a stepmother into her kids' lives; if not, keep your cool and say as little as possible. Be kind to those kids no matter what, and do your best to include them in the wedding. In short, be the better person. This may be extremely difficult to do when you're faced with an ex who seems like evil incarnate, but in the long run, mature behavior always pays off. Always.

Your Ex

If you were in a serious relationship in the past—either a marriage or something very close to it—do you owe your ex a call now, even if you don't have any children binding the two of you together? You don't want him to find out about your engagement on the street, but you also don't want to make the assumption that he would want to know. What is the right thing to do in this situation?

Well, if you left things on friendly terms, then by all means, call the guy and just be honest. Let him know that you wanted him to hear this news from you, not from a third party. You can't control his reaction, but if you tell him yourself, you won't have to wonder if he knows or how he found out about your engagement; you also won't have to wonder whether he's upset that you didn't have the courage to call him.

If your split was chock-full of animosity, then no, you do not have to call him now. Doing so would probably only dredge up old feelings on both ends of the phone. Honestly, if you got yourself out of a bad relationship, you deserve to be happy now, and you can't do that if you put yourself in the line of fire. He'll hear it about it sooner or later, and you can deal with it then, if you must. Don't borrow trouble for now.

Telling the World

After you've taken care of the kids and parents, you can start telling everyone you know that you're engaged. But keep in mind that you're probably not going to *invite* everyone you know to your wedding—so don't make promises that you won't be able to keep. Keep the topic of the actual ceremony off-limits for now, especially if you have no idea where you're going to be married or how many guests you'll be able to invite. It's natural and appropriate for you to be bursting at the seams with excitement right now, and really, that's all you need to say: "I'm so happy!"

If anyone asks about specifics of the ceremony that you haven't started planning yet, just be honest: "We're just so excited about the engagement right now. We haven't even started to plan the wedding." This is a perfectly natural and appropriate response.

Is it all right to walk into your office and announce your engagement? Of course; you want to tell your friends, so go ahead and let your coworker pals in on the news. Just don't expect the office to grind to a screeching halt, and don't expect more than a "congratulations" from coworkers whom you don't know well. You don't need to tell everyone in the office, by the way. Word will probably spread once you tell a couple of people.

Engagement Parties

One formal way to announce your engagement is with an engagement party. Traditionally, the bride's family has the option of hosting the first engagement party; after this celebration (or if the bride's family passes on the party altogether), the groom's family can host an event honoring the engaged couple. Engagement parties are usually held relatively soon after the engagement has taken place, and well before any other pre-wedding parties, such as showers, bachelorettes, and the like.

Who's Invited?

The same rule of thumb that goes for all pre-wedding parties also applies here: Only people who will be invited to the wedding should be invited to the engagement party. That means you'd better think long and hard about who you want on that final guest list, because there's no graceful way to back out of it once the parties get rolling. The one exception to extending the guest list to include people who won't be invited to the wedding is if you're having a very intimate destination wedding—just yourself, the groom, and immediate family. In that instance, *everyone* else is excluded from the ceremony, which evens things out. (It's not as though half of your engagement party guests are being invited to the wedding and the other half aren't.) And since gifts are not given at the engagement party, it's an opportunity for friends and family to celebrate without feeling as though they've only been invited so that they would bring a present.

What Kind of Party?

Engagement parties can be formal or informal, large or small. There's no need to send out engraved invitations or hire the best caterer in town, although there's no reason not to do these things, either. It all depends on who's hosting and what you and the groom are most comfortable with.

E--ssential

Since engagement parties are not common in some areas of the country, ask your host to help the guests prepare by including relevant information on the invitations, such as what type of dress is expected (casual, formal, black tie), and a "no gifts" tag line at the bottom of the card. According to traditional wedding etiquette, gifts should not be given at an engagement party.

Sometime during the evening, the parents of the bride and groom may wish to offer a toast to your future happiness. Play the part of the graceful bride, nod, smile, and remember—you and your fiancé *don't* take a drink when the two of you are being toasted! Rather, the two of you should express thanks for the kind words, and share a little kiss.

It's a Date!

Choosing a date for your wedding is a personal thing. For some couples, it comes down to choosing a specific date or time of year—the day they first met, for example, or the season they realized they were in love. For other couples, vacation time determines when they'll be able to squeeze in the nuptials. April through October are hands-down the most popular wedding months. This is probably due to the weather; spring, summer, and fall are just prettier, even in areas where winter doesn't cover everything in ice and snow. Some brides love the idea of a winter wedding, however, and will go to great lengths to make a holiday wedding happen.

When you think about holiday weddings, you might reason that everyone takes vacation around the holidays anyway, so that might be a perfect time to plan a destination wedding. Run down a list of all of the long weekends throughout the year: New Year's. Easter. Memorial Day. Fourth of July. Labor Day. Veterans' Day. Thanksgiving. Christmas. Are you more of an Independence Day bride or a bride who should carry poinsettias?

❁ E~Alert

Keep in mind that most people spend the major holidays with their families. If they have to choose between your wedding and seeing their relatives who are in town for the week, you might lose out. If you are planning to schedule your wedding near a holiday, be sure you give people enough time to plan accordingly. Who knows? They might enjoy going someplace new for Thanksgiving. ❧

There's no perfect date for every single one of your guests. Start by finding a few dates that work well for you and your fiancé in terms of vacation time. Then decide who must absolutely be able to attend your wedding. If your cousin has already booked her wedding during the same month as your first-choice date, then pick another date. Don't make family members choose between the two of you!

Sending Announcements

You've got the spot; you've chosen the date; now you want to send out announcements. Do people usually do this sort of thing, and if so, how? When? And why do people need to know so far in advance? They'll find out when the wedding invitations come, right? Well, when you're asking people to travel a long distance to spend a week with you before your wedding, it's a good idea to give them as much notice as possible.

Save-the-Date Cards

In this day and age, what most often serves as the formal announcement is the save-the-date card, which is sent out at least six months prior to a destination wedding. It gives all the pertinent details, including the names of the bride and groom, the date of the wedding (the exact hour is *not* specified), and the city where the wedding will take place. Basically, the save-the-date card serves as a memo: *This big date is coming up; please mark your calendar and plan on joining us.* There's no correct or incorrect way to word the save-the-date card, but it's usually informal:

Rachel Walls and David Muller
Have planned their wedding for
June 16th, 2008
at the Cozumel Beachfront Hotel
Cozumel, Mexico
Please plan on joining us during the week before the wedding!
Invitation to follow
Travel information enclosed

When a couple sends a save-the-date card for an in-town wedding, they can reasonably wrap it up with a line that reads, "Invitation and travel information to follow." You can't really hold back that kind of information for a destination wedding, though, because your guests need to know how much this trip is going to cost and whether they can take vacation time for your weeklong wedding extravaganza. It's also a good idea to include information about and directions to the rehearsal dinner. Your guests may have no trouble finding your wedding resort in Miami, for example, but may have a terrible time finding a restaurant downtown if they aren't familiar with the area.

E~ssential

To really get people excited about your wedding, include the resort information and a small travel booklet with your save-the-date cards. That way, your guests can get a good feel for your wedding site, and you might just persuade those who are on the fence about the whole trip that yes, they *do* want to come along!

What this all means is that before you send these cards, you *have* to have your wedding arrangements finalized. You not only have to let people know where the wedding will be, and when; you also need to tell them where hotel rooms have been reserved, and which airlines fly into the area. Make things as easy as possible for your guests, and they'll show up in droves.

Make Sure It's Final!

The save-the-date card isn't meant to say, "We'll see if these plans work out and we'll get back to you—if not Mexico, then maybe Miami!" This is a big no-no! Once people get these cards announcing the date, they'll start freeing up their time *and* money for your wedding. If you cancel for any reason other than a broken engagement, you're going to get some *very* nasty phone calls from people who've lost deposits and taken time off from work when they otherwise wouldn't have.

Naturally, you won't be able to control every little detail of your wedding, and some plans may change or fall through. Even so, careful planning before you send your announcements will help prevent problems as the big day approaches. Be considerate of your guests, and they'll be happy to come along on your wedding trip.

Save Some Money

Must you order save-the-date cards from a stationery shop? No way. In this day and age of digital photography and online card services, even the least technologically proficient couples can make their own announcements. All you need is a nice picture of the two of you taken with a digital camera. First, download that picture onto your computer. Now find an online picture-sharing service, such as Smugmug (*www.smugmug.com*) or Shutterfly (*www.shutterfly.com*), and browse through the card-making options. You can personalize your cards from beginning to end and preview them before you finalize your order. Quick, easy, and cheap.

Alternatively, you can create little save-the-date gifts for your guests—perhaps mugs, puzzles, or magnets.

Newspaper Announcements

Newspaper announcements are another notion many people overlook these days, but they're a nice tradition that family, friends, and neighbors who still read the local paper might really appreciate. The newspaper clipping will also make a nice addition to your wedding scrapbook. Additionally, since many newspapers now have Web site counterparts, you might be able to get your announcement on the Internet as well as in print. This will make it easy for you to e-mail the link to interested parties.

Newspaper announcements are generally a paragraph or two in length and include some key details about the bride and groom. Here's a sample:

Mr. and Mrs. Jason Hill announce the engagement of their daughter, Jennifer, to Robert Andrews, son of Mr. and Mrs. John Andrews. The future bride received her B.A. in journalism from Brown University and now does freelance writing for various publications. Her fiancé is pursuing his master's degree in engineering from Villanova University. The couple is planning a July wedding in Mazatlan, Mexico.

Some people wonder if they should embellish an announcement to make their lives sound more exciting or paint themselves as more "successful" than they actually are. This is a mistake. Don't lie about your life just because the information is going in the newspaper! It's silly to stretch the truth even just a little in the hope that your arch-nemesis will read the announcement and say, "Wow, I guess she's really more important than I ever knew." This probably won't happen, and it doesn't matter anyway. Your friends will read the fake announcement and wonder why you lied, and people who aren't your friends will know it isn't true anyway and will not be impressed, no matter what your announcement says.

Be proud of who you are, what you've accomplished, and the man you're going to marry! Chances are your family and friends are tremendously proud of you already. The confidence it takes to be honest about your life is an indication that you are truly ready to get married.

Chapter 6
The Guest List

Maybe you've always dreamed of having a wedding where everyone you've ever known shows up to wish you well. Or maybe you're more of a quiet, please-don't-gawk-at-me type of bride. Once you have that engagement ring on your finger, you're going to have to decide whether you want the big wedding or a smaller affair, and that decision alone can be one of the biggest factors in deciding how much you're going to end up spending on the wedding.

Proceed with Caution

One misconception is that destination weddings are small events. While that certainly may hold true for some couples, other brides and grooms invite all of the people they would have invited to an in-town wedding. Why not, they ask? If people have to travel to the wedding anyway, and the bride and groom have to pay for the food and drink no matter where the wedding takes place, why would they cut people from the list?

Decisions, Decisions

There are no rules on the size of a destination wedding, only limits on what may be possible at any given location. So if you decide that you *do* want 150 guests to join you for a week in Florida, all you have to do is work out the logistics (which is obviously easier said than done). But if you only want to include immediate family members, planning a destination wedding is the perfect way to keep the wedding small and yet incredibly special—probably more so than planning a tiny event back home.

Zip It Till You Know Your Numbers

Before you start telling everyone that you're having a great tropical wedding and you hope they have some vacation time coming up so they can join the fun, you have to know what kind of destination wedding you can comfortably afford. Although you are not responsible for paying your guests' travel and lodging expenses, you will pay for the reception—and some locations are much pricier than others. Also, some can only accommodate a small number of guests. Do your homework before verbally implying to anyone that they're going to make the cut.

If you find a place (such as a cruise ship or a large resort) that can handle every family member and friend that you and your fiancé can think of, there's no reason to keep them off the list, assuming that you want a large wedding.

Don't Invite Everyone

The etiquette surrounding invitations to destination weddings doesn't vary all that much from in-town weddings, with one exception: Don't invite mere acquaintances who wouldn't need to travel to your wedding if you were having it in town. If you live in Topeka and you're getting married in Paris, for example, chances are that coworkers you know only casually are not going to make the trip overseas, and may interpret the invitation to join you atop the Eiffel Tower as nothing more than an attempt to squeeze gifts out of them.

Not inviting those people may put you in a spot, especially if you would have invited them to an in-town reception. Don't lose sleep. First of all, people are fairly understanding about destination weddings—the general assumption (true or not) is that only close friends and family members will be invited. And most couples can safely assume that the majority of those who accept the invitations *will* be close friends and family.

E~ssential

Coworkers tend to be an understanding lot where invitations are concerned. Most will understand that you can't invite the entire office. However, if your final guest list includes everyone *except* two or three colleagues, issue them their own invitations too. It's just the classy thing to do.

There's always a chance that if you invite your whole office, several of them will show. However, it's just as easy—and acceptable—for you to not invite any of them. They are much less likely to be offended at not being included in a destination wedding than at not being invited to a reception down the street. And anyway, you have a perfect excuse for leaving them off the list: Your entire office can't be on vacation at one time, now can they?

Common Guest List Concerns

A generation or two ago, coming up with the family portion of the guest list was easy enough (except for when it came to inviting a nasty aunt or a drunken cousin, and even then, the consensus was for the bride to invite them and ignore their antics as much as possible). Nowadays, it's not uncommon for brides and grooms to struggle with their parents' remarriages, resulting in family tensions that lead to the inevitable question, "Should I invite my step-so-and-so to my wedding?"

Mom and Dad, Behave Yourselves!

When your divorced parents can't be in the same room without one of them hurling insults at the other, how can you be expected to invite both of them to an intimate island wedding? Does one of them need to stay home? And if so, which one?

Here's the deal: Your parents are adults, no matter how they behave in your presence. In the interest of what's best for you, their child, they should be able to bury the hatchet—or at least settle for a temporary indifference toward one another—during your wedding trip. If you know that your mom is more prone to outbursts than your dad is, for example, speak to her before the wedding and explain how much it will hurt you if your marriage week should involve horrible bickering. If she can't promise to behave (or you know she won't), then it's up to you to decide whether you want to include her in the ceremony. You can't parent your parent, after all, and definitely not when your parent should be babying you (that is, during the days leading up to your wedding).

Stepparents should be invited, no matter how you feel about them. It would be completely unacceptable for you to tell your dad that his wife is not invited to an in-town wedding; a destination wedding is no different. You would only put your dad in an awkward spot, forcing him to choose between you and his wife. (Guess what? His wife might say that you're being immature, and she'd be right. That doesn't make you look good.)

Don't try to say that the resort can only handle six wedding guests, and your stepmom just didn't make the cut. If that's truly the case, find a resort that can accommodate a few more people. When all's said and done, and you don't have to hear for the next fifty years that you left someone out of your wedding, you'll be glad you included her. Who knows? A week on a cruise ship might be just the thing that'll bring the two of you together.

E~Question

Why should I assume the role of referee between my divorced parents? They're adults!

It's in your best interest to let each parent know how their sparring hurts you and how upset you'll be if any bad blood trickles into your wedding ceremony. They'll take your words to heart simply because this is your wedding, and no parent wants to be responsible for ruining what should be the happiest day of his or her child's life.

Step Right Up, Stepsibling

What about stepsiblings? Should they be included in an intimate gathering? If you're very close to your stepbrothers and stepsisters, you probably don't need to ask this question. If you barely know them or you've never particularly cared for them, you don't need to invite them to a small destination wedding. Leaving them out of a larger gathering, though, is something of a slap in the face, so don't do it unless you're prepared to reap what you've sown. It's always better to err on the side of caution, particularly where weddings and family members are concerned. If it's within your means and you're inviting everyone you know, send your stepsister an invitation, too. Chances are, if the two of you really don't click, she won't come—but you'll still look like a decent person, as opposed to how you may be judged if you blatantly exclude her.

Showers, Engagement Parties, and Bachelorettes

Your final wedding guest list affects some other guest lists, too. During your engagement, you may be faced with providing someone (your mom or your maid of honor) with a list of people to invite to a shower or a bachelorette. Someone might also decide to throw an engagement party for you. Whose names should you include, and why?

Showers

The old standby rule about showers applies to the destination bride as well: Only invite people who are also going to be invited to the wedding. It's just not polite to invite someone to celebrate your upcoming nuptials, accept a gift from them, make them sit through the opening and flaunting of your loot and then not invite them to the wedding.

Does this rule mean that if you're planning a very small (immediate family only) destination wedding, you are completely out of luck as far as the shower goes? Yes and no. Your friends and/or extended family members may decide to fete you anyway, despite the fact that you're not including them in the wedding. Accept this party graciously, because it is above and beyond what they need to do for you. (What do they need to do for you? Nothing, really, in light of the fact that they haven't been invited to the wedding.)

If you're planning a large destination wedding, you can go ahead and invite anyone on your wedding guest list to the shower.

Engagement Parties

The bride's parents traditionally have the option of hosting the first engagement party; if they have no interest in doing so, the option passes to the groom's family. You and your fiancé are not supposed to host an engagement party for yourselves, but some couples don't care much for tradition and they host a shindig celebrating their betrothal anyway.

Engagement parties used to be kept to an intimate circle of guests, mostly members of the two families. Nowadays, these parties are sometimes very large affairs. It's truly a matter of preference—and the size of the wedding.

E~Fact

Gifts are not traditionally given at engagement parties, so save the registry cards for your shower invitations. If some guests do bring gifts, accept them graciously and open them either in an out-of-the-way area (away from guests who didn't bring gifts) or after the party. And don't forget to write a nice thank-you note for each one!

Anyone who receives an invitation to the engagement party should make the final cut of the wedding guest list. Again, it's just in bad taste to invite someone to celebrate *this* part of your relationship and not give them the option to attend the biggest celebration.

Bachelorettes

Bachelorettes are usually given by the bride's closest friends, so the guest list will most likely include women you know and love. One caveat here: If it's going to get wild, limit the list to women you know very well and are *completely* comfortable with. Don't invite your boss, for example, as a way of improving your relationship with her. She may freak out when she sees a male stripper dressed as Tarzan—or *you* might freak when she pretends to be Jane. In either case, chances are the two of you will never view your professional relationship in the same way, so it's best she stay at home.

A good rule of thumb for the bachelorette, no matter what the size of your wedding guest list, is this: Don't make this a get-to-know-you night. In other words, if you haven't been out socially with a person before, don't bring her along on the bachelorette evening. There are just too many volatile factors involved. For example, if the groom's sister is uptight and you and your friends love to swing from the chandeliers, do everything in your power to avoid inviting her. Your reputation in the groom's family may take a sudden nosedive if she attends.

Must everyone at the bachelorette be invited to your destination wedding? If it's a big wedding, yes. But again, if you're only inviting five people to witness the ceremony, your friends are likely to be very understanding—and unwilling to let this opportunity for a night on the town pass them by.

Destination Wedding Invitations

If you're having a very intimate ceremony that will include only immediate family members, you might be tempted to dispense with the invitations, reasoning that your mom doesn't need a reminder to show up in Honolulu on November 12 for your wedding. Fair enough. Just keep in mind that wedding invitations are more than the paper they're printed on—they become part of the whole feel of the wedding, something that marks this event as incredibly significant, and something that will become part of your prized wedding mementos.

How Destination Invites Differ

An invitation to a destination wedding offers the unique opportunity to reflect the theme of the wedding. "What theme?" you ask. "We aren't having a *theme*!" Yes, you are, even if you don't know it. The beach is a theme. A castle is a theme. The mountains are a theme. Las Vegas is a theme. Stationery companies have embraced destination weddings, so it should be easy to find an invitation that reflects your chosen location. You also should be able to find just about any type of card stock online or at your local printing shop.

Wording an invitation for a destination wedding is a breeze. Parents' names may take up several lines on an invitation to an in-town wedding, but most often only the bride's and groom's names will appear on the destination invitation.

For example:

Emma Lynn Brown
and
Derek Lee Smith
will exchange vows
on the beach
at the Honolulu Sheraton
Honolulu, Hawaii
on November twelfth, two thousand seven
at four o'clock in the afternoon
We invite you to join us
as we begin our lives together
as man and wife

Note that the site of the wedding can also be somewhat abbreviated if it is a major local landmark. If you've chosen a less popular spot, make sure that you include the street address, like so:

Emma Lynn Brown
and
Derek Lee Smith
will join in holy matrimony
on August twelfth, two thousand seven
at five o'clock in the evening
at Silver Leaf Winery
45 Kelleher Road
Sonoma, California

Invitations that clearly lean toward being formal and traditional spell out every single word—"street," "road," time of day (no "A.M." or "P.M."), and the date. The one area that is starting to fall into a gray area is the actual street address. The old rule of thumb was to spell out the number. However, more and more, formal-looking invitations will arrive with numerals in the street address. (It's really not that big a deal, and nothing that anyone will take you to task for.) Using the other common abbreviations, though, just doesn't look right on a formal card. Zip codes are never used on the invitation itself.

For a cruise ship wedding, give the name of the boat and its home port:

Emma Lynn Brown
and
Derek Lee Smith
will become man and wife
aboard the Crystal Wave
Miami, Florida
on August twelfth, two thousand seven

Offering Information

How will your guests know, for example, whether the cruise mentioned in the previous invitation lasts for one hour or five days? You can tack this information onto the invitation itself, but it would be infinitely more helpful to precede the invitation with a mailer that explains travel logistics. As mentioned in Chapter 5, this information really should be included with your save-the-date cards, which ideally should be mailed six months prior to your destination wedding so that your guests will have plenty of time to negotiate vacation time from work and find the best airline rates.

Assume that your guests know nothing about the place where your wedding will be held. Your goal is to let them in on any information that will sway them into accepting your invitation *and* make their trip as much fun (or as relaxing) as possible once they arrive. In order to do this, of course, you have to educate yourself. Embrace your role of travel director! You might be surprised at how much interesting (and little-known) information about the area you can come up with, which will only serve to make *your* trip more memorable as well.

 E~ssential

Your guests will always remember your wedding; just make sure it's because they had a great time, and not because they spent the week trying to find you! Provide guests with easy-to-read maps of the airport, the resort, and the surrounding areas. Create a wedding-week brochure listing local events and sights worth seeing. And remember, it's better to include too much info rather than too little! ♪

Ordering Invitations Versus Getting Crafty

There are various options when it comes to invitations. Many people choose to have them professionally done to avoid spending time and energy on this chore. Of course, whenever you have someone else do something for you, you end up spending money instead of time and energy. These days, with all the new computer and photography technology, lots of couples are choosing the do-it-yourself option. Your decision is based entirely on preference. Do you like the idea of sitting down for an afternoon of invitation preparation, or would you rather leave it to the professionals?

Do It Yourself

If you're having a small destination ceremony and you're wondering why in the world you should spend money on invitations, there's good news for you: With a little computer skill and some creativity, you can make close to 100 of your own overlay invitations (an overlay is a picture printed on vellum laid on top of a printed invitation) for less than $100.

Here's what you'll need:

- ✳ Card stock
- ✳ Vellum
- ✳ Roll of thin ribbon
- ✳ Scissors
- ✳ Hole punch
- ✳ Computer and printer

Creating the invitations requires nothing more than time and patience for trial and error. Give yourself more than an hour to figure out how to set your computer's picture-printing options and to experiment with different elements. You'll be looking for an online picture, for example, and you'll want to find one that doesn't block the text of your invitation.

✿ E~Alert

Most veteran crafters advise that you find decent, formal envelopes first and then size your homemade invitations to fit inside the envelopes. Imagine printing up odd-sized invitations and then having no way to mail them, or having to place your lovely invitations inside manila envelopes. ✍

Here's how to make your own invitations:

1. Decide on the wording of your invitations and type it up on your computer, using whichever font suits you best.
2. Do an Internet image search of the area you're headed to. Test the print quality of the picture with a regular sheet of paper.
3. When you've found a picture that will print well (it's not blurry or cut off at the edges), set your computer to print the correct size and number per page. This may take some trial and error, so practice with plain paper until you've got it right.

4. Insert the vellum into the printer and print your pictures.
5. Insert your card stock into the printer, and print the word portion of your invitation.
6. Lay vellum on top of the cardstock and trim edges as necessary with scissors or a paper cutter.
7. Using the hole punch, make two centered holes through both sheets of paper. Insert ribbon through the back of the holes and tie the papers together.

Voilà! Done, and on the cheap. This is *really* easy stuff as long as your computer is up to the task. If you don't have picture-printing software installed on your computer, now's the time to do it. Also, your invitations will work out best if you have a decent printer.

No Time for Crafts?

All right, so you don't want to be burdened with actually creating your own invitations. When ordering from a local printer, remember: An educated bride is far less likely to spend too much money on invitations. Before you walk into a print shop, here's what you should know:

Engraving is the most expensive form of printing invitations. The paper is "stamped" from the back by metal plates the printer creates, which raises the letters up above the surface of the paper as they're printed. Beautiful, yes, but pricey enough that most brides of average means actually laugh (or cry) when they're given the estimate.

Thermography is a form of printing that mimics engraving, but at about half the price. Chances are you've seen this type of printing on wedding invitations, as it's the most common form of printing done on mass-produced invites.

Calligraphy is a nice touch if you can swing it financially—but hiring someone to pen all those invitations by hand is going to be *mucho* expensive, and calligraphy is not the type of thing that an amateur (your maid of honor, for example) should attempt. However, as with most things these days, calligraphy can be faked with some decent computer software. Ask whether the printer offers this option.

Online Ordering

If you know all about paper quality, ordering invitations online can be very easy and inexpensive. But before you commit yourself to a couple of hundred invitations from an online retailer, invest a few hours doing research on paper weights, on the company you're considering, and on whether these invitations are standard-size or if they're going to cost you more than you're planning to spend for stamps.

No matter where you're getting your invitations, *always, always, always* check the envelope size against what the U.S. Postal Service considers "standard." Oddly shaped envelopes may cost more per letter to mail, even if they aren't over the weight limit. A quick check with your friendly post office is all it takes to prevent the major headache of having all of your invitations returned to you for insufficient postage.

Online retailers usually make the ordering process fairly painless. Most have sample wording, and many have a seemingly endless array of borders and fonts. If possible, get references from friends or friends-of-friends who have used an online stationer.

Order early, and order extras! (Why pay for a rush job two months before your wedding when you can order those invitations four months ahead of time?) Make sure that you have enough extras on hand so that if you make a mistake in addressing the invitations or you remember at the last minute that you haven't invited someone, you won't have to order another, smaller batch, which will be markedly more expensive per card than the initial, larger (bulk) order of invitations.

Invitation Details

Are destination weddings perceived to be so informal that you can reasonably throw caution to the wind and address your invitations any way you want? The jury is still out on this matter; however, since it never hurts to know which rules you're breaking, read on to learn how invitations are traditionally addressed and assembled inside the envelope.

Envelopes

Like the invitations themselves, the envelopes you choose can range from simple, with plain, high-quality paper, to fancy, with foil-laminated inner flaps or flaps with a colorful design. Beautifully packaged invitations are a nice touch, but as you might expect, the more you add to the envelope, the greater the cost.

If it's possible, save some money on the envelopes and put it toward the invitations themselves. Before you break the budget, keep in mind that the envelope is a throwaway item. Ask yourself if it really makes sense to spend extra on something most people rip to shreds and then toss in the garbage can.

E~ssential

Plan to have the return address preprinted on the outer envelope and on the response cards. Assuming that you and/or your groom are handling the details, have your home address printed on these cards. If your mom is the one doing the organizing, have them sent to her.

Reception and Response Cards

If the reception is at a different location than the ceremony, you will need to include these cards in your invitations. Remember to include the full address of the reception site and a map with written instructions included. Some people cannot read a map to save their lives, so pointing out landmarks along the way never hurts.

You'll also need to include response cards, which the guests send back to you so that you know who is going to show and who isn't.

The favor of your reply is requested
by the twenty-second of July

M_____

_____ *will attend*

Most resorts and hotels will only hold rooms until a certain date. Don't make your response date later than the reservation cut-off date.

✿ E~ssential

You need to include an envelope with a first-class postage stamp (provided by you) for the response cards, so keep these postage costs in mind when you're tallying up your wedding expenses. Here's another helpful fact: Response postcards are cheaper than the traditional response cards. For starters, their postage is cheaper, and you won't need to order envelopes for them. ✍

Addressing Envelopes

This is a huge chore—especially for a large wedding. Don't try to address and assemble two hundred invitations in one sitting all by yourself. It will quickly become one of those wedding memories you would rather forget. Corral a bridesmaid or two (preferably those with the nicest handwriting), uncork some wine, and get to work.

To address your invitations, you will need your box of invitations (obviously), several pens (preferably black ink, but blue will do—do not use red, pink, green, metallic, or any other color or type of ink), stamps, a list of your guests' addresses, and perhaps a couple of small sponges to help you seal all of those envelopes.

Although it's very easy to use the computer to address envelopes, resist the urge to take this shortcut if your invitations are formal. You've invested a lot of money in those invitations so far; complete the job the right way.

When you're writing the names of your friends and loved ones on the envelopes, it's most formal to spell everything out. (*Mr.* and *Mrs.* can be abbreviated, but that's about it.) Street names should take the long form (*Avenue* instead of *Ave.*, for instance), and formal names (Michael) trump nicknames (Mike).

And Guest?

Traditional wedding etiquette frowns upon using the term *and guest* on the inner envelope. In reality, brides do it all the time, and it's not such a bad thing to do. Here's why: The old way of thinking demands that a bride who is considerate enough to allow a single guest to bring a stranger to her wedding must also be resourceful enough to track down that stranger's name and address and mail that person a separate invitation. (This way of doing things dates back to the time when engaged women had very little else to do other than address their wedding invitations.)

Assembly Line

How on earth are you supposed to put formal invitations together? You opened the box to find several different cards, envelopes, and tissue paper. Before you start throwing things in the trash, thinking you don't need them, see if these steps don't just do the trick:

1. Place the response card face-up under the flap of the response card envelope.
2. Place a piece of tissue paper over the lettering on the invitation to prevent smudges.
3. Put any enclosures (reception cards, maps, directions, and so on) inside the invitation. The response card goes in here, too.
4. Place the invitation into the inner envelope with the lettering facing the back flap. *Don't seal* the inner envelope.

5. Put the inner envelope inside the outer envelope; again, the writing on the inner envelope should face the flap of the outer envelope.
6. Seal the outer envelope. Make sure the envelope is properly addressed and contains your return address.

Seal it, stamp it, and cross the addressee off your master list. Complete and mail all of your invitations in one batch.

 **E~Alert**

In addition to preparing invitations, you'll need to have thank-you cards printed and ready to go upon your return from your trip. It actually makes a lot of sense to take care of these at the same time that you order your invitations, since you'll want to start sending your thank-yous out soon after the wedding.

Ceremony and Pew Cards

In addition to standard invitations, many brides find that they need more from their printer. Ceremony cards are used when a wedding is being held in a public building—such as an art gallery or a historical home where tours are regularly passing through. These cards are shown to a person who works at the site and is assigned to differentiate between patrons of the building and wedding guests. Pew cards are reserved for your cream-of-the-crop guests. They flash their little cards to the ushers and are granted access to the best seats during the ceremony.

Programs

Many weddings include a little program that either gives detailed information about the ceremony, or tells something about the main players (who *are* these bridesmaids?), or both. You can actually print these at home on your computer. Craft stores sell the card stock, program covers, and ribbon that you'll need to assemble a beautiful guide to your special day.

Chapter 7
Choosing Your Bridal Party

When it comes down to giving people the nod to be included in your wedding as bridesmaids and groomsmen, you have to ask yourself two significant questions. First, if you're considering someone other than a family member, is this person someone you want to know (or want to remember knowing) for the rest of your life? And second, will this person live up to his or her duties or only make your life more stressful by having a role in your ceremony? This chapter attempts to lead you toward the good candidates and steer you away from the less-than-worthy.

Narrowing Down the List

Before tapping anyone for bridesmaid or groomsman duty, you and your fiancé must first decide on the size of your wedding. Obviously, if the two of you are leaning toward having a tiny ceremony with fewer than ten guests, you aren't going to have six attendants each. If you're on the fence about the size of your ceremony, don't extend the invitation to prospective attendants until you're 100 percent sure that you won't have to rescind it.

✿ E~Alert

Base your bridal party decisions on what you want, not what someone else wants. If your mother is upset because you aren't going to ask all four of your sisters to be in the wedding party, that's unfortunate for your mother. At the same time, don't exclude a family member just because you happen to be having a spat at that moment. If the person is important to you, chances are you'll both get over it eventually. In fact, asking the person to be in your wedding party might be a great way to clear the air and move on.

If you're having a large wedding and you aren't against having a big bridal party, it's easy to include your sisters, your best friends, and your fiancé's family in the bridesmaid lineup. It's much tougher to eliminate these same people from a smaller bridal party. Despite the fact that everyone should be adult enough to respect your decision and not make you feel guilty about having to streamline the parade of maids and ushers, this is where you may learn the hard truth about planning a wedding, which is this: Although weddings should only bring out the best in people, the opposite often holds true.

Somehow, some way, some people feel as though you're doing—or not doing—certain things to hurt their feelings. (Never mind the fact that you're agonizing over your choices in an attempt to keep everyone happy.)

Family or Friends?

In the event that you're having a small ceremony with just one or two attendants on each side, choose people who are very close to you. This probably goes without saying, but if you're torn between choosing your best friend and your fiancé's sister (whom you barely know), go with the best friend.

✿ E~Fact

You can always include the family and friends in a small ceremony in other ways aside from making them attendants, such as asking them to do a reading or bring gifts to the altar when required in a religious ceremony. This should appease anyone (read: parents of the bride and groom) who are tempted to be outraged by your choice of bridesmaid(s). ✿

Why would you choose a lifelong friend over a future relative? You're supposed to be able to lean on your attendants for all of your wedding-related emergencies. You know that your best friend will probably help you out regardless of whether you've assigned her to official attendant duty, but it's just silly to pass over her and make your future sister-in-law into some sort of bridesmaid figurehead if you know you're going to be uncomfortable asking her for favor after favor. Ask her to bring up the gifts or to do a reading during the ceremony instead.

Come One, Come All!

A large bridal party can include close friends and family members from both sides. Before you start asking anyone and everyone to stand up for your ceremony, though, realize that in addition to asking these men and women to help you through the planning of the wedding, you're also asking them to spend quite a bit of money on wedding attire (possibly), travel, and lodging. If you know that a certain someone on the list is going to do nothing but gripe about having to fly down to Cancun for your wedding, then leave him or her off your list.

Be aware that bridal parties can mushroom out of control. You ask this friend, so you have to ask that one. You can't ask your favorite cousin without also including her sister, even though you were never that close to her. It may be helpful for you, especially if you have a wide circle of family and friends, to set a limit to the number of attendants in the bridal party before you start asking; otherwise you may end up with fifteen bridesmaids and twenty-seven groomsmen (when your fiancé has a hard time choosing among his fraternity brothers).

You *do not* have to include friends and family members by default in your bridal party. This isn't some sort of barbecue, where you might feel the same pressure (you can't invite this person without also inviting his neighbor). It's also not some sort of popularity contest. Choose only the people who are most special to you and your fiancé, and those who will be helpful to you in the planning process.

❁ E~ssential

Your attendants are supposed to be people you can reasonably count on to uphold their duties to support and occasionally help you and the groom throughout the wedding planning. Don't choose acquaintances with the hope that this will bring you closer together. If you and/or your groom aren't close to prospective attendants *right now*, scratch them off the list. ❧

Every person in your bridal party should fall into one of two categories: Loved One and/or Little Helper. Ideally, they should fall into both, but in the case of a large bridal party, it's completely understandable that you'd include your groom's sister in your party of ten bridesmaids even if she isn't going to be particularly helpful to you. She's special to your future husband, after all, and excluding her from such a large gaggle of maids would be hurtful.

Attendant Duties

Traditionally, bridesmaids are held responsible for hosting the bride's wedding shower and helping her with her pre-wedding errand running and other tasks. You can call on your bridesmaids to help you address those wedding invitations, for example, or to come dress shopping with you. In the hours (or days, in the case of a weeklong destination wedding) before the ceremony, the bridesmaids help the bride with last-minute preparations for her big day.

E~Alert

Bridesmaids are expected to be pleasant enough toward the bride during the wedding season. The bride, in turn, promises not to treat the bridesmaids as though they are her actual property. If you are kind and considerate of your attendants, they should return the favor.

Generally speaking, the maid of honor and best man should be reliable enough for you to call on them for help with just about anything, so choose these two wisely. The maid (or matron, if she is married) of honor has special duties. She is expected to sign the marriage certificate as a witness and is held responsible for keeping the bride looking her loveliest during the ceremony. In fact, she should be prepared to keep the bride's dress looking picture-perfect the whole day through. The maid or matron of honor also is sometimes asked to hold the groom's ring until the officiant asks for it during the ceremony, though some couples expect their best man to hang on to both rings.

The groomsmen have their own set of duties. They are supposed to help the groom with his own set of pre-wedding tasks and errands (which, let's be honest, are not usually quite as extensive as those of the bride). Usually, they host the groom's bachelor party and show guests to their seats during the ceremony and also tend to any last-minute pre-wedding tasks that aren't otherwise covered (if the groom realizes on the morning of the wedding that he has forgotten to pack his tie, for instance, a groomsman or two can promptly be dispatched to rectify the situation). They are expected to be charming under any circumstances on the day of the wedding.

Bridesmaids and groomsmen agree to be in the wedding party acknowledging that it is almost always an expensive prospect, destination wedding or not. If your friends are of limited means, do your part to keep their costs down where possible. For example, if the resort you've chosen is on the pricey side, try to keep the cost of the bridesmaids' dresses low.

E~ssential

Be up front about your attendants' financial duties from the moment you ask them to be in the bridal party. This includes wardrobe, airline tickets, hotel costs—everything. If you have no intention of picking up the airline tab for everyone, say so. You don't want a simple misunderstanding to end up as a friendship-breaker six months from now.

If you're planning to have a small wedding party and you're having a terrible time choosing among friends and siblings, there may be a way for you to include everyone. As long as you're having a regular ceremony (as opposed to a short tying-of-the-knot by a justice of the peace), you have plenty of jobs to hand out, such as:

* Readings
* Presentation of gifts (in a religious ceremony)
* Handing out programs prior to the ceremony
* Distributing bubbles, birdseed, or flowers to be showered upon you after the ceremony

When assigning these duties, consider who's most likely to actually show up and who might bail on you at the last minute. Also, don't ask a friend to do anything too time-consuming, like being responsible for taking all of your wedding photos. For one thing, that's a big favor to ask of a guest (and you want everyone to have a great time at your wedding). For another, what if the pictures turn out horribly? You don't want to lay that kind of responsibility on a friend.

Little Ones

Flower girls and ring bearers. Chances are you're either set on having them at your wedding or you're opposed to the idea, depending on what kind of performances you've seen by children in these roles in the past.

Obviously, before you decide to include children in your ceremony, you have to consider whether your chosen wedding site is kid-friendly: Most cruise ships are, while resorts vary. Also, if you're asking a friend or relative's child to be in the wedding party, remember that this means added expenses for the parents of the child (who may not have brought their tyke on this trip otherwise). It might be nice for you to pay for the flower girl's dress or the ring bearer's suit as a way of cutting their costs.

E~Question

What do children attendants do?

Traditionally, the ring bearer walks down the aisle after the last bridesmaid, but before the flower girl. The ring bearer holds a pillow with rings tied to it. Most couples opt for decorative rings, as they don't fully trust this little kid (cute as he is) not to lose their wedding bands.

Traditionally, the bridesmaids walk down the aisle first, one by one; they're followed by the maid of honor, the ring bearer, the flower girl and (last but hardly least), the bride. However, you can have your littlest attendants walk down the aisle together or before the maid of honor. Just make sure you've made arrangements for very young attendants to be seated with a caregiver *who isn't part of the wedding party* during the ceremony. If the maid of honor is also the mother of your ring bearer and he's having a tantrum during your vows, you don't want her MIA when the time comes for someone to fix your crooked veil! Plan for someone else to take him for a walk and let your honor attendant do her duties.

Parents Are Part of the Party, Too

Mother of the bride. Father of the bride. Mother of the groom. Father of the groom. These are all official titles of those other members of the wedding party, and whether you're planning a big wedding or an intimate ceremony, you need to know the traditional roles of parents during the wedding season.

Your Mom and Dad

The mother of the bride has traditionally been the brains behind the wedding production. If you're very close to your mother and she's very excited about helping you to plan a wedding, this should be one of the most enjoyable times in your life. Her duties may include:

* Helping you make calls to prospective wedding sites and vendors
* Coming along on the wedding-dress shopping excursion
* Keeping your siblings, attendants, and other relatives in check
* Possibly helping the bridesmaids plan a shower
* Helping with the guest list
* Assisting you with your dress and veil on your wedding day
* Seeing that everything goes as planned during the reception

The mother of the bride used to plan the wedding while the bride sat back, gazing at her engagement ring and dreaming about married life. Of course, the bride's parents also paid for almost the entire wedding back in those days, so the bride was pretty much at her mom's mercy when it came to picking a caterer and a florist. Because today's average bride pays for a large portion of her own wedding, the mother of the bride has (in most cases) been relegated to "helper" status.

Even if you can handle all the details, though, you'll need Mom now and then for some support. That's really the main job of the mother of the bride these days. She should be supportive and ready to jump in and help at a moment's notice. (Really, who else can fill that job description?)

Make sure that you're aware of the changes that have taken place in wedding planning since your mom walked down the aisle. She may have visions of the two of you working side-by-side, choosing the appetizers for the reception, while all you plan to do is hand everything over to your wedding site coordinator. Try to find *something* for your mom to do if she's going to be heartbroken otherwise.

E~Fact

The mother of the bride is traditionally the last person seated by an usher before the wedding ceremony begins. Since she is such an important person at the wedding, and an official member of the wedding party, her dress should complement the bridesmaids' dresses in style and color.

The father of the bride used to simply sign the check and show up at the wedding looking dapper in his tuxedo. Nowadays, that's still about all you really expect of him; in fact he may no longer even be the one signing the check. He'll walk you down the aisle if you choose, he'll dance at the reception, and he'll impress your future in-laws with his wit.

The main duty of the father of the bride: Be charming. Mingle. Talk to people. He should be willing and able to show the guests where you got your sparkling personality.

Your Future In-Laws

The mother of the groom and father of the groom used to get off easily when it came time to plan the wedding. They would contribute names to the guest list, show up for the wedding, and have a great time at the reception. Since the bride's parents usually don't finance the entire wedding nowadays, the groom's family—and their wishes—are more likely to be included in the wedding. Although this new financial setup may not be great news for anyone except the bride's parents, it does make for a more complete wedding picture, one in which both families feel comfortable. No one is anyone else's guest; everyone has contributed something.

Stepparents

How do you include your stepmother in the wedding without making your own mom crazy? Very carefully.

Unfortunately, parents don't always behave as the adults we know (or suspect) they are. Though it's fair to say that the factors behind a bitter divorce are not something that anyone except the two ex-spouses can completely comprehend, it's also fair to have a minimum expectation of conduct from your parents on your wedding day. That includes a no-tantrum rule where parents and stepparents are concerned.

E~ssential

Though one shouldn't overuse the line, "I'm the bride and what I say goes," if there's any situation that merits its use, dealing with the remnants of your parents' divorce (and their potential effect on your wedding) is it. As an adult who's preparing to enter into her own marriage, you can't be put in the middle of your parents' defunct relationship—or their new ones, for that matter. ᶘᴥ

Now, remember that a wedding is a very emotional time for parents of the bride and groom. Right now, your mom and dad are wondering how it's possible that you're old enough to be getting married. They're probably also thinking about how their own marriage didn't work out so well, so they're already walking an emotional high wire. If your dad has a major issue with your stepfather and you're planning to include both of them in the ceremony, give your dad plenty of time to get used to the idea—and don't expect miracles (like the two of them standing peacefully side-by-side throughout the entire ceremony).

In the end, it's your decision to include whomever you want in the wedding party. However, you also have to learn to prioritize and how to say no. Let's say your mom and stepmom just don't get along. You like your stepmom well enough, but honestly, you could take her or leave her. Your dad is insisting that your stepmom be included in all of the traditional mother of the bride activities, such as shopping for your wedding dress. He says it'll bring the two of you closer, and it'll make him happy, too. Since you're only buying one dress and you can't go shopping with both of these women at once, *and* you can't shop for a dress forever (and you'd rather spend the time with your mom, anyway), speak up and say so. If your stepmom really wants to get to know you better, suggest that you meet for a leisurely lunch sometime during the pre-wedding months.

Gifting the Wedding Party

It's not enough to simply include people in your wedding party; you also have to thank them for their service. When shopping for gifts for your wedding party, consider a memento of the occasion—something useful that they'll have forever. Whenever they use this item, they can say, "I got this from Jane and Tom for being in their wedding. What a great gift this was!" You'll seem wise beyond your years.

For the Bridesmaids

Think about what your bridesmaids are doing for you: They've planned your shower, they've agreed to purchase a dress for your wedding, they're taking time off to spend with you the week before your wedding, they're traveling to your chosen locale to witness your vows and they'll be there to calm your nerves on the morning of the wedding. They're pretty good eggs, these girls, especially if they've done all of this with nary a word of complaint. They deserve a nice reward.

Consider:

* Jewelry (earrings or bracelets are especially nice)
* A leather-bound, refillable datebook
* Monogrammed key chain
* Monogrammed note cards
* Silver (or leather) picture frame
* Gift certificate for a restaurant or favorite shop
* Appointment for a massage or pedicure (or both) at your resort

This list includes several potential monogramming gifts. Customizing gifts in this way is a great option, and honestly, a lost passion. When in doubt, monogram it.

E~ssential

Traditionally, the bride also takes her attendants out for lunch in the weeks before the wedding as another means of thanking them for their hard work. If this has to wait until everyone arrives at the resort for the wedding, that's okay too.

Massages and pedicures are more modern ideas for bridesmaids' gifts, but they're a fun twist on a classic tradition. True, your bridesmaids can't pull out the massage years from now and reflect on its appropriateness, but it *is* something they'll never forget. Also, if you have a bunch of bridesmaids who don't know each other well, a group spa outing might make for a great bonding experience.

For the Groomsmen

Your fiancé should also be prepared to show his appreciation toward his groomsmen for all of their hard work, which probably mostly consisted of listening to the groom talk about how great you are and how lucky he is. They may have planned a killer bachelor party, as well, and they are going to have to travel to the wedding and act charming while they're there (or so you hope).

Some nice gifts for the groomsmen include:

* Money clip
* Watch
* Manly looking picture frame
* Travel or shaving kit
* Essential sporting or hobby equipment

Again, the goal is to choose something useful and timeless. Talk your fiancé out of the case-of-beer-as-a-thank-you idea. Although it may be useful, it's not timeless. (It also can't be monogrammed, which pretty much says it all.)

E~Fact

Gifts are usually given to the attendants at the rehearsal dinner, but do what works best for you. If you don't want to have to pack the gifts, then plan on handing them out *before* the wedding. This might make things easier on your attendants as well, since they'll all have plenty of stuff in their suitcases anyway. ✿

Parents Are Important

Don't forget about your parents and your fiancé's parents, too. It's a nice gesture to take them out to dinner or to otherwise show your appreciation for all they've done for you during your engagement. Parents sometimes get the short end of the stick here, so make sure you take the time to acknowledge their help and their support. Consider buying them a piece of nice artwork or something for their garden, like a sundial or a birdbath—something that will remind them every day how lucky they are that their children grew up to be so sweet and thoughtful.

Don't Forget the Younger People

Your ring bearer and flower girl also need to be thanked. We're going to forget about timeless and useful gifts and instead focus on something appropriate for the children in question. First, you have to take the child's age into consideration. A typical three-year-old flower girl isn't going to *ooh* and *ahh* over a beautiful pair of earrings that you've chosen for her, even if they're real diamonds and they're very close to what you've given to the bigger girls in your wedding party. No, your flower girl wants the doll she's had her eye on for a month now.

You might reason that unlike a plastic doll, those earrings are something that she'll have forever, but to her, forever consists of right now and next week. And she *wants* that doll. You'll be her hero forever (beyond next week, even) if you get her something she'll truly enjoy, and that's the point of a gift for your littlest wedding helpers. For help in finding something that'll wow the tykes, ask their parents. You'll probably end up with a list to choose from.

Chapter 8
Leaving Your Wedding to the Professionals

There are basically two ways to plan a destination wedding. You can either choose a resort or hotel, which will significantly narrow down your options and help with the planning, or you can pick a place where you'll have to do a large amount of the planning yourself. Many destination brides choose the former option, figuring that making life easier is one of the perks that a destination wedding has to offer. The biggest issue then becomes choosing the best possible location from the long list of potential sites.

Benefits of Going with the Pros

Why would you want to hand over control of your wedding to someone you don't even know? For the same reason you'd allow a surgeon to perform your appendectomy or a lawyer to fight for you in court: You may not know them personally (at least not yet), but these people know what they're doing. However, just as you'd never let just *any* doctor wheel you into the operating room, you shouldn't leave your wedding ceremony in the hands of fate. A wee bit of research can help you find out how well any given location is able to pull off an event.

Resorts, hotels, and other popular destination wedding sites have loads of experience dealing with out-of-town brides. The vast majority of these places already have safeguards in place for making sure that everything goes according to plan. Also, while it's true that you may have to choose flowers, for example, from a standard booklet or pamphlet of package offerings, chances are you're going to find that what's offered meets or exceeds your standards of beauty. (Again, these people know how to make brides happy!)

✿ E~ssential

Although most places offer some sort of package deal for flowers, music, and food, some destination wedding sites may be willing to work with you to create truly unique elements of your wedding. ﷯

Many destination wedding sites offer unique add-ons, which truly make each wedding feel like a once-in-a-lifetime event. In Las Vegas, for example, you can arrive at your wedding in a helicopter. At some seaside resorts, you can make a grand entrance on a yacht. The key to enhancing your wedding in extraordinary ways is to know your budget first, then do some research. Even though some of your standard ceremony and reception elements may be limited in one sense (only one color of linens to choose from, or the absence of your favorite hors d'oeuvres from the menu), some of your other options may be nothing short of incredible. You might have to make some tradeoffs—but you'll probably do so with a smile.

Digging up the Details

If you visit the Web site of any destination wedding resort, you're going to find glowing testimonials about how professional its staff is and how beautiful and unique its weddings are. Here's an obvious piece of information that's far too easy to overlook when you really, really *want* to like a place: These Web sites aren't run by consumers; they're run by the resorts, whose primary interest is making money. Now, if you were a business owner (or, more likely, a marketing director), would you really post negative comments about your business, even if they were true? Not if you wanted to keep business flowing.

Seeing Is Believing

The very best way to check out any destination wedding spot is in person. It's just too difficult to objectively evaluate a spot you've never been to. Many couples choose a place where they've vacationed in the past. Even if the brochures and pictures on the Internet are nothing short of stunning, you have to realize that a good photographer can do wonders with even the worst surroundings.

If a visit is out of the question, another relatively safe way to choose a spot is to rely on the word of a friend who has been there. One caveat here: Make sure this friend is someone with whom you share common viewpoints. If you're ultra-traditional, in other words, don't base your choice of a ceremony spot on the advice of your wild, non-conventional pal. Although she may mean well, she may not be able to put the place into the context that you're looking for. She also may forget to tell you about the clothing-optional part of the ceremony, which might not be something *you're* interested in—but what if the officiant *is*?

Taking a Chance

Only the bride with nerves of steel chooses a spot sight-unseen. This isn't to say, though, that doing this is at all unusual. Again, because destination wedding spots are run by professional wedding planners, most brides wind up having a happy experience. Nevertheless, when you're considering a site that you've never actually been to, it's essential that you do some in-depth research on the place. Here are some steps to follow to ensure that you're getting all the information you need:

1. *Play the part of the skeptic.* Be on the lookout for things that sound or seem amiss. Although brides often don't want to look at life this way (they're happy, happy, happy!), it's the best way to protect yourself when you're entering into a business transaction.
2. *Check out the Web site.* Does this place offer the basics of what you're looking for? You may not be able to have it all, but are the major elements in place?
3. *Do an Internet search.* Type the name and location of the site and the words "destination wedding" into your search bar, using a search engine like Google. Then try various skeptical qualifiers to find out whether there are numerous negative comments about the place. For example, type in "Happy Hotel Miami Fla. destination wedding terrible" or "Happy Hotel Miami Fla. destination wedding bad experience." Get creative with those qualifiers and see what pops up.

Another way to check out any business *in the United States* is to log on to the Web site of the Better Business Bureau (*www.bbb.org*). Be aware, however, that as long as the business responds to a complaint, the business may *not* receive a negative rating, even if the consumer's complaint is valid. (This, ironically, is one complaint that people sometimes have about the Better Business Bureau. Businesses can pretty much lie about their part in a transaction and try to make the *consumer* look guilty or crazy.)

Take your time doing your research! Read any consumer complaints posted either on the BBB's site or elsewhere on the Internet, look for a pattern of similar complaints, and judge for yourself whether you feel comfortable with a particular resort. If you've read one complaint too many along the lines of "The food was horrible and the minister was drunk," it's time to start looking elsewhere.

 E~ssential

If there are bad reviews of destination wedding sites out there, you *will* find them on the Internet. The Internet has become a sounding board for consumers of all types, and brides are the *last* group of consumers that would remain silent after a horrible experience. In some cases, you can even contact the reviewers to get more information.

Choosing the Experience You Want

One of the considerations in choosing a spot is narrowing down what kind of wedding experience you're looking for. This goes beyond the ceremony itself. Because the destination wedding often turns into a weeklong event spent with guests *before* the ceremony and a weeklong honeymoon *after* the ceremony, you want to make sure you're headed somewhere that's right for you. You don't want to be in a loud, hustling, bustling city if you're looking for peace and quiet; conversely, you don't want to spend your time in a secluded area if you constantly need to be on the go.

Seclusion

If you want to be alone with your groom and immediate family members, you may want to look into some of the less-developed islands in the Caribbean. St. John, for example, is a quiet paradise, free from hustle and bustle. Now, that also means that there's very little to do other than relax and spend time with your loved ones. You can hop a catamaran over to St. Thomas for some shopping and more in the way of nightlife, but on the island of St. John itself, you will, for the most part, be blissfully free from noise and other people.

You also can find seclusion at a bed-and-breakfast. You often can book an entire B&B for a week or a weekend, leaving the cooking and cleaning to the proprietors. Instead of sharing living quarters with strangers, you'll be hanging out with your family. And since there are B&Bs out there to suit almost every taste, you might choose an ornate Victorian mansion or a simple country home.

If you're really looking for seclusion, think off-season. You might look into the ski resort towns out West for a summer destination wedding. These locations are beautiful in every season, but when the snow melts, prices drop—and the crowds evaporate.

Like the Nightlife?

Fortunately for couples looking for some action and nightlife wrapped into their destination wedding experience, there are plenty of options to choose from. Almost any booming metropolis—Las Vegas, New York, Chicago, Houston, Los Angeles, Miami—has a lot to offer in the way of dancing and partying.

How will you ever narrow down the choices? Go with your gut and choose a place you know and love. Even if you've only been to Las Vegas once, for example, you know whether it's the right kind of place for your wedding. And since most cities are divided into distinct areas—New York, for example, has midtown, uptown, downtown, the East Side, the West Side, the Theater District, and so many other sections, such as Soho and Greenwich Village—you can really choose the atmosphere that best suits your wedding. One bride might dream of walking down the aisle in St. Patrick's Cathedral, while another might dream of a Central Park wedding, and yet another can envision a ceremony in a grand hotel.

Cruises are another great option for lively destination weddings—they're filled with round-the-clock, instant entertainment. With casinos, shows, and nightclubs galore to choose from, you and your guests will have a rollicking time!

E~Alert
Make sure you're booking the correct type of cruise for your wedding! Many cruise lines offer trips that are family-oriented, and you probably don't want to be reveling with a bunch of eight-year-olds (nor will you want to deal with their parents' complaints about your out-of-this-world partying).

With all of this excitement to look forward to, don't overlook the wedding! When booking a cruise ship wedding, your first priority is to look into what types (big or small, civil or religious) of wedding ceremonies the ship offers. Many ships offer a choice of two or more chapels or reception sites, each with its own ambiance.

Sun and Fun

If you're looking for a little R&R, loads of sun, a swim-up bar and—oh yeah—a wedding, you'll find an abundance of sites to suit your needs. Some of the most popular beach wedding sites include:

* Jamaica
* Aruba
* The Bahamas
* The U.S. Virgin Islands
* The Dominican Republic
* Hawaii
* Cancun, Mexico
* Puerto Rico
* Bermuda
* Florida beaches (Miami, Key West, Siesta Key, and others)

There are countless other beaches to choose from: The entire East and West coasts are lined with picturesque towns that are perfect for destination weddings. Maine is a popular—and beautiful—spot for die-hard fans of New England, while the coast of Oregon is breathtakingly gorgeous and a nice choice for nature lovers.

Popular Spots for Every Taste

Where else are destination wedding couples headed, if not to the beaches? Oh, just about everywhere. Destination weddings have become so popular in the last decade that you can plan one anywhere and no one will think you're crazy. We already covered some of the most popular beach spots. What if you're thinking of something totally different, though? What if you want something really romantic, or elegant? What if you're the outdoorsy type and you want to get married in a forest? Try these places on for size:

* *European castles.* What's more elegant and romantic than tying the knot in a place where royalty once ruled? Book through a travel agent or do an online search ("European castle weddings") to find your fairy-tale wedding site.
* *Mountain lodges.* The Poconos in upstate New York have long been a popular wedding spot; the Rocky Mountains are beautiful any time of year; and the Smoky Mountains have a down-home atmosphere that will make you feel like you fit right in with the locals. All of these areas are well prepared to handle the destination bride and groom.
* *Nature's glory.* Niagara Falls is another popular wedding spot. You can actually hold a ceremony while looking out at the great cataracts.
* *Wine country.* Vineyards are situated in rich, fertile valleys and provide an almost indescribably gorgeous backdrop for a wedding ceremony.

✳ *Oceanside.* If having sand in your wedding shoes doesn't sound like your idea of fun, look for a cliff overlooking the mighty sea.

Actually, if you take another look at this list, you'll note that every option is romantic, natural, different, and elegant in its own way. Choosing the right spot depends on your personalities and personal preferences. Because there are so many exciting, unique approaches to planning a destination wedding, and because these events continue to grow in popularity, you can be certain that there are resorts and planners in almost every picturesque corner of the world just waiting to help you plan the wedding of your dreams.

How Much, How Many?

Although you're off the hook for paying for everyone's transportation and lodging, you are going to pay for a reception, which may be every bit as expensive as an in-town affair. Add your airfare and lodging to that cost, and you may not be saving a penny by leaving town. For some couples, saving money isn't the point of a destination wedding—but for others, it definitely is.

Know Your Budget

Before you sign any type of wedding contract with a resort, know how much you're willing to spend on the entire event. (For information about budgeting, read Chapter 3: Money Talk.) Then touch base with the site's wedding coordinator. Let her know that you are working within the confines of *this much money.* She should be able to present you with a couple of different options: either a scaled-down reception for a large number of people, or a fancy reception for fewer friends and relatives.

When you plan a wedding in a resort, you'll have various packages to choose from, which will help tremendously with sticking to your budget.

Still, sometimes even within the packages, you have many other options to choose from, and this is where you can start losing track of how much you've spent. The name of this game is *prioritizing*. We talked a little bit about this in Chapter 3, but let's recap here, in one concise sentence: Choose the areas of the wedding that are most important to you and spend your money there. If it's most important to you to invite as many people as you can think of and you're working with a limited budget, you may have to choose the least expensive items on the reception menu. Weddings usually involve tradeoffs of this kind; you aren't the only bride to have to make concessions in the name of remaining financially solvent. Start thinking about those choices now.

❀ E~Alert

If you find that every destination wedding site option you're presented with is way, way over your budget, start looking elsewhere. You can always find a less expensive site to suit your needs. Starting off your married life without two nickels to rub together is not the best idea. ❦

Wedding Coordinators

Some women hear the term "wedding coordinator" or "wedding planner" and immediately think to themselves, "I don't need a planner. I'm smart. I'm savvy. I can do this myself." Well, you can be smart and savvy (and sassy, to boot) and still find yourself completely overwhelmed by trying to plan a wedding on your own. Even brides who get married in their hometowns often rely on planners to do their legwork; it's just so much easier to hand over the details to someone who deals with this kind of thing day-in and day-out.

If you book a wedding at a destination wedding resort, the coordinator is often thrown in as part of the package. It's easier for the site to have just one contact person running interference and pulling everything together, rather than have you speak with the dining room manager, the concierge, and the off-site florist individually, trusting that they will all eventually touch base with one another.

If you're planning a destination wedding on your own, you may want to hire a local wedding planner to make things easier on yourself. You'll read more about finding a planner in Chapter 9.

Packages

Booking your wedding at a site that wheels and deals in weddings means that you will be presented with some sort of wedding package. Keep in mind that packages vary wildly from place to place. For example, some include lodging for the bride and groom and some don't. Some include a free wedding if you book a certain number of nights at the site. Some are only able to accommodate ten or twelve guests, while others can handle as many as you can think of.

The pricing of packages, as you can imagine, also runs the gamut from ultra-cheap to mega-expensive. You can book a wedding in Las Vegas that includes the officiant, flowers, photos, limo ride, music, cake, and champagne, all for several hundred dollars. On the other hand, you can book a full-size wedding at a resort for tens of thousands of dollars. What's the difference?

Well, obviously, there's going to be a significant difference in the length and formality of the service; the quantity and quality of the pictures; the type of floral arrangements provided; the type of music that's played; and so on. Plus, you aren't getting a full reception with the Vegas deal, which means that your reception will consist of you, the groom, and perhaps three or four witnesses or guests. Your costs are minimal, even though all the basics are pretty much taken care of.

Is there one package that's right for every couple? No. What sounds like heaven to one couple might sound like a living hell for another. It all comes down to the type of wedding you prefer. That's the great thing about destination weddings: They've become a sub-industry of the wedding business, which means there are resorts and packages to suit every couple, just about anywhere they'd like to take their vows.

The best advice about packages is to take things slowly. Give yourself plenty of time to do your research and compare locations and prices.

❀ E~ssential

Some couples find that a large destination wedding actually costs less than what they figure they would have spent on a wedding in their hometown. This is obviously a couple-by-couple evaluation. ❧

"All right," you're thinking, "this is all fine and well, but what do couples *typically* pay for destination weddings?" Well, it's impossible to nail down even an average figure, because destination weddings encompass so many different types of ceremonies, receptions, and locations. A wedding that's held just an hour or two from the bride's hometown is considered a destination wedding—but so is one held halfway across the world. The wedding held closer to home could even (theoretically) end up being more expensive than the one held in a far-off location.

Cost boils down to these elements:

* *The site itself.* Some sites just charge more for ceremonies.
* *The season.* Off-season weddings are often less expensive but come with a risk of inclement weather.

* *The number of guests.* More people eating prime rib at your reception equals a bigger bill for you.
* *The number of "extras."* These add-ons include such things as a huge photo package, the biggest cake in the world, arriving by helicopter, and the type of food served at the reception.

Admittedly, this is nonspecific information. But this is actually good news for couples who are afraid that a destination wedding is going to cost them big (*too* big). Lose the extras and cut the guest list and you may find that you're able to afford a wedding in your dream location!

Help Is Just a Phone Call Away!

If you feel overwhelmed about narrowing down your choices for a destination wedding, talk to a travel agent. The benefit of working with a travel agent is obvious: less research for you to do. The potential downside is that your travel agent might point you only toward the businesses she works with on a regular basis, which may or may not measure up to your expectations. Be upfront from the beginning about what you're looking for in your wedding trip.

 E~ssential

When you contact a travel agent, ask her what types of fees she charges for planning a wedding. Some charge standard fees (per airline ticket; per hotel booking); others charge by the hour for big jobs, including weddings. 🐦

If you're thinking about skirting the travel agent and checking out your favorite online travel site for a deal, you're not going to have too much luck. Booking a resort destination wedding through an online travel site is really not an option. Because you'll be purchasing a package through the resort, you'll have to deal with the resort directly.

Chapter 9
Off the Beaten Path

While many brides choose to plan their destination weddings at hotels and resorts that specialize in ceremonies and receptions, other brides decide to have their weddings elsewhere. Some may pick a truly out-of-the-way and hard-to-find location, but most choose a simple everyday town or setting that speaks to them somehow (even though it isn't necessarily a hot spot for out-of-town brides and grooms). The reasons behind their choices may vary, but for these couples, the true test of their love and commitment to each other is their ability to plan a wedding in a new land.

Why There?

It's hard enough for some people to accept that you aren't getting married in your hometown. However, it might be easier for your friends to understand that you'd want to get married in Hawaii or Cancun than to comprehend why you've chosen a small town in Minnesota, considering that you don't live there now and have never lived there in the past, but just fell in love with it when you were passing through on your way to somewhere else.

E~Alert

Every bride chooses a spot for her wedding based on personal feelings, so don't feel you need to justify your reasoning to anyone beyond doing a little friendly arm-twisting to get them to attend your ceremony. It's your big day, and it should take place where *you* want it to.

These are reasons why couples may choose an out-of-the-way spot:

* It's where they met.
* It's where they spent a memorable vacation.
* It's where they got engaged.
* It's where one of them went to college.
* It's a central location for most of the guests.
* The bride and groom are taken with the beauty of the area.

You can probably flesh out this list with a couple of your own reasons, but you get the point: The place you choose means something to you and your groom, and it's where you want to say "I do." If your friends and family don't quite get it, don't get defensive—and don't be shy about sharing the reason why you've decided on this place, even if it's as simple as loving the general look and feel of the area. Your guests are sure to be intrigued by your decision to marry out of town in the first place, so make this a game for your own enjoyment: Do your best to sell them on the place, and watch how many of them show up.

Benefits of Out-of-the-Way Places

The biggest bonus of steering your wedding away from touristy spots (including big cities) is that you'll probably get more wedding for your buck, which is not to say that you'll pay next to nothing for the caterer and florist, but *per person* your costs are likely to be lower than they would be in a major metropolis or in a resort. Another perk of planning a wedding in a less popular place is that you'll feel like an individual bride. Some brides go out of their way to avoid places that specialize in destination weddings, fearing that they will feel like one of a cast of a dozen brides who will walk through the wedding chapel doors on a given day.

Squeeze Us In!

On the other hand, small towns are . . . small. If you have your heart set on getting married in a little village chapel on July 1 and there are already three weddings planned there on that weekend, you're going to have to choose another date or another place. The same is true of the reception halls in the area. Your choices will be somewhat limited.

E~Fact

Most couples plan weddings between April and October, which is why it pays to plan early or plan your event for the off season! In many areas—particularly those where weddings are not an industry—rates in the less popular months are much, much lower than they are during the peak of the "I do" season.

Early planning and the ability to be flexible can salvage plans dashed by other engaged couples who beat you to the punch (or, more accurately, the reservation book). If July 1 is booked, maybe July 8 is open. If you're planning a year in advance, you should have no difficulty taking vacation time on either weekend—and you can also give your guests plenty of notice. If you've left the planning until mid-April, however, July 8 will probably be a goner, too.

The Balanced Bride

The most difficult part of falling in love with an offbeat wedding spot is planning a wedding from miles away with vendors who aren't used to dealing with out-of-town brides. Fortunately, technology has made this much less of an issue. E-mails, faxes, and phone calls are almost as good as sitting down face-to-face with a business owner. The downside is that sometimes you can't get a good feel for a product (flowers, for example) unless you're able to see it in person.

Generally speaking, if you're thinking about planning an out-of-town wedding, you should have exceptional organizational skills and a disposition that includes the ability to take things in stride. If you can't reach your caterer a week before the wedding, for example, you should be able to say to yourself, "He's just out talking to a client. I'm sure he'll return my call before the day is over," instead of, "I know he's taken my money and left town! How am I going to feed a hundred people at the reception? Oh, why, *why* did I ever try to plan this wedding out of town?"

Test Yourself

Not sure if you're ready to plan a faraway wedding? Take this personality quiz and find out:

1. Your desk at work reminds you of:
   (a) A well-oiled machine. All the pieces are in place.
   (b) A forest. You can navigate your way through the undergrowth.
   (c) The news. In particular, last week's natural disaster.

2. Generally, you return e-mails and phone calls:
   (a) As soon as possible.
   (b) Within forty-eight hours.
   (c) When the other person calls or e-mails you again—and again.

3. If no one showed up at your wedding, you would feel:
   (a) Fine—as long as the groom was there.
   (b) Sad, but you'd understand some people couldn't make it.
   (c) Devastated, enraged, and out for revenge.

4. You like to plan things:
   (a) Alone.
   (b) With your fiancé or a good friend.
   (c) You've never followed a plan in your life.

5. Your best friend would describe you as:
   (a) Very structured.
   (b) Structured, but able to let your hair down.
   (c) The least structured person on the face of the earth.

6. When things don't go your way, you:
   (a) Find a way to make them go your way.
   (b) Retreat and think up a new plan.
   (c) Cry. And then cry some more.

7. You like adventure.
   (a) True.
   (b) False.

8. If someone questioned your choice of wedding site, you'd most likely respond by saying:
   (a) "You'll *love* it once you get there!"
   (b) "I know it's not everyone's cup of tea, but give it a chance."
   (c) "You're uninvited."

Here's the answer key:

* *Mostly a's:* You're going to hold up just fine when planning an out-of-town wedding. You're well organized and ready to face the tasks that lie ahead.
* *Mostly b's except for number 7:* Although you could certainly work on your organizational skills, they are solid enough to carry you through this wedding-planning adventure. Good luck!
* *Mostly c's, and b for number 7:* Don't do it! Being disorganized and unable to deal with stress are not mortal sins—but don't put yourself through the emotional wringer by taking on the task of planning a long-distance wedding.

Analysis

You might think it's silly to determine the type of wedding you end up planning using a personality test. But here's the scoop: Planning a wedding is a *big* deal. It's time-consuming, it can be exhausting, and it can take over your entire life. Organized women can usually take everything in stride. That's not to say that problems won't pop up even for these brides; it's just that they're more likely to do a thorough job of researching vendors before they hire them. Nevertheless, unforeseen trouble sometimes arises. An organized, calm bride will immediately look for the solution instead of letting her emotions carry her away, thinking that this is the worst thing that has ever happened to anyone. A less-organized bride might not know how to even go about beginning to look for a solution, which results in panic, which, in turn, results in misery.

If you know that you are disorganized and/or that planning is not your strongest quality, don't try to plan a wedding out of town by yourself. Choose a destination wedding resort or hire a wedding planner based in the town you're headed to, and let the professionals take over. You'll learn more about this option in the last section of this chapter: "Long Live the Wedding Planner!"

Vendor Search Procedure

As you know, brides who plan in-town weddings usually depend on word-of-mouth referrals to get their planning started. A best friend, coworker, or neighbor will recommend a caterer, a florist, or a vocalist, the bride checks out the vendor in question, and wedding history is made. Many times, it really is *that* easy for in-town brides to find good wedding help—but where does that leave *you*? Can you hire a caterer from your hometown to come halfway across the state (or country) with you to your wedding? Are you supposed to grow and transport your own bouquet? Will you end up singing at your own ceremony? Of course not. Finding decent out-of-town vendors isn't hard to do if you just know where to start looking.

The first rule of checking out wedding vendors is to prepare yourself for interviews and research. (In other words, get organized!) Have a notebook handy to jot down important facts when you talk to a banquet manager, a baker, a florist—whomever. The second most important thing is to put away any tendencies toward shyness and ask all the questions that you need to have answered!

E~ssential

Visit the Better Business Bureau's Web site (*www.bbb.org*) before booking a vendor. Look for a pattern of similar complaints against the business. Complaints are not always legitimate, so ask the vendor for his take on any that you find—and proceed with caution. If you find multiple similar allegations, there's a good chance they're true. Move on to someone else.

Most couples start their planning by booking the reception site, which is where most of the wedding-fund money will be spent. For this reason, you won't commit to a reception site without first checking it out and making sure it's a legitimate business that suits your needs. You can find this kind of information by talking with the catering or dining room manager, asking the right questions, and checking referrals.

Here's what you'll need to find out:

* *Is your preferred date available?* No sense going any further until you've determined whether this place is available.
* *What is the total occupancy of the site?* If the site can't accommodate your large family, you'll have to move on.
* *Does the facility also allow ceremonies to be performed on site?* Most will.
* *What kind of food does the site specialize in?* You want to get an idea of whether the site can meet your specific desires here. If you're looking for a vegetarian meal and the location you're considering serves only spit-fired pig roasts, it might not be a good fit.
* *Is there a dance floor? How large?* Can your boogying friends and family all fit into the space?
* *What about the bar? How large is it, and how many bartenders will be on duty?* You don't want parched guests standing in line for thirty minutes waiting for their booze.
* *Will you pay for coat checkers and valet parking attendants?* In upscale places, the answer is usually yes.
* *How much will you pay for the site per hour? What's the fee for running overtime?* Obviously, these fees vary from place to place.
* *Does the site charge a cake-cutting or wine-corking fee? How much?* Many places do charge for these services, so don't be surprised to hear you'll pay for someone to slice up your dessert.
* *What other charges can you expect?* Sales tax? Linen rental? Centerpieces?
* *If the site doesn't serve food, can the staff refer you to a caterer?* We'll get to this in a moment.

These questions will give you a good idea as to whether this place is right for your wedding. You'll learn a lot about the accommodations, the service, and the price. If you like what you hear, ask the manager to send you some literature so that you can read everything in black and white.

Once you've checked out the place, ask for referrals—and call those people! It doesn't take a whole lot of time to contact brides who can either put your fears to rest or tell you to steer clear of a place. Ask them what they liked best about the place, but also ask them what didn't go according to plan—because there's usually *something*. If it's a small thing (like the coat-check girl giving out the wrong coats) that's nothing to worry about. If you hear the same major issue from all of the brides you speak to—such as the food was cold and the service was slow—that's reason enough to start looking into other options.

Finding and Choosing Vendors

The great thing about finding one good wedding vendor is that you've found an "in" in the local wedding scene. Businesses that regularly host social events (like weddings) can refer you to other reputable vendors. So don't be shy, and don't put it off too long. You've got a lot of calls to make!

Caterers

If you find yourself having to hire a separate caterer for your reception, you'll want to know more than what kind of food he or she serves. Caterers typically charge rental fees for everything: Chairs, silverware, china, glassware, linens, candlesticks, chafing dishes, a tent—you name it, you're paying for it. But that's only fair, since the caterer is hauling everything to your reception site.

 E~ssential

The caterer will probably also provide the servers for the reception, so ask how many will be in attendance, what their duties will be (will they serve appetizers on trays, or will they merely make sure the snacks are replenished frequently?), and how they will be dressed. 🌛

Food is the major issue with the caterer, so find someone whose skills match your taste, literally. Are you looking for a sit-down meal or stations (or a buffet, which is very similar to a station setup)? Does the caterer specialize in any particular type of food? Does this business seem to be a good match for you?

Contracts

As with the reception site (and every other vendor), ask for literature so that you can look over prices and services and make the best (*non-rushed*) decision. Ask for and check references, and don't sign the contract unless it's 100 percent correct! It's not difficult for a business owner to line out a mistake, initial and date it, and fax the contract back to you, so be firm on this rule: No signing until the contract is finalized. No exceptions.

Remember—business is business. You can bet that if a contract were incorrect in your favor (charging you too little for a service, for example), the business owner would correct it on the spot. He has to watch out for his bottom line, after all. You're watching out for *your* bottom line, so no matter how nice a vendor seems, don't take his word for it that he'll correct a mistake after you sign. You'll have no recourse at that point.

Long-Distance Obstacles

Most couples experience a couple of glitches in their wedding planning, and distance usually doesn't have anything to do with it; it's just the nature of trying to work with several different vendors at once. If you were planning a wedding next door to where you currently live, you could reasonably expect a problem or two to crop up over the course of your engagement. They might not be major issues, but things that need to be dealt with as soon as possible to make sure that the wedding goes along as planned.

That phrase "as soon as possible" is where the distance thing can bite you. If you have a problem with your florist, for example, and both of you are in the same town, you can deal with it fairly easily, even in the worst-case scenario. Long distance can be a whole different story.

Let's say you're planning a wedding in your hometown and a friend has told you that your florist has closed shop and left town. You find that difficult to believe, of course, because . . . well, because your wedding is coming up, and your florist wouldn't forget about that! You call her right away, just so you can dismiss this silly rumor. No answer. You call later. Still no answer. After you try eight times without even getting a recording, you drive over to the shop on your lunch break and find that your friend was right: Your florist has disappeared.

This is a worst-of-the-worst-case situation, of course. Most brides don't end up dealing with crooked vendors (especially not if they've done their research). However, it can be easier to clear up unforeseen circumstances if you're a short drive down the pike instead of a hundred miles away.

Is this some roundabout way of telling you you're crazy to plan a destination wedding outside of the relative built-in safety of a resort? No. You just have to be willing to keep on top of things from week to week—or hire a local wedding consultant.

Long Live the Wedding Planner!

If you're planning a destination wedding on your own, consider hiring a wedding planner based in that area to help you out. While a planner can be worth every penny you pay her when you plan an in-town wedding, she can be absolutely *priceless* when you're planning an out-of-town wedding in an area that you aren't all that familiar with.

A good wedding planner has several vital tools to work with:

* ❋ She knows which vendors are good, which are reputable, and which are difficult to work with.
* ❋ She may be able to work out some sweet deals for you because of her previous relationships with particular vendors. (She brings them business; they give her clients a break.)

* She has the time to talk with these people; this is her *job*.
* She may also know of some talented, inexpensive start-up companies (for instance, someone who has worked with a particular florist for years and is now in business for himself).
* Because wedding planners see all kinds of ceremonies and receptions, they know their stuff. Her ideas might be right up your alley, or they may inspire you to come up with some creative notions of your own.

A well-connected planner is often worth her weight in gold. How do you find this miracle worker? You can check out the Association of Bridal Consultants (*www.bridalassn.com*), which requires its members to have formal training in the field of wedding planning. That way, you know you're dealing with someone who has experience and not someone who woke up last week and decided that this wedding planning business is *easy*! If you have your heart set on a particular reception site and you've already contacted the person in charge there, you can ask for a recommendation for a good wedding planner.

What Does She Do, and What Does It Cost?

You can usually hire a wedding planner to do as much or as little as you want her to do. Some couples feel as though they really only need someone to help with the ceremony; others want someone to run the reception; and some couples like to hand over everything to someone else.

 E~Fact

You should be the one paying the consultant. You don't want to hire someone who gets kickbacks from vendors. You might just end up hiring a caterer who's all wrong for you, for example, because your consultant is working on commission with this guy. ✿

Typically, if she plans the entire ceremony and reception, a wedding planner is paid a percentage (usually 15 to 20 percent) of the final bill of the event. For that kind of money, she gathers pertinent information about vendors and passes it along to you; she advises you on how many flowers the reception hall will need and what type of arrangements will work best; she'll contact the musicians and make sure they know what they're supposed to play and when. In short, she'll take care of business. She'll be present during the ceremony and reception, leaving you to concentrate on looking pretty and having a smashing time.

How to Interview a Wedding Planner

If you're thinking of hiring a planner, make sure you ask her these important questions:

* *How many weddings do you take on each weekend?* One full wedding per weekend is plenty; any more than that, and some bride is going to get the short end of the stick.
* *Do you have an assistant?* If she says yes, ask who will attend your wedding—the planner or her partner?
* *What happens if you get sick?* It's a good idea to know that she has someone who can pick up the wedding ball, so to speak, and run with it in case of an emergency.
* *How much or how little are you willing to plan?* Some planners will only take on full events; others will do à la carte services (such as planning only the ceremony or reception).
* *How do you charge?* By the hour? Flat fee? Percentage?
* *Can you provide me with referrals from past clients?* If she's eager to get you in touch with her past clients, and the clients give glowing reports, chances are you've found a keeper.

Also ask her if she can work with your budget! Most planners are incredibly knowledgeable, creative people who can put on a beautiful event without going way over cost. If you get the sense that a particular interviewee is not thrilled with your budget (because she groaned when you told her the monetary amount you're working with), save yourself from months of anguish—arguing over which dinner to serve, which flowers to choose, which musicians are best. Find someone else.

A Perfect Match

It's very important for you to get a sense of how well you and a planner will work together. Most wedding consultants are wonderful, open-minded people who truly find joy in their clients' wedding-day happiness. As you well know, though, personality types differ wildly. Just because you're paying someone to do a job for you doesn't necessarily mean that you're going to be the boss.

This is why it's so important to check those referrals! An out-of-control planner may feel as though she's putting herself on the line by striking a deal that's going to cost her a favor with a vendor; the bride, who didn't want this particular deal in the first place, then becomes the object of the planner's ire when she turns it down! On the other hand, brides can drive consultants crazy by constantly changing their minds on major issues, whining about almost everything, and treating the consultant as though she's under contract to be a personal servant.

Most bride-consultant relationships do not turn out badly, thank goodness, but the key to preventing hard feelings is finding someone with whom you can speak freely, someone you aren't intimidated by, and—perhaps most important—someone who is going to listen to *you*. Now turn all of those good qualities around and make sure that you are as open-minded with your consultant as she is with you, treat her as respectfully as you expect her to act toward you, and the two of you will be a match made in wedding-planning heaven.

Chapter 10
Dressing for the Occasion

What's more fun than shopping for your wedding dress? Not much, as long as you enter into this project with helpful information. From knowing what kind of dress to purchase to purchasing it in the right place to making sure it arrives at your destination in time, you'll learn how to cover all the basics of the wedding dress in this chapter. You'll also learn about dressing the attendants and how to request that guests show up at your ceremony in appropriate clothing.

10

...g dress can be one of the easiest tasks
... a time-consuming, nail-biting experience.
...erience lands somewhere in the middle. It
...ne kind of dress you're looking for before
... to know this, you need to know where your
...place; so until you book your ceremony, the

...e to shop for a dress? Do people still go to bridal
...t has made everything so convenient? What kinds
o... ... to look out for when making a purchase of this
magnitude... ...tion will give you all the information you need to
have in order to be an educated bride in search of the perfect dress.

Church Bells or Sea Shells?

Before you can even think about making appointments at dress shops
and trying on gowns, you have to know where you're headed for the ceremony. Your destination is the number one factor in deciding which kind
of dress you'll wear.

"Well, that's just silly!" you say. "I can wear whatever I want! It's my
wedding!" In theory, this is true. It also might make sense to you to go
looking for a dress before you finalize any other plans, especially if your
mom is only in town for one weekend, or if you know it will take you
months to find the right look. Your destination is *part* of the look, however, and you have to make sure the dress suits the setting. You just cannot wear a brocade gown with a twenty-foot train to your beach wedding.
Not only will you be *way* overdressed, but you'll also probably faint from
the heat. If that particular kind of dress has always been your dream and
is the one thing you can't do without, then choose a more appropriate
location (like a grand cathedral), where it will blend in with the setting.

If you're choosing a very long or large dress, really give some thought
as to how well you'll be able to deal with shipping the dress ahead of you.

If you just know that you would be a nervous wreck waiting to see if the dress makes it to your wedding on time, go with something simpler that you can pack in your suitcase.

E~Alert

When choosing a gown for your destination wedding, look for an easy-to-care-for fabric. Satin can be an absolute nightmare to de-wrinkle, for instance, but linen, cotton, and even silk can be smoothed out relatively easily by the resort's staff once you arrive at your location. Check with your wedding coordinator to ensure that the resort offers on-site pressing services.

Bridal Salons

You'll probably be pleasantly surprised to learn that many labels are embracing the destination wedding trend and designing less formal gowns that pack and travel well. It's best to call a bridal salon before stopping by. These shops usually have a fairly small staff, and you want to make sure that someone will be available to hunt through all of the dresses and narrow down your choices for you. The dress consultant will ask about your wedding so that she knows which dresses to bring to you, so again, before you go dress shopping, *know where you're headed for your wedding*!

What do you need to watch out for in a salon? Price gouging. Some salons will remove the tags from gowns for two reasons: first, so that you can't go down the street to another salon and compare prices; and second, so you don't know what size you're trying on. In a very worst-case scenario, a salon may try to increase its profit margin by convincing a woman that a certain dress tends to run small, so the bride should order it two sizes larger than she would normally wear. When the dress arrives and is falling off the bride, she has no choice but to pay for extensive (and ultra-expensive) alterations.

Full-service bridal salons tend to be more expensive than their cut-rate counterparts. Yes, it's nice to sit on a plush settee and sip champagne and eat pastries while you're talking to your mom and sister about which dress is prettiest, but you're paying for all of the niceties in the dress markups. That's not to say it's a good thing or a bad thing; it's just the way it is.

✿ E~ssential

You can reduce the risk of dealing with a disreputable dress shop by asking for references from friends who have recently purchased their wedding gowns. They can tell you which shops are good, and which ones you should stay away from. ✿

Before you sign a contract for the dress, read through it carefully. Take special note of the following information:

* *Deposit and balance.* How much did you put down, how much do you owe, and when do you need to pay the balance? It should be there in black and white.
* *Delivery information.* When will this dress be delivered? The date should be on the contract.
* *Shipping address.* The dress should be shipped to the shop, not to you. If it arrives at your home damaged, you're going to have a heck of a time getting a replacement or refund. If it arrives damaged at the shop, it's their problem.
* *The size.* Make sure the correct size is on the contract! You don't want to end up paying for alterations because a too-big dress was ordered. Likewise, if a too-small dress arrives and your signature is on that contract, that dress belongs to you.

It's advisable to use your credit card when paying for your dress. If something goes awry, you've got added protection in the form of your credit card company, which will help fight a monetary dispute for you (at least to some extent).

Discount Shops and Department Stores

Discount bridal shops are a booming industry. Brides have come to their senses and now ask themselves, "Why am I paying so much money for a dress I'm going to wear once?" The dresses in these shops tend to be last season's models or dresses with slight imperfections. They still look great; they just cost less. The drawback here is that you may not find exactly what you're looking for. You may be tempted to go with a dress because of its low price and not because it's particularly flattering. We'll talk more about choosing a dress that suits you well later in this chapter.

If you're looking for a fairly simple dress, you may also be able to find one in a nice department store. The downside here is that unless the dress fits you perfectly, you may have to hunt down your own seamstress and pay for alterations, which will pretty much offset any money you've saved by shopping in the mall. Chances are, though, that you're going to have to pay for alterations on *any* dress, so it's a wash.

Internet Shopping

When you buy a sweater online, do you wonder if it's going to look as good when it arrives as it does online? You can't really tell if it fits until you get it, and even if it does fit, the fabric might just be a little chintzy.

Some brides are so brave that they shoot right past the sweater shopping and order their wedding gowns on the Internet! While this may seem like a good way to save time and money, you really shouldn't take this kind of chance unless you've already done a good amount of research and you know the exact brand, style number, and size of the dress you're after. You really need to try on dresses to make sure the sizes run true, which means you probably have already invested some serious time in this venture. Therefore, the theory of saving time is out.

If the dress you've ordered online arrives damaged (or is the wrong size or style), you might have some serious problems on your hands, depending on the Web site's shipping and return policies, so make sure you check them out *extremely* carefully before ordering a dress in cyberspace. At the very least, if you need to make a return, you'll probably be out some shipping charges, which can be very expensive when you're talking about insured, weighty packages.

Bottom line: This is not the best way to buy something as significant as your wedding dress. If you do decide to go this route, find out which state the business is based in and then do another Internet search for that state's Better Business Bureau. Type the company's name into the search box and see what pops up.

Dressmakers

For that one-of-a-kind dress that you design yourself, look for a reputable dressmaker in your area—but look early. A good dressmaker may be booked a year (or more) in advance. Make sure she knows that your dress will travel with you so that the two of you can choose the best style and fabric for your gown.

Important Considerations

Here's one big mistake that brides make: They go after a particular look without stopping to consider whether the style is flattering on them.

Certain body types look better in certain dresses. A petite bride can wear a sheath dress, no problem; in fact, she'd be overpowered by a big, poofy gown. A tall bride might not necessarily want to look her height; she might choose a tea-length, A-line dress to make herself appear smaller.

Color is another common mistake. Some women (blondes with blue eyes, for example) look best in white; others (brunettes, typically) look their best in various shades of off-white. Maybe you normally can't wear white, but you plan on having a great tan by the time your wedding day rolls around. It's still a wiser choice to go with a dress that flatters your complexion on a typical (non-tanning) day. After all, what if you arrive on your tropical wedding island a week ahead of time only to learn that rain is in the forecast?

Don't go dress shopping alone, and don't take along someone who has never disagreed with anything you've ever said. And while you can take their ideas under advisement, don't rely on the word of dress shop employees. Although they may be very good at what they do, they don't know you on a personal basis; they don't know your style or what you're most comfortable in. While a salesgirl might go on and on (and on) about the gorgeous—stunning!—dress you're currently modeling, your family members are more likely to give you an honest appraisal if need be— something along the lines of, "It's a beautiful dress, but it's just not you."

Footwear

Rule of thumb: The less you see the shoes, the less important they are. If your dress is floor length, you really don't need to spend big money on the perfect pair of bridal shoes, because no one is going to see them. If, on the other hand, you're wearing a tea-length or shorter dress, you have to make sure your shoes are dazzling. They'll be on display the entire day, and they have to be just right.

Is it ridiculous to drop big bucks on a pair of shoes for your wedding? Not at all. Shoes make or break an outfit. You've put all this time into finding the right dress; don't mar its appearance with junky footwear. Think of it this way—if you can see the shoes, you were probably able to save a little money on the dress (at least as compared to the typical long dress with a train attached). Take that money and put it toward your shoes.

Undergarments and Accessories

Undergarments are another expense that might seem to be a waste of good money, but they aren't. If you aren't wearing the right bra, panties, crinoline, girdle—whatever your dress requires—the dress isn't going to fall right on your body. And then it isn't going to *look* right. So make the investment, even if it pains you at the time, and know that you're going to look as good as you should in that killer dress.

Once you've decided on the dress, choose your accessories carefully. At informal weddings, brides often go without a veil and wear flowers in their hair instead. Tiaras are a nice, simple alternative to long veils, and they're easy to pack and take along.

Make sure your jewelry complements the dress and isn't either too overpowering or too small to notice. Very delicate jewelry may look nice up close, but it will all but disappear in photos. Finally, choose something that suits you well, instead of letting someone else persuade you to make a purchase you might regret later.

Transporting the Dress

Choosing the dress is such an emotional process; you want to know that it's going to make it to your wedding intact and looking as good as it did in the bridal shop. The very idea of packing and/or shipping a wedding dress is enough to give some brides the shakes—it's as if they're sending their child off in the mail. This section will give you some tips for making sure that your dress has as nice a trip as you do.

Pack It Up

If you choose a simple enough ensemble, you can pack it and take it along to your destination yourself, but do so carefully. Ideally, your dress should be boxed and wrapped in tissue paper. If you're driving to your wedding site, make sure you have plenty of room for the dress box in the car. (In other words, don't plan on piling luggage on top of the box or—heaven forbid!—strapping it to the roof.)

If you're boarding a flight to your wedding and taking your dress along, you may have a couple of options—call your airline to get the best recommendation. The best way to make sure your dress makes it to your destination is to never let it out of your sight. Ask your airline if you will be able to hang the dress in a garment bag and place it in one of the closets on the plane. If this isn't possible, ask how you can best prepare your dress to be a carry-on item. If hanging it is out of the question, you may be able to at least lay it flat in an overhead compartment.

❈ E~Alert

Most airlines try to accommodate the needs of a bride on her way to the altar, but as you well know, we live in a zero-tolerance world. So although boxing your dress is the best way to keep its shape, this may not be an option if you want to bring the dress onboard with you. To eliminate any last-minute issues with your dress at the airport, call ahead and ask for recommendations. ❧

You really, *really* want to avoid checking your dress with your luggage. You can stand at that check-in counter and explain your situation to the airline agent using very strong language, and you might even receive his personal guarantee that your dress will arrive at your location with you. But guess what? There is no such guarantee unless you personally walk out onto the tarmac and load your luggage into the cargo bay yourself (something that is not recommended, as you're likely to be arrested for being in restricted territory—that zero-tolerance policy extends to brides, too). Even if it's never happened to you, you no doubt know somebody whose luggage was lost, never to be seen again. How awful would it be to arrive at your destination only to discover that your dress has taken off for parts unknown?

All right—you don't want to hear this lost-luggage admonition? You have faith in the airline and you just want to know how to pack a big old dress? Box the dress. Wrap it in tissue paper to lessen its chance of wrinkling. Buy a big suitcase that can hold the dress box. (If you simply check the box at the ticket counter, there's a chance it could be crushed en route.) Luggage is inspected these days for the presence of weapons and the like, so cross your fingers that the x-ray machine does its job well and that no one needs to go into your suitcase, open the box, and paw through the folds of your dress looking for anything suspicious.

Shipping Options

If you're going to send your dress to your site through the mail or through another shipping carrier, plan for it to arrive good and early, at least a week to ten days before your scheduled arrival so that any delays that may occur don't send you into a complete frenzy. Depending on where you live, you may have countless shipping options, or only one or two. No matter. Follow the same directions no matter who you're handing that dress to:

❋ *Protect the dress.* Wrapping the dress in tissue paper helps to stop massive wrinkling. Wrapping the dress in plastic will help to protect it from moisture. Do both.

- ✳ *Box the dress.* The shop you bought the dress from will have a box for you. Don't take no for an answer.
- ✳ *Rebox the dress.* Put the dress box into a shipping box so that the inner box doesn't get crushed. Add whatever cushioning is available to protect the inner box from excessive shifts during shipping. Professional shipping stores have foam peanuts or bubble wrap on hand for this purpose.
- ✳ *Insure the dress.* When you're shipping a book or a pair of shoes, do you really care if they get lost? No; you can skip the insurance with those. In this case, though, you want assurance that your dress will arrive where and when it's supposed to—and that someone else will pay for it if it doesn't.

When you walk in the door of the shipping store, tell the clerk what you're sending and then let her take the lead. She may have even better ideas or options than those discussed here.

Your resort's wedding coordinator will be able to receive and store the dress for you. If you're not planning a resort wedding but you will be staying in a hotel, the concierge can sign for your package and put it in a spot for safekeeping. Make sure to call ahead to make these arrangements.

 **E~ssential**

When shipping your wedding dress, it's a good idea to choose a shipping company with real-time tracking information available. Many companies offer this service through their Web sites. This will allow you to follow your dress throughout its journey and make sure it's headed in the right direction at all times. ⌇

One more word of advice: Before you try to ship your dress to a foreign country, be sure to check its customs policy. Some countries charge very expensive fees on foreign packages, and some countries may have restrictions in place on what types of goods can come into the country in the first place.

Buying a Dress at Your Destination Spot

Is it a good idea to purchase your dress ahead of time in the same town where you'll be having your wedding? That depends. If you know you're going to be back in town frequently enough for fittings, then it might be a good idea to do this kind of one-stop shopping.

These circumstances tend to be on the rare side, however. It's not recommended that you choose a dress from a random dressmaker when you happen to be in town once, and then trust this stranger to make the dress look perfect in a matter of days when you roll back into town for your wedding.

It's possible to have fittings done at the very last minute, but you have to be dealing with a dress shop and seamstress you trust implicitly. Alterations are usually easy for a professional, but keep in mind that there are good seamstresses and bad seamstresses, and some dresses are just harder to work with than others.

E~Fact

Some destination wedding sites have rental dresses available for brides who just don't want to be bothered with handling a gown of any sort. If this idea works for you, call your wedding site and ask if they have dresses available for one-day use.

Generally speaking, it's best to have your dress nearby so that you can have it ready for the wedding as early as you choose. You don't want to arrive at your destination only to discover that the bodice of your dress is four sizes too big—and then find that no one can fix it.

Groom Attire

Here comes the bride, all dressed in white . . . and there stands the groom in his dirty old swim trunks and a tank top that has apparently been used as a napkin (is that steak sauce or chocolate smudged across his midsection, you wonder?). Instead of saying "I do," the bride shouts, "Time out!" Play will resume once the groom finds an appropriate wedding outfit.

Let's face it: Many men don't care about what they're wearing—ever. Sound like your fiancé? Is he telling you that it's the ceremony that's important, and not what he chooses to wear? He's right—to a degree. However, there are some events in an adult male's life for which he should make the effort to dress the part. A man's wedding is one of those events.

E~ssential

Linen suits are all the rage for beachfront ceremonies, for good reason: Linen is lightweight and relaxed, yet still dressy enough for the occasion. Some men choose to forgo the suit jacket in favor of a gauzy light-colored shirt. It's a matter of personal taste.

What a groom ends up wearing to his wedding is dictated by the ceremony itself. Obviously, a very formal, traditional ceremony (one held in a cathedral or a castle, for example) calls for very formal, traditional wedding gear, which means a custom-made suit or tux. Since most destination weddings turn into less formal events, couples find they're free to play around with their choices a bit more.

Let's say you choose a short, sleeveless, lacy little number for your resort wedding. Your groom's ensemble should complement yours. Think lightweight, light-colored, and casual. An ultra-structured suit just looks out of place on the beach. Linen and cotton blends work especially well for grooms in tropical climates. As for shoes? Sandals or bare feet are completely acceptable for seaside ceremonies (for both of you).

What if you're planning to walk down a sandy aisle in a sarong and a halter top? Do you have to let him wear those swim trunks and his tank top? No! Dress him in linen shorts and a tropical-print shirt and you two will look like a match made in paradise.

What's Everyone Else Wearing?

Other people will look to you for fashion advice: What should they wear to your wedding? While not every guest will beat down your door for your input here, your attendants and parents certainly will. Since you don't want them showing up in formalwear if you're going to be in a decidedly more relaxed outfit, don't take this conversation lightly. Many people are honestly at a loss when it comes to dressing for a destination wedding, and you'll need to be able to steer them in the right direction.

Attendants

Once you've dressed yourself and the groom, the attendants' outfits are easy to choose. The men should be dressed similarly to the groom, so if your fiancé is wearing a suit, the other men should, too. If there's only the best man to consider, then it's all right if the groom wears a tan suit and the best man is dressed in black. If there are several attendants, they should at least be dressed in the same family of colors—all dark or all light. You don't want them to look like Catholic schoolboys lining up for Mass, but you don't want a rainbow of suit jackets at the altar, either.

The trend in bridesmaids' dresses nowadays is for the bride to choose the color and allow the girls to choose the style of dress they'll wear. This is really a nice option, because then everyone is happy—you choose the level of formality and the color scheme, and they get to wear a dress that actually fits well and that they can very likely wear again. And if you're having just one bridesmaid, the two of you can go shopping together to look for a dress you're both happy with, or you can let her choose on her own. (After all, you *must* trust her if she's your only bridesmaid.)

The best part of allowing bridesmaids and groomsmen to wear clothing of their choice is that they can do their own bargain shopping, and you won't ever have to hear that you forced someone to buy a $400 dress.

Parents

There are a couple of rules of thumb for the parents of the engaged couple to follow when choosing outfits for the wedding:

* The bride's mother should not outdo the bride.
* The mother of the bride should choose a dress that complements the bridal party's dresses in formality and color—but it shouldn't match exactly.
* The bride's mother chooses her dress first and the groom's mom then chooses a complementary dress for herself—but not the same color as the bride's mom's dress.
* Similarly, dads should rise to but not exceed the level of formality of the men in the wedding party.

So what does all of this really mean? Mothers choose something that will make them shine (they're stars of this show, too) but not make them look like outcast members of the wedding party. Dads should show up looking as dressed-up as the groomsmen are. If your dad is going to give you away, he should really make an effort to look extra-dapper on your wedding day. If you need to go suit shopping with him in order to ensure that he doesn't show up in cutoffs, then do so.

Guests

And speaking of cutoffs, how do you politely tell your guests that they are not to show up at your wedding in their swim trunks? This is sometimes a problem with "vacation"-type weddings: Because the wedding experience is a weeklong, fun-filled experience, guests assume that the wedding itself will essentially be something else that's going on that week—nothing really serious, just another diversion on the trip.

If you're planning a formal wedding in an otherwise informal setting, such as a beach resort or a cruise ship, include this information in your invitations. In the lower left-hand corner, add a line that reads: "Please, no shorts or swim trunks at the ceremony. Business casual attire requested." (Of course, this is only an example. You'll substitute your own wedding's level of formality.) You may feel funny doing this, but you're really doing yourself and your guests a big favor. You won't have to chase your brother out of the ceremony when he shows up with his snorkeling gear (fresh from a dive), and he won't have to suffer the humiliation of *being* chased while wearing flippers.

Your Hairstyle Is Important, Too

From the moment you got engaged you have probably been thinking mostly about the dress. True, your wedding dress is a major part of your big day, and it's something that you should feel beautiful and comfortable in. Shoes and jewelry are also a big part of the package, and you'll need to consider all of your choices carefully when you're planning your ensemble. However, there's one more thing that brides often overlook until it's too late: Hair! Your haircut or style is just as important to your appearance on your big day as are your gown and accessories. And like the other aspects of your wedding, hair deserves some planning.

Cutting It Close

Here's the rule: Do not make any drastic changes to your hairstyle in the two months before your wedding. If you've always had shoulder-length hair, don't crop it to within an inch of your scalp just weeks before the big day. If you've always been a brunette, postpone going platinum until after the honeymoon. Honestly, if you've waited to make major changes until now, you can wait a while longer.

You just can't fix serious hair mistakes quickly. A bad dye job can follow you for months, even if a professional tries to correct it. (Hair dye can damage hair beyond recognition, so you shouldn't fool around with going from very dark hair to a very light coif on your own, anyway.) A too-short cut can take months to grow out to a length you're comfortable with, depending on how "too-short" you went. Even though you might adapt a healthy attitude and come to terms with everything that's gone wrong on top of your head, you don't want to look back on your wedding pictures and think to yourself, "That hair! I can't bear to look at it!"

❀ E~Alert

Any woman who's lived through an unfortunate hair experience will tell you it's nothing you want to relive, which means you'll be faced with trauma every time you look at those wedding photos. ﾉ

If you have just recently set a date for your wedding and you have almost a year between now and the big day, go ahead and experiment, but only with a trusted colorist or stylist. When it comes down to the home stretch, do what you've always done. If you know that the hairs on your head need a good week or two to chill out and regroup after a cut and color, then don't pop into the salon three days before the wedding. Give your head enough time to settle down and look its best for the big day.

Capturing That Perfect Look for Later

You probably won't have your stylist with you when you take off for your wedding, but this doesn't mean that you should arrive at your destination without a plan for your wedding-day hair. If you're wearing a veil or headpiece, take it in to your hairdresser at least a couple of months before the wedding so that the two of you can talk about what type of hairstyle will look best. Bring a picture of your dress; talk openly with her about the ceremony and how formal or informal it will be. She should have some good ideas about what might work best for your hair. Be prepared to make several visits to work out the best style.

Once you've perfected your wedding-day hairstyle, you have to plan a way to achieve that look on your wedding day! When you get home from the salon, have your maid of honor (or your mom, or your future hubby) take some pictures of your perfect 'do.

Then, about two months before the wedding, find a stylist or a beauty shop near your ceremony site (your wedding coordinator will be able to give you a recommendation; if you're planning on your own, ask a female wedding vendor for the name of a good hairstylist in the area). Book two appointments for yourself. The first one will be a consultation as soon as you hit town so that you can meet face-to-face with the hairdresser and discuss your hairstyle for the wedding. Bring along those pictures from home—and your headpiece—to this meeting. The other appointment will be on your wedding day, so don't be shy during the first meeting—make sure that the stylist understands exactly what you want before you leave the shop.

Finishing Touches: Makeup

As important as it is for your hair to look its best on your wedding day, it's just as necessary for your face to show that you're glowing with happiness. Though some women have the ability to throw on a little lip gloss and mascara and look their absolute best, most of the rest of us need a little help smoothing out the rough edges and perfecting that look of imperfection. Our tools: the cosmetic bag and its contents.

Subtle Magic

Some women are opposed to makeup on principle, thinking that it's ridiculous for society to expect its female members to paint their faces when men can walk around looking pale and drawn and no one seems to care. If this sounds like your set of beliefs concerning makeup, this book isn't going to argue the point. But when it comes to your wedding day, maybe you could open your mind just a little to consider these points:

* You're going to have your picture taken over and over and over again throughout the course of the day.
* A little bit of well-placed makeup can effectively camouflage flaws, such as dark circles under your eyes or redness on your cheeks—flaws that tend to show up more in pictures than in real life.
* This doesn't have to be a lifelong commitment; just try it to see.

No one is suggesting that you go from wearing no makeup to caking it on. Remember, you want to look natural—and like yourself—on the big day and in the photos. Experiment with just the basics first:

* *Concealer.* Choose a shade that's close to your skin color and use it to hide under-eye circles.
* *Foundation.* Use a makeup sponge to apply foundation to your cheeks. It should just even out the skin tone. A little foundation goes a long way; just make sure it's blended at the jawline so that your neck and face appear to be the same color.
* *Lip color.* The rest of your face can appear bright and youthful, but if your lips are colorless, you'll end up looking washed out in pictures. If lip color isn't your thing, choose a subtle shade of lip gloss and try it out for a few days. When you're comfortable, experiment with other shades of gloss and with lipstick.
* *Mascara.* If you're not a regular user of mascara, you'll be amazed at how long your lashes can appear with one swipe of the wand. Always use a brow brush to separate lashes (and get rid of clumps) after applying mascara.
* *Blush.* A carefully blended dab of blush on each cheek, and you're all set. Again, a little goes a long way with these products, and you can make yourself look *finished* without appearing overdone.

* *Eye shadow.* A smidge of color is all you need to make your eyes appear brighter and more open. Darker colors go on the lid and in the crease; lighter shades are blended up to the brow bone.
* *Eye liner.* No one's suggesting that you outline your eyes with a black kohl pencil. A light lining of the lower lid defines your eyes and really makes them pop in pictures.

If makeup is relatively new to you, start experimenting with colors and products well before your wedding day. Ask your friends and family for their honest evaluation—and their help!

Get Professional Assistance

Maybe the idea of experimenting with makeup on your own leaves you feeling shaky. You don't know the first thing about color or application, and you don't really trust anyone you know to show you how to do the job the right way. Get your handbag and your shoes; we're going to the cosmetics counter.

When you enter the store, choose a consultant whose makeup looks like what you'd like to achieve with your own face. She will be more likely to listen to your concerns about not looking overly made-up than will the woman whose eyes are done in three very distinct shades of eye shadow. Your consultant will have ideas of her own for your face; if you have any thoughts on the issue of color, speak up before she starts applying products. Also, it's courteous to purchase something from her when she's finished with your makeover; just make sure it's something you want to own.

When you've achieved the perfect balance of natural glow and woman-made beauty, note which products you like best and then practice, practice, practice! You really will get the hang of it fairly quickly, and your wedding pictures will show your expertise.

Chapter 11
Wedding Photography and Video

Been practicing that perfect smile? Good, 'cause you're going to need it. Whether you're a real ham or you hate having your picture taken, all flashbulbs will be on you on your wedding day, and your pictures could come out looking like a magazine spread—or like your thirteen-year-old cousin was fooling around with your camera and trying to catch you at your very worst moment. In this chapter, you'll learn how to find the right photographer and how to look your very best in your wedding pics.

Find a Pro

Right off the bat, it's important for you to know that a good photographer is usually worth every penny you end up paying him or her. A professional photographer can make you look like a model, or at least come very, very close to doing so. Since you're going to be looking at these photos for many years to come, you want them to look as flawless and flattering as possible.

E~Alert

While it may seem like a great way to save money, it's actually not a good idea to ask a friend or relative to act as chief photographer at your wedding. That's a lot of pressure to put on someone who was expecting to relax and enjoy himself throughout the day. You may also be very disappointed with the pictures, adding unnecessary strain to your relationship.

A skilled photographer sees things that other people don't. He knows what kind of lighting will work best with your skin tone and coloring. He can envision the backdrop of a group photo just by looking at a particular space. He observes you from all angles and decides which one is most flattering. This guy is an artist in the truest sense of the word—he's able to find beauty where you might think none exists. (So if you think you always look terrible in family pictures, blame the picture taker, not the image in the mirror!)

There's no magic involved in taking great pictures, only talent. What makes the difference between good pictures and bad ones? Lighting, setting, composition, and even the type of film or camera the photographer uses. You'll read more about these topics throughout the chapter. Just know for now that strapping a very expensive camera around someone's neck doesn't necessarily make him a professional in the truest sense of the word. He's also got to have the ability to see you in the best light, even if you're currently standing in the worst light.

Resort Photographers

If you're marrying in a resort or someplace where a photo package is included in your wedding, you won't have a choice of photographers. And that may be fine with you—it makes everything easy. You'll choose from packages offered in various sizes and prices. Before you choose, though, do ask if it's possible to see samples online. While digital pictures sometimes appear grainy when sent through cyberspace, you can get a fairly good idea of what kinds of pictures you can expect. For example:

* Are the bride and groom standing in a dark hallway? Can you make out their faces?
* How do the colors appear? Are they vibrant or washed out?
* What kind of composition did the photographer use? Is the wedding party nicely arranged, or does it look as though your Aunt Dottie ambushed them with her instant camera?
* Generally speaking, are they nice-looking pictures?

You may not have any choice when it comes to who takes the pictures; however, if the sample photos look amateurish, this speaks to the quality of photographers that your wedding site hires. You don't want to blow a lot of money on an album that is filled with pictures of similar (bad) quality, so you'll be better off purchasing the smallest package available.

E~Fact

If the setting seems to be the problem in most of the poor-quality photos you view, you may be able to request that your photos not be taken indoors, in front of a particular statue, and so on. Just make sure you make such requests as soon as possible in order to avoid less-than-ideal options.

If the sample photos are really bad, you might want to rethink (or at least re-research) your wedding destination. You have to go on the assumption that they've sent you the best samples they have; if the pictures are bad, how bad will the food be? And how about the musicians?

Finding a Photographer on Your Own

If your wedding isn't an all-inclusive package, it's up to you to find the right man or woman for the job. When a bride is planning a wedding in her hometown, she has the luxury of depending on word-of-mouth referrals about which photographer is unbelievably talented, which one is overpriced, and which one is a little wet behind the ears but has amazing potential. But even with word-of-mouth recommendations (and warnings), brides still make mistakes when choosing photographers, mostly because they haven't done enough research on the topic.

 E~ssential

While you can't depend on recommendations from friends and relatives when planning an out-of-town wedding, you can ask your reception and/or wedding site coordinators for their recommendations. Doing this will at least narrow down the list of candidates to a manageable number.

Just because you're trying to find a photographer in a faraway location, you're not really at a disadvantage. In fact, if you know what kinds of questions to ask of a potential photographer, you're better off than someone who *thinks* she knows what she's talking about, but doesn't. Do you follow? Read on.

Independent Photographers

An independent photographer has her own studio. This person answers only to herself and her clients, not to a manager and/or some larger national company. The upside of hiring an independent is that as a group they're usually pretty creative and willing to work with you on unique poses and shots, whereas someone working with a big studio may not have that kind of leeway, even if she agrees with your ideas.

A good independent photographer is usually fairly expensive. She sets her own prices, and if she's as good as people say she is, she isn't hurting for business (which means she probably isn't open to a lot of negotiation on price). The downside can be that independents are sometimes *very* independent, and will make no bones about telling you that they're only available from noon to six on your wedding day because they have other things to do in the evening, which means you're just going to have to work your wedding-day schedule around their plans. That's a tough pill to swallow when you're paying top dollar for this person's services—and the day is supposed to be all about you!

Studio Photography

Another option is to work with a studio. The benefit of going this route is that you can usually find a package to meet your budget. The downside is that you'll choose from a list of poses and shots, which may or may not include the kinds of pictures you're looking for. Also, some studios won't commit to sending a specific photographer to your wedding, so there's no way to know who you'll be working with on the big day, *or* what kind of pictures you'll end up with. You can do all of your research, go into the studio, look at countless wedding photos, ask all the right questions, but if the studio can't tell you who is going to show up to take your pictures (which means you won't see samples of your photographer's work) then you have little to go on, really. *You need to see samples of your photographer's work before you sign a contract.* Otherwise, it's about as good as hiring a stranger off the street to take your pictures.

Gathering Information

Unless you're locked into a package photo deal, you'll have to assume the role of interviewer when talking to potential photographers. Many of the topics you'll cover are the same, whether you're speaking to an independent or a studio. This section covers the different ways to find out if a photographer is the right one for your wedding.

Asking the Right Questions

While you can't demand this person's social security and tax identification numbers, you can and should ask about his background in photography. Here are some questions you might ask:

* ☀ Is this a profession or a hobby for you?
* ☀ How long have you been in this business?
* ☀ How many weddings have you done?
* ☀ Can you show me some of your most recent work?

What kinds of answers are you looking for? Chances are you'll know when you hear them. First of all, you want to know that this person is a dedicated professional, and that picture-taking isn't just something he does for kicks once in a while. If his bread and butter depends on the quality of his photos, he's more likely to be dedicated to doing great work, and also to keeping abreast of the latest techniques, which is something you'll read more about shortly. You also want to know that he has some sort of formal education in the arts—preferably in photography. A good photographer needs to know about color, composition, and lighting. These are things that the average Joe usually doesn't give much thought to (which is why Joe's pictures turn out so badly).

E~ssential

A start-up photographer should have plenty of experience apprenticing with a professional before he does his first solo gig. Although you may want to be nice and give someone his big break, you have to realize that you won't get a second chance at getting these pictures right. Do what's smart for you and let the photographer worry about his own career.

When it comes to how long a prospective photographer has been in business and how many weddings he's done, different brides are comfortable with different answers. Someone who is just starting out might be more eager to prove himself by taking some really interesting pictures and working much harder than a seasoned pro would; on the other hand, the seasoned pro has done a thousand weddings and may not need to work so hard to get the same results.

In addition to asking lots of questions about his background and experience, also ask to see samples of the photographer's most recent work, and *really* take note of the quality of the pictures. Again, you're looking for color, composition, and lighting. You want to see a variety of poses, crisp colors, and a combination of flash pictures and natural lighting (which always looks more natural). Consider these questions:

* Do the colors look realistic or just horrific?
* Does the bride appear pale with circles under her eyes?
* Does the wedding party appear to be smashed into the frame— or is the picture taken from so far away that you can't see their faces?

If the answers to these questions are yes, it means that you're looking at poor-quality pictures. Then do yourself a favor: Thank the photographer for his time, and move on to the next name on your list.

Photo Styles

One thing you need to know before you book a photographer is what style he tends to use. There are three main styles: traditional, photojournalistic, and illustrative (sometimes also called creative).

* *Traditional.* These are classic wedding shots. Everything and everyone is posed. The photographer gives you a "shot-list" of poses and pictures that you want in your wedding album. After you choose your specific poses, the photographer takes charge of the day, telling you where you need to be and when.
* *Photojournalistic.* These pictures are decidedly un-posed, spontaneous, and candid. The photographer basically takes pictures that tell the story of the day, and they could include anything: A shoe. Wine glasses. The back of your flower girl's dress.
* *Illustrative.* This style calls on the photographer to come up with something more creative than the traditional poses, but less avant-garde than photojournalistic shots. So—sort of traditional, but with a more unique twist.

You have to see the photographer's work to know whether he's capable of pulling off the style he claims to have mastered. Photojournalism is a particularly tough art to polish. An experienced photojournalist can do a bang-up job taking pictures of shoes and flowers and backs of heads; an unskilled photographer will present you with a picture of a wine glass, and you'll react by asking, "What is *this* supposed to be?"

Although good photojournalism is becoming more popular with marrying couples, parents of the bride and groom are sometimes disappointed to learn that there won't be any family pictures or more traditional shots.

So it may be worth your while to ask whether your photographer is adept at combining two or more styles.

Techie Talking Points

If your initial questions are answered satisfactorily and the pictures seem to be up to par, the next thing you want to know is how this person works. In this day and age, you should be hearing some sort of digital answer. Some photographers use a combination of film and digital cameras, but most will agree that digital photography has come a long way in terms of quality in just the past few years, so much so that some picture-takers have gone completely digital.

Why Digital?

You may be old-fashioned at heart and think, "I hate technology. Give me film!" Well, consider this: Digital cameras let the photographer see how well the pictures have turned out on the spot. All you have to do is ask someone who's been married for at least ten years whether some of their most desired poses turned out badly (because of blinked eyes or someone shifting in a group photo), and they'll tell you: Do the digital.

 E~ssential

Digital photography is less expensive in the long run for you. Film is simply more expensive to work with—it's less forgiving in the sense that pictures have to be developed before they can be evaluated. You're paying for that film, whether the pictures are acceptable or not.

When you sign a contract with a photographer, you'll choose how many pictures you want in the end; the photographer will tell you how many proofs she'll take. The proofs are the original pictures that haven't been enlarged or retouched. You might end up with three times as many digital proofs as film proofs to choose from.

Important Digital Facts

What do you need to know about pixels? Well, they're the tiny dots that make up digital pictures. The more pixels, the better the definition of the photo, especially when the picture is enlarged.

Photographers talk about pixels in several different ways. They may say that a picture is 2000 x 1800 pixels, or they may say that the picture has 3.6 million pixels (this is the same thing; the latter measurement is just the earlier numbers multiplied). They also talk about dots per inch (dpi) or pixels per inch (ppi). The higher the number, the better, as a higher number means the picture will appear crisper and clearer.

You'll choose digital pictures off a CD-ROM (*so* much easier than flipping through stacks of film proofs), which you'll also be able to purchase (if it's not already included in your photo package).

Another option, aside from going with film-only, is doing a combination of digital and film. Why would you want to do this? Well, some settings and colors just naturally respond better to film. Where pixels might have a meltdown in front of a sunset, for example, film can step in and handle the job. For this reason, many photographers still tote their old handy film cameras around.

Hiring a Videographer

You've see them: the bad wedding videos that elicit laughs for all the wrong reasons. Bad shots of the wedding party. Cheesy special effects. Pop something like this into your DVD player and suddenly everyone is rolling on the floor while you're trying to relive the magic of your wedding day.

Just as it's vitally important to see samples of your photographer's work before you hire her, you need to see what a videographer has done in the past to know what he's capable of doing for you.

No More VHS Tapes

Most videographers work in the digital medium these days for the same reasons that photographers have embraced the technology: It's easier to work with in many cases, especially when editing and adding special effects. From your point of view, a wedding DVD will be infinitely easier to view—and to share with friends. Unlike videotapes and standard photos, digital images can be downloaded onto your computer and sent across cyberspace (with your photographer's or videographer's permission, of course).

Check Out a Sample

Although videographers differ in their style and skill, you can expect to find some similarities among them as a group. Many videographers, for example, will use at least two cameras when filming a wedding, which is a good thing. In the editing process, you'll get the best possible shot of each part of the event.

E~ssential

Videographers offer various packages (with various prices). One package might offer ten hours of taping with two cameras, while another might offer ten hours of taping using three cameras plus a video montage of you and the groom as children at the beginning of your DVD. 🌢

No matter how much you like the videographer or how low his price may be, ask to see a sample DVD before you sign a contract—and watch the entire thing! Since the same video can appear perfect to one couple and horribly cheesy to another, your evaluation of it will be a highly personal thing.

Following are a few things to watch for, though, no matter what your personal taste.

* *Editing.* Is the video smooth, or are there sudden cuts in the action that jump to an unrelated scene?
* *Sound.* Can you hear the bride and groom reciting their vows?
* *Color and picture clarity.* Fuzzy, yellow-toned people are not acceptable.
* *Special effects.* Subtle or over the top?
* *Special elements.* Did all of the guests have a chance to wish the newlyweds well? Did the video capture the bouquet toss and the cake-cutting? Do there seem to be large chunks of time that are missing?

Given that your wedding is going to take place out of town, you may think that your only option is to find a videographer who works near your wedding site. This may not necessarily be true. With the growing popularity of destination weddings, many photographers and videographers are willing to make the trip with you—at your expense, of course. If money is no object and you've found the perfect person for the job in your hometown, it can't hurt to ask if he or she might consider hauling the video camera down to the Caribbean!

Chapter 12
Nosegays and Bouquets: The Flowers

Decorating your ceremony and reception sites with the right flowers seems like a simple enough task. They're flowers, after all; by their very nature, they're all pretty, so how can you go wrong? You may not realize that flowers can be one of the biggest expenses of your entire wedding, and that's just for basic arrangements. If you're planning on plastering posies all over your canopy or the altar, it's best to know what you're in for financially before you sit down with the wedding coordinator or florist.

Pick Those Flowers

Are daisies your thing? Do lilies just make you swoon, or daffodils send you over the moon? Identifying the type of flowers you'd like to use for your wedding is a good way to start this process. If you're not really a flower person and don't have a favorite, you can go by color scheme, or you can incorporate flowers into the bouquets based on their traditional meanings. The most common flowers and plants and their meanings are:

* Red roses: love
* Lily: majesty
* Iris: affection
* Lily-of-the-valley: happiness
* Ivy: fidelity
* Gardenia: secret love

Consider the Season

Thanks to modern advances in greenhouse techniques, most flowers are available year-round. However, their prices may vary according to the season. The price of red roses, for example, spikes around Valentine's Day, when demand is at its highest; meanwhile, the price of lily-of-the-valley drops in May, when these blooms are naturally in season.

E~ssential

For a holiday wedding, you might want to incorporate traditional poinsettias into the bouquets. These will provide a burst of color and give your wedding a special seasonal feel. After the ceremony, you can use the bridesmaids' bouquets on the head table as decorations during the reception.

You'll want to keep the season or location in mind for the sake of appropriateness, also. If you're planning a wedding in the South Seas, use the natural flora found there; it's part of your décor, anyway. Meanwhile, if you're planning a Christmas wedding in a mountain lodge, think twice before ordering hibiscus bouquets, even if they are your favorite blossom; they just won't look or feel right.

Where Do the Flowers Go?

Perhaps you're wondering what the big deal is about wedding flowers. A couple of baskets of flowers here and there and you're all set. Well, depending on the site of your ceremony and reception, you may be faced with filling a lot of empty spaces with prettiness. Think about:

* *The church or synagogue.* Is it big or small? Will the pews look barren without anything on them? What about the entryway?
* *The canopy.* Is it decorative enough on its own, or does it need some sort of decoration added to it?
* *Your reception site.* Is it a tent, an outdoor patio, an indoor hall? Can you envision topiary trees, plants of any sort, ribbon strung from here to there?
* *The tables.* They'll need centerpieces. Will candles of various sizes work, or might candelabrum do the trick? If you're having a seaside wedding, might you be able to fill bowls with various shells and use them as your ornamentation?

You get the idea. Your goal is to fill empty space with wedding-themed paraphernalia. Think about adding tulle draping to the pews, or ivy garlands to stairway banisters. Grapevine wreaths are easy to put together; they can be used as homespun centerpieces for less formal weddings.

Consulting the Experts

For a partially or entirely preplanned resort wedding, you may be presented with various options from which to choose from. This makes your life easier, but it also limits you to the offerings you're presented with. If you're choosing vendors on your own, however, the ball is completely in your court. The downside is that you have to search for and interview florists on your own, which can be a time-consuming process.

Resort Offerings

If you're planning a wedding at a resort, the wedding coordinator on-site will give you several options, which will almost certainly include local flowers. If you just have to have something that isn't presented to you in her brochure, it can't hurt to ask. However, in the event that you don't find what you're looking for, you probably will not be allowed to import your own flowers. The resort very likely has a florist under contract, which means you're limited to what this florist can offer. It's always possible that she can special-order what you're looking for, but it's never a foregone conclusion.

✿ E~Question

Is there any way to find out about the floral options at destination wedding sites before actually visiting in person?

When checking out destination wedding sites, do some digging on each resort's Web site. Most have pictures of their floral options, along with package details and pricing. While flowers shouldn't be the only factor in your wedding site decision, especially lovely floral packages might help narrow down your choices. ✿

Rest assured, most resorts offer stunning floral arrangements as options for their weddings. Remember, this is one of the perks of having a destination wedding: Most of the planning is cut back to manageable choices.

Digging Up a Florist

If you're planning an à la carte destination wedding (that is, you're marrying outside of your hometown but you have to find each vendor on your own), you need to start looking for a florist at least six months prior to the wedding, if you have that kind of time. (If you're short on time, then start looking now.) This is not a task that you should shrug your shoulders about, thinking "Hey, I'll go out and pick flowers myself if I have to. No big deal." It *is* a big deal. You want to find someone talented, reliable, and reasonably priced. You don't want to get stuck using any florist you can find (who ends up being a big advocate of using roadside weeds in her arrangements—at exorbitant prices, no less) just because you didn't get with the program early enough.

Normally, the way to find a great florist would be to ask people you know for recommendations and to check out functions where the florist's work is on display. So how do you track down this perfect florist when you don't know anyone in the area? Assuming you've chosen a site for your wedding (which is really the best place to start—if you haven't booked a site, you can't very well book any other vendors), ask whomever you've been dealing with there to recommend someone. Chances are, that person will be able to lead you in the right direction.

E~Alert

Even with a stellar recommendation from another vendor, ask your florist for the names and numbers of other clients (brides who have gone before you, or churches or businesses she regularly creates arrangements for). Take the time to make a few phone calls to ask if these people have been consistently happy with the florist's work.

If by some chance you aren't able to get a recommendation for a florist from your contact at the ceremony site, ask one of your other vendors. Caterers, musicians, and florists often work the same party and wedding circuits, so your other vendors should be able to recommend (or steer you away from) a particular person or business.

Along with checking a florist's references, make sure you see her work—either in person or in photos—before you sign a contract. Digital photography has made sending pictures so easy that there's just no excuse for not doing this.

Choosing a Florist

When you call a florist for an initial consultation, you'll need to provide her with the date and site of your wedding so she can check it against her busy schedule. (If you don't have a date yet, don't bother calling. No sense in both of you wasting your time if she ends up being booked on the date that you eventually choose.)

You want to start out asking some standard questions, such as how long she's been in business, what her background in horticulture is, how many weddings she typically handles at that time of year, how many assistants she has backing her up, her prices, and so on. Then you can get into issues specific to your wedding. Here are some sample questions:

＊ *Are you familiar with my ceremony and reception sites?* It will help if she has some idea of the size of the space(s) she's dealing with. An intimate space needs far fewer floral decorations than does a mighty cathedral.

＊ *With my wedding site in mind, what kind of decorations would you recommend?* Visualize what she's saying, and use your best judgment to determine whether you agree with her. Obviously, she's a pro and you aren't, but you can get a fairly good sense of whether she's filling the space well—or just overfilling it.

＊ *What types of flowers are in season in the area at the time of my wedding?* Again, in-season flowers most often translate into savings for you. If there's anything on her list of in-season blooms that you can live with, use it.

The "right" answers to these questions vary from bride to bride. Some women have no problem hiring a start-up florist, for example, while others want only a veteran of the floral world handling their wedding. This is where those references will come in handy. Even the greenest florist in the garden should be able to give you the name of someone she's worked wonders for. When all's said and done, you should be completely comfortable with all of the information you've gleaned from your conversation with a prospective florist. If she simply refuses to quote even a ballpark price for a fairly standard wedding-issue nosegay, ask if she'll send a written quote for all of your floral needs. You should have some idea of what this person is going to charge *before* you book her.

Make It Official

Once you find a florist who meets your needs, be prepared to sign a contract with her. When you're looking over the contract, double-check the date of the wedding; the delivery time and address(es); and the number of arrangements, bouquets, and boutonnieres. In short, make sure that everything you've discussed and agreed upon verbally is in front of you *in writing*. You'll also be charged rental fees for vases, stands, the runner for the church, and things of that nature, so don't be surprised to see those charges on a written binder.

If something is missing from *any* contract, don't sign until it's been corrected and initialed by the vendor, which in this case is the florist. If there are multiple errors, *nicely* ask for the contract to be entirely redone. It'll give you peace of mind, and send a clear message to the vendor that you mean business.

Other Important Details

The date, times, and address(es) of the ceremony and reception site are of particular importance when making arrangements for your flowers because you have to take your photographer into consideration. If he's planning on taking pictures of the wedding party at four o'clock on the day of the wedding and your ceremony is at five-thirty, you'll want the flowers by three o'clock.

Make sure to give the florist the correct address of the wedding site and also of the place where you'll be preparing for the wedding. If she delivers twelve pedestal-topper vases to 401 Elm Street (because it's the address you gave her) and the wedding is taking place at 401 Elmwood Drive, that's not her fault. (And we won't get into whose fault it is. Just triple-check the addresses on the contract and leave it at that.)

Your Flower Budget

Just because they're fresh flowers that will likely have to be thrown away within a week's time doesn't mean that they won't be costly. Flowers for the wedding can be one shocking expense that you never saw coming. Flower arrangement is an art and a service, so you're not just paying for the flowers themselves.

Before you call any florist, have an idea of what types of arrangements you're looking for. Look through your bridal magazines or do some Internet searches and find out the difference between a nosegay and a cascading bouquet. Check out some different options for decoration the church and reception sites—do you want gardenias floating in a crystal bowl with votives underneath, or do you want mammoth vases of exotic flowers on each table?

Ask your friends what they paid for their wedding flowers and what that price included. Visit a florist in your hometown armed with a list of wedding ideas and get a quote from her. This is not to judge the honesty of a given florist (because along the way, you may note variations in prices), but to give you some idea of what florists typically charge for their arrangements.

Once you have a fairly solid idea of what your flowers might cost, you can set a realistic flower budget. It's just not wise to be thinking that you can decorate a huge tent with floral arrangements on each table for about

$700 (which, to someone who hasn't done her research, sounds like an awful lot of money for decorations that are grown in dirt).

✿ E~Alert

If you're planning your wedding in a metropolitan area, don't use your small-town research as a base for budgeting. Expect to pay more for just about everything in such a locale, including flowers. And remember: Allowing for a little extra spending is better than budgeting too little. If you don't end up spending it all, you'll be pleased to be left with some cash still in your pocket. Drowning in debt, on the other hand, always makes for an unhappy ending. ✿

Have a budget in mind when you talk to a prospective florist, and be firm in your resolve to stick as close to it as possible, because it's just too easy to go way over on this expense. A really creative florist can work with you and make your wedding beautiful on almost any budget.

Snipping Costs

There's no real way to completely do away with flowers at a wedding, because the pictures would look bare without them. Flowers add that last touch, that color in the background that reminds everyone that this is a special day (because people don't lay money out on such beautiful flowers for nothing). When dealing with a resort or cruise line, you'll look at several plans and packages at various prices and make your final choices from there. When planning a destination wedding elsewhere, you'll be able to get more creative with the decorations, and cut costs in the process.

Be Creative

If you're already thinking that there's no way you're going to get creative (just because you've simply never considered yourself a crafty, think-outside-the-box person), think again. All you need is some time and inspiration—and an open mind.

If you happen to have a really creative friend or family member, don't squander that resource! Get her involved and ask her for ideas. Crafty people love to share their visions and they also like to try new things. But before you give anyone carte blanche to start spending your wedding money and creating centerpieces for you, make sure that you both have similar ideas about how your wedding is going to look. You don't want your aunt to be making down-home accent pieces while you're imagining something more elegant.

Should You Fake It?

You might be tempted to use fake flowers in your wedding décor, reasoning that these phony buds will last forever, so you'll at least get your money's worth when you use them to decorate the house.

If you just love silk floral arrangements and you know for sure that you will use them, then this might be a very wise choice. Just be aware that the more realistic looking the silk, the more expensive it's going to be. If you're going this route just to save money on fresh flowers, you might be completely shocked when you realize how much money you've spent on fake peonies.

This isn't an encouragement to go as cheaply as you can on the fakes, however. There are beautiful silk flowers—but there are also some really bad reproductions that are poor excuses for real flowers. One rule of thumb: If you can't find the flower in nature (for example, a truly blue rose), don't include it in your wedding bouquets or other decorations.

Plant It

Large potted plants or trees are another reusable non-floral option for your ceremony and reception sites. Ferns are always a classy touch, as are topiaries. Before you go out to purchase real or silk plants, make sure to measure the area where you're going to place them. A too-large plant will look out of place to even the least discerning eye, and a too-small plant is likely to be trampled, knocked over, or otherwise destroyed.

Don't forget to take into consideration your ceremony and reception sites and the plants themselves when purchasing the pots for the plants. A topiary is a fairly expensive and upscale plant, for example. It belongs in a beautiful planter—not in a terra cotta pot. (The planter itself will be another added expense.)

Planters lining the stairway into a reception hall or ceremony site add a nice touch. Again, choose plants of an appropriate size, and planters that match the décor. If you choose plants that are large enough, you can probably even place the planters on every other step.

Filling the corners of an empty reception area with trees is a nice touch, as long as the trees aren't going to look dwarfed and puny, as they will in a room that's wide open (such as a fire hall). Decorate those trees with white or clear lights, and your guests will feel like they're watching the stars come out.

Nonfloral Options

To get ideas for nonfloral decorations for your wedding, look at bridal magazines. Look online. Go to other weddings and study what other brides and grooms have done. Consider the season and the setting. Nothing is really out of the realm of possibility as long as you can transport it.

For example, gourds, pumpkins, and Indian corn make great decorations for fall weddings. Ice sculptures are a nice choice for winter. Colorful fruit baskets are also a fun nonfloral choice, and these can be used year-round.

E~ssential

At a recent autumn wedding, the groom and his ushers carved pumpkins for the table centerpieces. Purchasing twenty-two pumpkins was far cheaper than ordering the same number of floral centerpieces, and each table had a similar—yet different—focal point. Carving the pumpkins also served as a fun bonding activity for the groom and his friends.

Balloons are a popular decorating option, and can be placed here and there around the reception site (large groups of balloons tied to a shiny Mylar base) or as major points of attention (an arch stretching over the entranceway). If you're going with balloons, try to make them as classy as possible. This means don't go balloon crazy. If your reception site is rather large, you'll need more balloons, obviously, but avoid making your reception look like a circus.

Though you might be tempted to use red and black balloons (because your bridesmaids are dressed in red and your groomsmen are in black), the classic wedding colors just look nicer. Stick with white, gold, silver, or a combination of these colors.

Choose What's Right for You

When it comes to narrowing down wedding options, there's one piece of advice that works 99 percent of the time—get out there and see what you like and then fit it to your budget. However, when it comes to choosing flowers for the bride, you have to look beyond what your best friend carried down the aisle when she got married—you have to consider what's going to flatter your complexion, dress, and body type the most.

All-white bouquets are popular in some areas. While they're extremely pretty (and minimalist, something that destination brides are often looking for), they can be very hard for a fair-skinned woman to carry off. If your skin color can best be described as alabaster, these flowers are likely going to make you look washed out and pale in the wedding pictures, and that's obviously not the look you're going for.

Stick with Your Palette

It's easy enough to find out which colors work best with your skin tone. There are two major color groupings in the world of beauty—warm and cool. Women who fall into the warm tones have more olive-colored skin, while the cool tones tend to more fair skinned. (One supposedly sure way to tell: Look at the veins in your wrist. If they look greenish, you're a warm color; if they're blue, you're cool.) Women whose skin is warm-toned look good in certain colors; those with cool tones look better in others.

E~Fact
Warm and cool color groupings used to be referred to as *seasons*. Your mom and her friends used to sit around and talk about whether they were autumn-, winter-, spring- or summer-colored, as in, "What color are you, Betty Sue?" To which Betty Sue would reply, "Oh, I'm a winter!"

So which colors work best for each group? Warm colors should lean toward earthy tones, including orange, yellow, deep green, dark red, rich browns, and off-white. What does this mean for your bouquet? Well, if you're getting married in the tropics, where the flowers are often orange and red, you'll look right at home!

Cool colors, meanwhile, look better in pinks, purples, and blues. Since many beautiful flowers come in these colors, too, there's no reason to envy your warmer sisters.

What Body Type Has to Do with It

If you're a short bride, a good florist will talk you out of a two-foot cascading bouquet. It's just too overpowering and will only serve to make you look shorter. On the other hand, if you're up around the six-foot mark, you need a substantial bouquet to see you down the aisle in style.

If you're round-ish, don't go with the biggest, roundest bouquet you can find; if you're lanky and have a long face, avoid drawing yourself into an even straighter line with a cascading bouquet. Tied calla lilies are very popular right now, and for good reason: They look good with almost any body type.

When you're working with a florist and choosing your wedding flowers, ask her about your complexion and body type. She should have some answers ready to go (and better yet, she should broach the issue before you do). If you think something won't look right on you, then it probably won't. And if you don't trust your own instinct, get a second opinion from a brutally honest source, like your mom, who isn't about to keep mum and let you look bad on your wedding day.

Chapter 13
Choosing the Cake

What's a wedding without cake? Before you give this question too much thought (and honestly, any amount is too much) the answer is that it would still be a beautiful, special day, but your guests would spend a lot of time asking, "Where's the cake?" The cake usually ends up being a focal point of the reception. Though most brides choose to go with the traditional towering confection, there are alternatives to the traditional wedding cake. In this chapter you will learn how to choose the right cake as well as how to avoid choosing the wrong cake, and you'll also read about other desserts you may want to consider.

Package Deals

When you choose a resort or cruise line for your wedding, you'll be given choices for your reception dessert. Out of consideration for the fact that most brides still lean toward serving wedding cake, most destination wedding spots are prepared to offer cake as an option. You may also be given the opportunity to choose from pastries, fruit plates, cookies, and so on, depending on the location. Your choices may be limited to what the resort normally serves at its weddings. Even the smallest sites will have a couple of different setups for you to choose from, but you may not be able to order the cake of your dreams if it includes some types of filling and frosting that either aren't available or that the baker can't work with.

Also, when you're working within a package deal, the cake will automatically be sized for your wedding. In other words, if you're having a very intimate ceremony and reception (just eight to ten people), you won't be able to order a cake that will be assembled with fountains, pillars, and the like. Most of it would only end up in the garbage anyway. Things to keep in mind when ordering your cake from a package deal:

* *Flavors.* Most sites offer fairly standard flavors (white cake, yellow cake, white frosting) as a means of pleasing most brides. However, if you're getting married in a location known for its fresh fruit and you're presented with a cake that features this fruit as a filling, that's definitely something to consider.
* *Size.* Your wedding coordinator should advise you on this, but make sure that you're only ordering as much cake as you and your guests can eat. You're not going to fly the leftovers home.
* *Other options.* Ask your wedding coordinator for other ideas. Replacing the cake with pastries shouldn't be a big deal.

Going with a Baker

If you're not working within a package deal at a destination wedding site and you're planning this wedding without the help of a wedding coordinator, you might wonder how in the world you're going to find the right baker for your wedding cake. It's really not that hard, but it does take some effort to make sure that you don't end up with a gorgeous cake that tastes like cardboard.

Compiling Options

If you're not an aficionado of pastries, doughnuts, and breads, then finding a baker right in your hometown—never mind finding one hundreds of miles away—might seem like a daunting task. What you're looking for in a wedding-cake baker is someone who can create a cake that's both delicious and beautiful. Meeting one criterion without the other just won't cut it (pun intended). So now that you've raised the bar, where are you going to find a baker who can combine good taste with good looks?

Start with your reception site coordinator or the banquet manager—whomever you've been talking with there. When you live in town, it's easy to ask friends, relatives, and coworkers for recommendations, but in this instance, you've got to rely on the judgment of anyone you trust in the area, so your choices are pretty limited. However, you chose your reception site for several reasons—ideally, one of those reasons is because it has a good reputation for putting on a beautiful event. Ergo, you can safely assume that the vendors the site deals with are top-notch.

If you're given several names, you might feel more overwhelmed than you did before you asked for a recommendation. Narrowing down these options is something every bride goes through, although most brides have someone right in town who can taste-test the cakes and pastries to make sure they pass muster. Although you might think that this is unnecessary and more of a hassle than dealing with an unsavory cake on your wedding day, it really is the best way to weed out acceptable vendors from their lesser brethren.

If it's within reason, it's a good idea for you to plan a trip to the area before the wedding and set up appointments with the various vendors you're employing so that you know who you're dealing with and exactly what kind of service to expect. This goes for the cake baker as well as all the other vendors.

If visiting the area is not a possibility, you'll have to rely solely on the advice of your contact at the reception site and any investigative work that you can do. For example, ask if the bakery has a Web site or if the baker can send pictures of his previous work. You want to make sure that this guy knows how to frost a cake so that it actually resembles the basket-weave topping you're dreaming of. Then get some references! Ask for the names of previous brides—and then make some calls to make sure that these women were happy with their cakes.

The Interview

When you initially speak to a baker, what kinds of questions should you ask? Well, for starters, you'll want to know if he's available on the day of your wedding. Then tailor your questions to your specific wants and needs. Tell him what kind of cake you have in mind and ask if it's something he's done in the past. If he can't create it, call someone else on your list.

Normally, brides are advised to bring along a picture of the cake they envision for the reception when they sit down to meet the baker. For this same meeting, the bride would also be encouraged to bring along fabric swatches of the bridesmaids' dresses to make sure that any decorations on the cake will complement the wedding colors. There's no harm in mailing these things to the baker, but make sure to follow up on it, and be as specific as you can. You don't want him confusing your pictures with something another bride sent in. He should put these things right into your file.

It All Looks So Good!

When you start actually choosing a cake from a list of flavors, toppings, and fillings, things can become confusing. Unless you're a die-hard fan of basic yellow cake and standard frosting (and there's nothing wrong with going traditional on the cake), you might find yourself lost in a daydream of all the possibilities!

What kinds of choices will you be faced with?

* *Shape.* These days, bakers are doing incredible things with their confections. Aside from stacking tiers upon tiers, you can also have cakes created in the form of a pretty gift box, for example, or a seashell, or a tropical flower.
* *Cake flavor.* Flavors range anywhere from the basic yellow, white, carrot, and cheesecakes to cherry, pistachio, and beyond. This is the big choice, as it will also affect your filling and frosting choices. Choose something that most of your guests will enjoy.
* *Fillings.* Possibilities include fruit fillings, crème fillings, and fillings that include nuts.
* *Frosting.* You'll choose the frosting in conjunction with the flavor and fillings. Frosting for wedding cakes is usually butter-based and fairly consistent from baker to baker.
* *Decorations.* Gumpaste flowers. Silver beading and garland. Fresh flowers. Pillars. Fountains. Some of these decorations are edible; obviously, others aren't. You'll be charged for both. (Technically, you'll be *renting* those plastic pillars.)

One major consideration when it comes to the cake: Choose something that will withstand the elements. If you're getting married on the beach and having an outdoor reception in the glorious warmth of the Caribbean, don't choose a cheesecake. It will droop, wilt, and be completely inedible by the time dessert rolls around.

Before you become attached to any particular cake, talk money with the baker! Although logic would dictate that a cake is a cake and it shouldn't cost you thousands of dollars, wedding cakes are a breed all their own. They're pricey, and the more you add to them, the more expensive they are.

Pricing and Contracts

Like many other details of your wedding, the cake is a significant expense. The price doesn't have to be overblown, but added decorations and fancy fillings—not to mention a very long guest list—can cause the dollars to add up quickly. The cake is another aspect that will require a contract. As with any contract, make sure that you thoroughly review and completely agree with your baker's contract before you sign it.

Cake Costs

Before you can figure out how much the cake is going to cost, you have to determine how much cake you'll need. The standard measurement among bakers is to figure on a three- or four-inch slice per guest; the cake is then priced per slice. Let's assume you're going with a cake with no filling and standard frosting. The base price per slice for that, we'll say, is $5. If you add a filling, that might increase the price to $5.50 per slice. Adding a decorative basket weave to the frosting takes it up to $6.25 per slice, and so on, and so on. (These prices are just examples of how cake is priced. Your baker will have her own price list.)

This is how wedding cakes top out over the $1,000 mark, even for a reasonably sized cake. Now, to be fair, the baker is providing you with his artistry and expertise—and the result is a knockout dessert. But it's up to you to decide from the get-go how important it is to have a cake with all the bells and whistles, which might shoot the price up to about $10 per slice.

E~Fact
Delivery is usually included in the price of a wedding cake—within a certain radius of the baker. If your wedding is outside the delivery area, however, you'll most likely be charged a fee.

If the price of the cake is getting out of control and you're looking to cut costs, ask your baker if she can provide you with a small, decorative wedding cake for display at the reception—and a sheet cake to serve for dessert. A standard sheet cake serves about forty people, and is much less expensive than an ultra-fancy wedding cake. If you can work this out, you just might be able to have a really unique wedding cake without going broke.

Signing the Contract
Delivery is a standard part of the cake contract, and for good reason: Cakes need to be transported and set up in a certain way. You can't count on your little brother to pick up three separate tiers, keep them intact in the trunk of his car, and assemble them at the reception site. Leave this to the baker; he and his employees do this sort of thing on a regular basis. They have a vehicle to safely transport your cake from their kitchen to the reception, and they know exactly which pillars are going to support which tiers. Plus, if they drop the cake, it's their problem. (Emergency contingencies are a standard part of the contract.)

What else should be in the contract? Delivery time and the reception site address, so that the cake will be all set up and ready to go before guests start arriving for the reception. The baker will have to coordinate this setup time with the reception hall; if they do business together on a regular basis, it shouldn't be a problem. In any event, it's the baker's responsibility to have this conversation, not yours.

Take a good look at the cake worksheet before you sign. Make sure everything is correct: the size, shape, flavor, fillings, decorations, and so on. You've put a lot of time into choosing this cake; it would be terrible if something completely different were to end up on the cake table at your reception!

The contract will also spell out the amount of your deposit (due at the time of signing), the outstanding balance and when it will be paid, and any terms of cancellation. If you end up canceling the wedding during the month after you place your order, for example, you'll probably lose your deposit, but you won't have to pay for a cake that will never be baked, let alone delivered or eaten.

Cake Placement Is Important, Too

Whether it's your baker or the staff at the reception site, someone will be responsible for placing the cake somewhere. While you may not consider this a sticking point, it is actually quite important that the cake be in a good location. The cake is a focal point for your wedding pictures, so you don't want any bizarre images (like a bathroom door or a garbage can) anywhere in the frame.

To eliminate this possibility, talk to the reception site coordinator about where the cake will be placed when you're doing the entire reception rundown. Be aware that you may not be able to put the cake just anywhere—for example, the spot that you love may be directly in the path of the servers—but the two of you should be able to find a spot that will display the cake nicely without tripping the waiters.

Alternatives to Cake

Some brides just don't like cake. Some brides find cake dull. Some brides are looking for something else to serve their guests. At large weddings, it's not at all unusual to see a wedding cake early on in the evening and a pastry table later to provide nourishment for guests who are exhausted from shaking their groove things.

Cupcakes, Éclairs, and Cookies . . . Oh My!

First things first: If you're planning a very small wedding (twenty or fewer people), you don't need a pastry table. It's just going to be too much food. Either save your money or spend it on a more extravagant cake.

If you're having a larger gathering, however, you may want to think about keeping the goodies coming all night long. Pastry tables were once only seen at Italian weddings; they're so common these days that they've almost become as standard as the wedding cake. This is not to say that you should feel obligated to set up a dessert table, but if you're wondering how it will be received (will everyone think it's too much? You're not the least bit Italian . . .), chances are that your offerings will be devoured.

What should you put on a pastry table? Consider what you've done with the cake. If you went with a really unusual flavor or filling, make sure that the pastry table includes some commonplace treats, like sugar cookies. If you stuck with a fairly plain cake, then the pastry table is the place to really sock it to your guests—ask the baker about his specialty cookies and pastries.

Whether you decide to serve up the pastries later in the evening or to go with a dessert table in lieu of a cake, here are some options:

* *Wedding-themed cookies.* Little brides and grooms laid out on a plate, or hearts with your names ("Sue + Johnny") emblazoned across them.
* *Cupcakes.* Everyone loves a good cupcake, and what's more, these can be stacked to resemble an actual cake.
* *Chocolate-covered fruits.* How often do people get to indulge in this decadence? Huge, chocolate-covered strawberries are something your guests will talk about for years to come.
* *Fountains.* Alternatively, what about a chocolate fountain? You can provide the guests with fresh fruits and cookies of all sorts for dipping.
* *Coffee, tea, chai.* Whatever your guests might need for a little extra (nonalcoholic) fuel on the dance floor.

The pastry table is also a good place to lay out those ethnic treats your family is so fond of (such as shortbread for Scottish clans). You're giving your guests the opportunity to share in one of your favorite treats without forcing it on them, and you're also tying your heritage into this special day, thus truly personalizing your wedding.

The Groom's Cake

The groom's cake is more of a whimsical treat, as it often reflects the groom's hobbies and interests. This was originally a Southern tradition, and although it has caught on in other areas of the country, you're still most likely to see a groom's cake at a wedding involving a man from south of the Mason-Dixon Line.

Bakers are truly artists, and you won't see evidence of this any more clearly than in wedding and groom's cakes. If the groom is a bowling fanatic, for example, a baker may just be able to create a dessert that resembles a 3-D bowling lane. A groom who is a football fanatic might end up with a cake shaped like a football helmet. Hard-rocking men might want a guitar-shaped cake.

If you've found a baker to do your wedding cake, he should also be able to do the groom's cake. Ask if he can send pictures of any really creative cakes he's done in the past. (They don't need to be groom-specific; if he's done a cake for a bowling league, chances are the same design will suit your pin-happy hubby-to-be.) And remember: Fun is the name of the game when you're choosing the groom's cake. Leave the serious stuff for the wedding cake.

Traditionally, the groom's cake is served at the wedding reception. However, with the advent of pastry tables and incredibly ornate (and expensive) wedding cakes, you might want to think twice before allowing this cake to upstage your carefully designed, multitiered wedding cake. Many brides and grooms opt to serve the groom's cake at the rehearsal dinner, which is a great idea. The groom gets to show off his cake by itself, for one thing. This also lets you serve your guests a really cool dessert, which helps to get everyone in the mood for what promises to be a truly unique wedding the following day.

The Do-It-Yourself Option

Let's say this right off the bat: Baking your own wedding cake—or asking your mom or sister to do it for you—is not the best idea, especially if you're planning a wedding out of town. Even if your wedding is just a couple of hours down the pike and your mother is a world-class baker, there's just so much that can happen between *here* and *there*. Flat tires, engine trouble, fender-benders, a bad sense of direction—anything could spoil your masterpiece before you even arrive.

There's really no good, easy way to bake your own wedding cake for a destination wedding, even if you're driving to your site. Carefully consider these questions: Where are you going to store the cake once you arrive? If you're thinking about creating a multitiered number, how on earth are you going to assemble that puppy in a strange location?

If these considerations elicited nothing from you except a shrug, and you're still set on baking that cake yourself, then you must have nerves of steel and a real knack for baking. No one would even consider such a thing otherwise.

✿ E~Fact

The wedding cake is part of the package deal at a resort. Hence, you will not be able to bring along a cake to a resort destination wedding. Consider this a blessing; it's one less thing you have to worry about! ✍

If you are not planning a destination wedding in a resort, then you're going to have all sorts of loose ends to attend to before the big event. Don't throw the assembly of the cake into the mix. It's just so much easier to order something from a local baker.

If cost is your main concern, then skip the fancy wedding cake and go with a big tray of cookies delivered from a local bake shop. Here's what you don't want: a wedding cake that did not weather the trip very well. Not only will no one want to eat it, it will be a pathetic topper to your otherwise beautiful day. Cutting wedding costs where possible is always a priority; this is not one of those "possible" areas. Leave it to a pro.

Chapter 14
Dance to Your Own Tune: The Music

Whether you thrive on hearing good music or music is a complete afterthought in your day-to-day life, you'll want to make great musical choices for your wedding ceremony and reception. In order to do that, you have to decide whether you want to go live (with a band, vocalist, or string quartet) or if a disc jockey might be better. Whichever direction you choose, you'll also be faced with selecting just the right music for the occasion.

Setting the Tone

The music for your ceremony and reception provides the mood for the event. Think about every movie you've ever seen: How did you know when something bad was about to happen? During sad scenes, what made you cry even harder? When something funny was happening, was there anything that added to your hysterical laughter? The music!

Music can lighten a mood, underscore the solemnity of an event, or just make everyone feel good. The right music can make a wedding. The wrong music sends the wrong message and kills the mood. If the people at your reception just can't groove because the DJ is playing music *sans* rhythm, or if the band has taken umpteen bathroom breaks, then your guests won't be having fun on the dance floor. It'll probably too late to address these problems at the reception, which is why it's so important to hire the right musicians in the first place.

 E~Fact

Musical packages for a destination wedding vary from resort to resort. Some of the larger places have musicians on standby, waiting for your signature on the dotted line before they jump into action. Others have a limited number of musicians to call on. If your wedding music is important to you, check out the available options as soon as you start looking at prospective sites.

Because music is such an important contributor to the atmosphere of your wedding, you want to make sure that the music you choose is appropriate for both the occasion and your guests. While you may enjoy heavy metal at home, your wedding is probably not the place to blast these tunes. Your Great Uncle Milt is not going to appreciate having a wild song rattle his teeth, and any older guests who are wearing hearing aids won't be able to tolerate the noise.

In addition to very loud music, another thing that can chase away your older guests is an overabundance of music that they can't dance to.

Your grandparents are probably of a generation that is used to dancing cheek-to-cheek, not crowd-surfing. It's your wedding, but it's smart to make sure that the playlist includes music that *everyone* will enjoy.

Music for the Ceremony

A small ceremony consisting of only the bride, groom, and immediate family members may not need a lot of punctuation from musicians, but a larger, more traditional wedding certainly does. There are various points in a long ceremony that definitely need *something* to offset the silence. We'll talk about those moments—and the type of music that might be appropriate for each—in this section.

Prelude to the Big Show

When guests are arriving at the ceremony and waiting for the ceremony to begin, do you want them sitting in silence, staring at the clock, or would you rather they were reflecting on the joyous occasion of your marriage? Complete silence makes a chapel or ceremony site feel a lot like a doctor's waiting room, except instead of waiting nervously for a shot, everyone's counting the minutes until they get a peek at the bride—and if you aren't right on time and you haven't given these people anything in the way of entertainment, you're going to see some guests who have ants in their pants. If you've thought ahead and provided your guests with some gentle tunes to help pass the time, you could be five or ten minutes behind schedule and no one will even notice (or at least not much).

Music that is appropriate for the prelude may include:

* Brandenburg Concertos, Bach
* *Jesu, Joy of Man's Desiring*, Bach
* Air on the G String, Bach
* *The Four Seasons*, Vivaldi
* *Water Music*, Handel

Choosing music for the prelude—in fact, for the entire wedding—is not always as easy as your telling the musicians that you want them to play a particular piece. The musicians you hire may or may not know that piece; but even if they don't know it, good musicians will be able to substitute something that's appropriate. If it's very important to you to have specific musical selections, discuss this with prospective musicians during the interview (we'll cover this in more detail later in this chapter).

The Processional

When it's time to send your bridesmaids down the aisle, you need to choose a piece of music that fits the feel of your wedding. If you're young and hip and working with a DJ, you might choose a contemporary love song. Just make sure you try out modern songs in a trial run before you commit to using them during your ceremony. There's a reason that traditional tunes are used over and over (and over) again—it's because they work well for wedding ceremonies.

You might just love a newer song and feel that it's perfect for your wedding, but if your bridesmaids have to walk awkwardly in order to catch the beat, and the DJ can't do anything but end it abruptly once you arrive at the altar, your guests are going to notice (and comment on it amongst themselves). Maybe you need to find something different.

E~Alert

Before you choose a contemporary song for the processional, have a bridesmaid walk back and forth across the length of your kitchen or living room while the music plays. Is she able to walk with a somewhat normal gait, or is she practically running—or crawling—to match the beat?

You can choose one piece to play as your bridesmaids walk down the aisle and another one for yourself. If you're a traditional type, Wagner's

"Bridal Chorus" might be what you're thinking about for your entrance. This is the music that everyone thinks of when they think of weddings: *Here comes the bride, . . .* Some other traditional pieces include:

* *Trumpet Voluntary*, Stanley
* Canon in D, Pachelbel
* "Hornpipe" from *Water Music*, Handel
* Lute/Guitar Concerto in D Major, Vivaldi
* "Wedding March" from *The Marriage of Figaro*, Mozart

Of course, there are countless others. You may have your own favorite classical music that will work perfectly for the processional. If you've hired a DJ, you can provide him with a copy of the music you've chosen; if you're working with live musicians, however, you'll need to consult with them about their playlist before you set your sights (and your ears) on any music in particular.

The Ceremony

Choices for music during the ceremony are usually based on whether you're having a religious or secular wedding. The length of the ceremony also plays a part in the songs you choose or whether you choose to have any music at all. A fifteen-minute ceremony focusing mostly on the exchange of vows doesn't really need a whole lot of music during the ceremony itself (which is not to say that you won't perhaps want to work a song or two in there anyway); a full-length religious service, on the other hand, not only includes plenty of opportunities for song, it *needs* music to pass some of that time for your guests.

 E~Fact

If you're having a Catholic ceremony, your selection of music will be limited to that contained in the Mass books. 🎵

Choosing contemporary music for your ceremony is not hard because you're familiar with these tunes. You can tell if they're going to work well and whether they're appropriate. However, contemporary music isn't always permitted during a religious ceremony. If you're faced with choosing among songs that you've never even heard of, you can depend on these selections to accent your ceremony nicely:

* ✳ "Ave Maria," Schubert
* ✳ "The Wedding Song," Stookey
* ✳ "Wedding Prayer," Artman
* ✳ Selections from *The Four Seasons*, Vivaldi
* ✳ Cantata No. 29, Bach
* ✳ "Toccata," Monteverdi
* ✳ Irish Wedding Prayer (traditional)

To hear these tunes, look for sound clips on the Internet or visit your local library and check out a few CDs.

The Recessional

After you've said "I do," it's time to make your way back down the aisle as husband and wife. This is a time of exuberance, so your music should reflect that! Mendelssohn's Wedding March is the song you hear in movies and at countless weddings when the newly married couple is ready to leave the altar. Some other traditional choices include:

* ✳ Finale from Handel's *Water Music*
* ✳ "Spring" from Vivaldi's *Four Seasons*
* ✳ "Trumpet Tune," Purcell
* ✳ *Sinfonia* ("Arrival of the Queen of Sheba"), Handel

You'll feel as though you're floating on air, so choose a song that will carry you out of the ceremony on a cloud of joy!

Finding the Musicians

As with every other wedding service, you won't have to find your own musicians if you have booked your wedding at a resort. Packages at resorts vary, usually in direct accordance with the size of the facility. Larger places are able to offer couples a choice of strings, a live band and/or vocalist, or a DJ (with all of the musical choices that are inherent to each). Smaller places may only be able to offer a vocalist, a guitarist, or a small string ensemble.

Looking for the right musicians on your own is like finding any other wedding vendor. Start by asking your reception site (or baker, or florist—whomever you've secured in your corner at this point) for several recommendations, and go from there.

Disc Jockeys

Hiring a disc jockey seems like an easy enough task. After all, all the guy has to do is show up with his equipment and play the list of songs that you've given him. How hard can it be to find someone to do that?

It's not hard to find just *any* disc jockey; finding one who will do exactly what you want him to do (and who will *not* do the things you've asked him to refrain from doing) takes a little more research. The first step is knowing what you want from your disc jockey. Ask yourself:

* Do I want him to play only a certain type of music? (Oldies, swing, or contemporary?)
* Am I looking for extra fun for the guests, like karaoke or group participation dances?
* Will it bother me if the DJ speaks at the conclusion of every single song he plays?
* Am I willing to leave most of the musical selections up to the DJ?
* Would I like the DJ to also play the role of emcee at my reception, introducing the wedding party, announcing when dinner will be served, when the cake will be cut, and so on?

These are major questions that you need to answer before you hire someone to play the music for your wedding! If you're imagining everyone dancing to big band music and the guy you've hired plays mostly hip-hop, you're going to be one unhappy bride on the day of your wedding.

Questions for the DJ include:

* What kind of sound equipment do you use? How many CDs can you be cueing up at one time? Is your equipment ample for the space I've rented?
* How many hours does your price include?
* How do you dress for the event?
* Can you provide me with a typical playlist? (Take a look to see if your musical tastes are in sync.)

Take note of this guy's personality when you talk to him. If you're looking for someone lively to whip your guests into party mode, don't hire someone who speaks in hushed tones. On the other hand, if this guy seems like he's out to sell his own slightly wacky personality, you'd better be completely comfortable with that idea before you set him up with a live microphone at your reception.

As with all wedding vendors, ask for references. Make sure to ask other brides about the issues that concern you most: Did the DJ play the correct songs for the special dances (like the one you'll have with your dad, and the one for the groom and his mom)? Did he talk too much or too little? Did the guests get up and dance? Was the sound good or was it muffled? Adjust this list—and add questions of your own—to ensure that you know exactly what you're getting with this particular DJ.

Bands

It's hard to hire a band without hearing them for yourself in an environment similar to your reception site. Your best bet is to rely on the judgment of your reception site contact, assuming that live bands have played there in the past. He or she can tell you which bands sounded great and which didn't work out so well. You can then narrow down *those* choices according to your specific tastes.

E~Alert

Acoustics can do crazy things to a band's sound, so hearing them on a demo CD and hearing them inside the tent at your reception can be different auditory experiences. If you audition the band, try to imitate the acoustics in the final location as best you can. If this isn't possible, make sure you at least give the band the rundown on your location ahead of time.

Some of the questions you'll want to ask the bandleader include:

* How long will you play?
* Can you play instrumental music during the cocktail hour or before the ceremony?
* Can I see a sample playlist?
* What types of music do you like to play the most? Which type do you like least?
* Can the bandleader also serve as the emcee during the reception?
* How does the band dress for weddings?

Before you sign on the dotted line, make sure the correct time and date are noted on the contract, and don't hire *anyone* without first checking those references!

Strings, Vocalists, and Everyone Else

If you're getting married in a church, the priest or minister can probably give you some recommendations for ceremony musicians, whether you're looking for a harpist, a string grouping, an organist, a pianist, a guitarist, a trumpeter, or a vocalist. If your wedding is going to be at the reception site, ask your contact person there for assistance in this matter.

Musicians tend to work with and know of one another, so if by chance the minister or reception site coordinator doesn't know a harpist, ask him or her to put you in contact with another musician, who may be able to help you find what you want.

Music for the Reception

Gathering up the musicians is a major accomplishment! Now—what do you want them to do? Professional musicians know the wedding ropes well enough that they can proceed without specific instructions, but you need to know what to expect so that you can put the kibosh on anything you find corny or unsettling.

Start at the Beginning

When guests begin to arrive, they'll be milling around, looking for drinks and appetizers. During this cocktail hour, there should be some background music going on as the guests arrive; you don't want your band or DJ setting up and doing noisy sound checks at this time. The cake is usually cut before dinner, especially if it's going to be served for dessert; the emcee will announce this to the guests so that they can take pictures of you and the groom feeding sweets to one another.

You may want to have some light music playing throughout dinner, but this depends on the size and layout of your reception site. Larger halls sometimes don't need the background noise, as the music is drowned out by the acoustics and all of the chitchat going on. Ask the banquet manager for his or her recommendations and find out what other brides have done at that facility. After dinner, the dancing begins, usually in this order:

* Bride and her father
* Groom and his mother

* Bride and groom together
* Wedding party

After those dances, the floor opens up to everyone. You may choose to combine or skip some of the traditional dances. If you do choose to include them, consider the song suggestions that follow.

Dancing with Dad

Choosing the right song for dancing with your pop is important. You don't want to choose something mushy if the two of you don't have that kind of relationship, and even if you're very close, you don't want to make him break down in tears on the dance floor. Pick a song that reflects on the joys of the past and the great job he's done raising you, such as:

* "Isn't She Lovely?" Stevie Wonder
* "The Way You Look Tonight," Frank Sinatra
* "Forever Young," Rod Stewart
* "Little Miss Magic," Jimmy Buffett
* "My Girl," Temptations
* "Because You Loved Me," Celine Dion

Whatever song you choose, make sure to listen to the lyrics to make sure it's appropriate for a father and daughter to dance to. In other words, make sure it's not a love song that would be more appropriate for your dance with the groom—otherwise, you could end up creeping out some of your wedding guests. Alternatively, ask the bandleader or DJ if he can provide you with instrumental music for this dance.

Mother and Son

If you've given yourself and your dad some time in the spotlight, extend the courtesy to your mother-in-law also. Appropriate songs might be a little harder to come by, but some nice musical tributes to her relationship with her son might include:

* ✳ "You Are the Sunshine of My Life," Stevie Wonder
* ✳ "Close to You," Carpenters
* ✳ "A Song for Mama," Boyz II Men
* ✳ "The Perfect Fan," Backstreet Boys

Let your mother-in-law choose the song if she wants to—she may have sung the groom a particular song time and time again when he was a little boy, for example, and that would mean more to the two of them than some random song chosen from a playlist. But again, make sure the lyrics are appropriate for a dance with her son.

First Dance

When you dance that first dance as man and wife, you want the song to be perfect, so don't be pressured into choosing something that your DJ wants to play, or a song that your mother loves—choose something that fits your relationship with your new husband. Some suggestions:

* ✳ "At Last," Etta James
* ✳ "In My Life," Beatles
* ✳ "I'll Be (The Greatest Fan in Your Life)," Edwin McCain
* ✳ "That's All," Michael Bublé
* ✳ "You and Me," Lifehouse
* ✳ "From this Moment," Shania Twain
* ✳ "My Best Friend," Tim McGraw
* ✳ "I Knew I Loved You (Before I Met You)," Savage Garden
* ✳ "True Companion," Marc Cohn

The song for the first dance is usually fairly easy to choose, because you probably have several songs in mind already. Because this is a public event, steer away from anything with racy or explicit lyrics—save those for the CD player back home.

Enter the Wedding Party!

This is one group song that you should have some fun with. Your attendants have been working very hard to make your big day special, so let them cut loose on the dance floor! These are some songs they can get their grooves on to:

* "We Are Family," Sister Sledge
* "Ain't No Mountain High Enough," Marvin Gaye and Tammi Terrell
* "Everybody Have Fun Tonight," Wang Chung
* "Silly Love Songs," Wings
* "Let's Get it Started," Black Eyed Peas

Cue the music and watch those attendants let loose! You can choose any music that seems appropriate for this dance, but since your attendants are being corralled into dancing with one another, try to keep the tone light enough so that no one feels uncomfortable (as happens sometimes when near-strangers are coupled up on the dance floor).

Keep the Party Going

There's almost nothing sadder than the reception that dies out early, or—worse—never really gets hopping in the first place. The music, without a doubt, is the do-or-die element for a decent-sized reception as far as most of the guests are concerned. Sure, some of your friends and relatives will sit at their tables for most of the night and talk (or drink), but most people expect to get up and dance. If that dance floor has momentum, if the music is drawing people in, if everybody out there is laughing together—then you know your reception is a hit.

Karaoke

Some couples choose to go with karaoke at their receptions, which can be a lot of fun. There's an old adage that works well in most areas of life, and it holds true where karaoke is concerned, also: everything in moderation. While off-tune singing might crack *you* up, it might not seem all that funny to some of your guests.

Put a limit on the amount of karaoke—say, three or four songs in a row and then back to real music for at least thirty minutes. And don't let any one guest hog the microphone. This is really your DJ's responsibility, but if you notice that your brother is gearing up to sing yet *another* disco hit while three or four others are vying for their time in the spotlight, tell him to move it along.

Dance, Chicken, Dance!

What about those group numbers, like the Chicken Dance? Are they hokey, or do people really like them? And what about those dances like the Electric Slide, the Cha Cha Slide, and the Macarena? Are they worn out, or can you still reasonably incorporate them into your reception?

The current thinking on this issue is that these dances are old news; however, this is *your* wedding. Don't be pressured by what's *en vogue* (or, more correctly, not *en vogue*). The one real piece of evidence that these numbers maybe aren't so worn is the fact that when they're played, everyone gets up to dance. You'll have to decide at your own peril whether to include them, but if you do believe that you really need the Hokey Pokey, leave the Chicken Dance and the YMCA out. Remember: everything in moderation.

Chapter 15
Writing Your Own Vows

There are two different reactions that people have when someone suggests that they might want to write their own wedding vows: either they think it's the best idea they've ever heard, or they think it's ridiculous. Why try to improve on what's already out there? Standard wedding vows can actually be lovely, and they certainly get the job done, but writing your own vows really, truly personalizes your ceremony. Since you're already flouting convention and having a destination wedding, why not try something new with your vows?

Write Now!

If you have counted yourself out of the vow-writing game simply because English was your all-time least favorite subject back in school, you have to change that attitude. Remember, not only were you far less mature back then than you are now (or so we hope), but in those years you also were being led through a curriculum. In many schools, there isn't a lot of room for creativity or even a whole lot of discussion in English classes. For these reasons, a lot of potential writers (and readers) are turned off at a relatively early age to the whole idea of expressing themselves on paper.

If that's your attitude, it's about to change. You can rediscover any spark you may have once had for writing, and what better way to do this than by writing about your future spouse?

E~ssential

Give yourself at least two months to make revisions and outright changes to your vows. At some point, what you've written may be extremely close to perfection, but it still might not sound exactly right. You can't rush the creative process, so don't leave this until the night before the wedding, or your greatest fear (the one about sounding like a nitwit at the altar) may very well come true.

What You Need to Write Amazing Vows

You don't have to shoot to be the new, female Shakespeare, and you don't need to invest in a lot of equipment. In fact, here's a list of what you'll need:

* A pencil with an eraser
* A pad of paper
* An open mind
* Ample time

The only other thing you need is the confidence that you can write a decent set of wedding vows. You don't need to buy ten books on how to write well, and you don't need any special software for your computer. As long as you can formulate a coherent sentence, there's no reason why you can't do this.

Keep It Classy

What are you supposed to *say* when you write your own vows? Well, your ultimate goal is to have your words sound sincere without being maudlin and to be personal without getting into too-intimate details. In other words, you want to remain on the correct side of the classy/trashy line. And you also want to keep it short enough so that your guests aren't falling asleep while you read a twenty-page dissertation on your fiancé's finer points.

This advice may seem to go against your better judgment. After all, this is your wedding, and you should be able to say whatever you want and speak for as long as you care to, right? Yes and no. There's no reason to cross some of these boundaries, especially when you're talking in front of a group of people. None of them need (or want) to hear about your amazing sex life, for example, so that has no place in your wedding vows.

✿ E~Question

I'm writing my vows for my fiancé. Does it matter what my guests think?

Your vows should focus mainly on your fiancé, that's true. But since you've invited these people to witness your vows, try to avoid shocking them or making them extremely uncomfortable during the ceremony. ✿

If your main goal is to elicit tears of joy from your fiancé, you'll probably also encourage eye rolls in the pews. Which is not to say that your fiancé *shouldn't* cry at your words—it's just that very few writers have the ability to compose something that makes people cry without also making them feel a little uncomfortable. So when you do sit down to write, write from your head and your heart. The tears will come naturally.

Finding Inspiration

Every relationship has its highs and lows. Obviously, when you write your wedding vows you want to recount more good moments than bad ones. Any moments that you mention in your vows should be either monumental or minute—both in a good way. For example, you might want to mention the moment that you knew you loved him, and you might want to talk about the way he touches your shoulder when he leaves for work. These are significant in their own ways—one was a huge defining moment, the other is a defining characteristic of his love for you.

Don't Even Go There

Since you want your vows to focus on the positive aspects of your relationship, skip over anything negative. This includes things like:

* *Doubts or misgivings about the relationship.* This is not the time or place to mention that one of you had cold feet a month ago.
* *Differences among family members.* You don't dig his mom or his kids' attitudes? Don't even attempt to joke about it in your vows.
* *Negative attitudes toward your union.* If friends and family members have been against this marriage from the start, you don't need to add a "So *there*!" element to your vows.

Your wedding day is supposed to be a happy time. You don't want to dredge up bad feelings, and you certainly don't want to set yourself up for target practice in the coming years (when your mother-in-law repeats that little "joke" you made in your vows—you know, the one about how hard it was for *you* to cut the apron strings between her and your hus-band). If something seems like it's even coming close to the line, nix it.

Fair Game

Now that you know what *not* to talk about when you write your vows, we'll move on to happier topics.

Aspects of your relationship that you may want to talk about in your wedding vows include:

* ✳ *What first brought the two of you together.* Was it his sense of humor, the wild look in his eyes, or a long-standing friendship that blossomed into something more?
* ✳ *The little things you love best about him.* The way he always makes the coffee in the morning even though you're the only one who drinks it, or the fact that he'll fold the laundry for you because you hate doing it—any highly endearing qualities.
* ✳ *His best "partner" points.* The reasons that you know he's going to make a great husband—he's loyal, honest, giving, and so on.
* ✳ *His human points.* Is he quirky, messy, silly? Again, these are his endearing qualities, the things that may drive you crazy once in a while but ultimately only make you love him more.

How would you incorporate this kind of information into a short, sweet public declaration of love? Consider something like this:

Rick, today I pledge my love and my life to you. I knew from the first time we met that there was something unique about the way you and I fit together. Your laugh was what first attracted my attention, but I soon came to realize that there is so much more to you than your sense of humor. I have to admit that I was surprised to find what a deeply caring person you are—the type of person who brings joy to the lives of so many others with just a smile or a touch. Your loving, caring nature has taught me to be a better person. In our many years together, we'll share laughter and tears, but I know we will persevere because of your strong nature and your love for life. I love you with all of my heart, and I am honored today to become your wife.

Obviously, when writing your own vows, you want to tailor your vows to reflect your feelings for your own fiancé. Three rules of thumb:

* ✳ *Hit the high points and move on.* Don't ramble.
* ✳ *Be sincere and natural.* If poetry isn't your thing, don't start spouting couplets at the altar. You'll feel strange, and you'll *sound* strange.
* ✳ *Don't try to ad-lib.* You won't be in your element, and you'll probably be nervous. Have a solid idea of what you're going to say, and don't stray too far from that plan.

If you follow these three guidelines, you'll sound like a professional writer *and* speaker—just when it matters most.

Poetic Pitfalls

Professional writers sometimes have a difficult time doing their jobs well, so it's no wonder that people who hate to write often avoid the task. When it comes to your wedding vows, however, you just may be willing to give it a shot, because, after all, they're only words. How hard could it be to put a few of them together and come out smelling like roses?

You can definitely do this. This section will point out a couple of common pitfalls and how to avoid them when you get down to work.

Don't Be a Chatty Cathy

Although it's nice—and necessary—to throw some details into your vows, you don't need to talk on and on and on about every date you and your fiancé have ever gone on, all of the pet names you have for one another, and your special technique for working the kinks out of his neck. Get to the point: You love him, and you want to spend eternity with him.

But *why* do you love him so? Give him three good, solid reasons, and call it a night (or an afternoon). Do you see what this limit does? It forces you to choose only the *very best* of his stellar attributes.

 E~ssential

Everyone knows that you love him, but if you take the time to recite twenty amazing qualities, your vows are going to lose their "oomph." Less is more, especially when you're speaking to a crowd. Keep it sweet and simple.

You may be thinking, "But this is our wedding! This is *absolutely* the time to list *every single one* of his amazing points!" No, it's not. Three good points. Four if you must. Any more than five, and you're *really* going to start to sound insincere, as in, "*Everything* you do is just perfect!" You may feel that way, but your vows will lose their intended effect if you go way overboard here.

And remember, you still have the entire reception to speak freely about what a great guy he is. You can also write your feelings about him in a journal and present it to him as a wedding gift; that way, he'll know that you truly *do* appreciate every little thing about him.

Cool It on the Comedy

If you and your fiancé crack jokes, you want some of that levity to come through in your vows, but you also want to honor the sanctity of this occasion. Even though it may feel unnatural, make sure to tone down your vows at some point to reflect the magnitude of this moment.

At the very least, wrap up your vows with a sincere sentiment, such as, "I know I am so lucky to have found the perfect man for me to share my life with. I love you more than I can say." Easy, sincere, to the point—and a salve to your laughter-free guests.

Find an Early-Bird Audience

If you've never spoken in public, it's especially important to rehearse your vows before reciting them on the altar. Even if it's going to be a small ceremony, you want the words to come naturally, and repetition beforehand is the best way to ensure that you won't leave out a major point. Also, you want to know well in advance whether some part of what you've written sounds awkward or just silly. You're going to recite these vows in front of the guests at your wedding, so it's essential that you're comfortable with the whole setup. If you're hesitant to read them in front of a friend, perhaps you should rethink this and go with standard, prewritten vows.

Choose a Trusted Friend

At least a month before the wedding, have your maid of honor or your mother or another trusted friend listen to the vows you've written. Choose someone who is honest but not overly critical. If there's something about your vows that just doesn't sound right, you want to be able to take the advice of a reasonable person who isn't out to make you feel bad. If this person has a strong objection to what she's hearing, listen to her criticism and try to be objective about it. Maybe you used the word "magnificent" too many times (actually, using it twice is once too many); perhaps the vows run on for three single-spaced pages and could be cut back considerably; or maybe the sentiment is just off and you need to adjust your writing to focus more on your fiancé and less on yourself.

Narrowing the Focus

Don't feel as though you've failed if your first draft doesn't work out. One of the hardest things for people who don't love to write is first finding the inspiration to write about something worthwhile. You already have that in the form of your husband-to-be. Another very common problem is staying on point and not digressing into issues that don't directly tie in to what you're talking about. But this is exactly why you need to run your vows past a goodhearted listener before the wedding!

For example, if your sister tells you that she doesn't understand part of your vows, chances are you've gone off-topic (because, really, if you're talking about the love you have for your fiancé, that shouldn't be difficult to understand). A set of vows that mentions careers, other family members, and things that happened way before the two of you ever met is in serious danger of completely losing its focus! Get back to talking about the two of you, your feelings for one another, the moments you've actually shared, and the life you're going to create together. Period.

Religious or Secular Vows

If you're having any sort of ceremony involving a clergyman, the presence of God will be acknowledged at some point. Even if you forget to include Him in your vows, your officiant will certainly mention Him, and ask Him to bless your marriage. However, if you're having a civil ceremony and you're not a religious person, you may have a hard time deciding whether to mention a higher power in your vows. The same advice that holds true for writing your vows is appropriate here: Do what feels right for you.

There's a reason for that old adage, "Never discuss religion or politics in mixed company." Each person has a truly unique and highly personal belief system, whether that includes believing in a higher power, belonging to an organized religion, embracing one without the other, or cringing at the thought of any of these. When it comes to your wedding vows, however, you should express your true feelings on the issue.

If you want to mention God or otherwise refer to your religion, then by all means, do. If not, then don't. Don't worry about who is present and how you will be judged. While marriage is one rite of passage into adulthood, asserting your beliefs is another.

A Little Help from the Masters

In the event that you sit down to write your vows and draw a complete blank, you can always turn to the great poets and lyricists who have gone before. This is a commonly used idea, and it works very nicely.

One caution, though: Before you use anyone else's words to express your devotion to your fiancé, make sure they're appropriate. Some poems whose titles sound like love poems spiral downward into a story of obsession or other unhealthy emotions; song lyrics can also be misleading. And try to avoid using an entire *lengthy* work belonging to another writer. An excerpt that underscores your own feelings is usually enough, especially if you've chosen a long song or poem to quote.

It's one thing, for example, to work the opening lines of a beautiful love song into your vows; it's another to stand on the altar and read the entire thing, especially if it runs about twenty verses. That could be interpreted as a lack of planning on your part, as though you didn't care enough to punch up the vows with your own heartfelt words. So choose to use someone else's words wisely, but also use them (relatively) sparingly.

Some of the all-time best romantic poetry comes from:

- George Gordon, Lord Byron
- Edna St. Vincent Millay
- John Keats
- Emily Dickinson
- Elizabeth Barrett Browning
- Dante Gabriel Rossetti
- William Shakespeare

Of course, there are countless others, but if you have very little experience with poetry, researching the works of these poets is a good starting point. And remember, you can also look for words of wisdom in modern-day poetry and song lyrics; just don't try to pass the words off as your own (you can count on someone calling you out on it).

Chapter 16
I Do! The Ceremony

With all of this talk about planning a trip out of town, it's easy to overlook the real reason why you're doing all of this in the first place: You're getting married! Because the ceremony is the most important part of the wedding, you don't want to leave anything to chance. This chapter covers all the major points of the ceremony, including the ultimate run-through: the rehearsal.

Make Sure It's Legal

Regardless of where you're getting married or what kind of ceremony you're planning, you need to obtain a marriage license, which is the government's way of ensuring that only people who are legally eligible for marriage (basically, residents of this country who are of legal age and not currently married) actually end up getting married.

How Hard Could It Be?

Generally speaking, it's not that hard to obtain a marriage license. It's not like you have to pass some sort of Marriage I.Q. or compatibility test before you're allowed to become husband and wife. But you do need to know when and where to apply for the license and what to bring with you to prove that you are, indeed, who you claim to be.

 E~Fact

There isn't one specific government office that issues marriage licenses. In some towns, the town clerk may perform this duty; in another city, you may need to visit city hall, the county clerk, or the marriage license bureau.

When you apply for the license, you'll need to bring proof of your United States citizenship (a birth certificate will do, if you were born here; naturalization papers will suffice for immigrants) and a valid picture ID, like your driver's license. Almost every state charges a fee (ranging from about $30 to $100, depending on the state), and a few states still require that you bring along the results of a blood test (a screening tool for sexually transmitted diseases).

In most states, marriage licenses have a limited shelf life—that is, they're only valid for a certain period of time before they expire. If you don't marry within that time, you'll have to reapply. Nevada is one state that issues marriage licenses that are valid from the application date until the end of time, which seems fitting for a state that hosts so many weddings.

Past Marriages

Who knew there was so much to know about marriage licenses? Well, there's even more! In addition to proving your identity and residency, you'll also have to prove that you aren't currently married. If you have been married before, make sure you bring a copy of your divorce papers when you apply for your new marriage license. If your first marriage ended in the death of your spouse, bring a copy of the death certificate.

You'll also need to know whether the destination you've chosen for your wedding has a waiting period between the time you apply for the license and the time you're permitted to get married. It's about an even split here in the United States: Around half of the states have a waiting period, and the other half don't. Wisconsin's waiting period is the longest at six days; the District of Columbia is a close second with a five-day wait.

Foreign Relations

If you're headed overseas for the big ceremony, check with the U.S. embassy or office of tourism in that country regarding the requirements for marriage of non-citizens. Most countries permit foreigners to wed while visiting there, but some don't. You probably wouldn't plan an entire wedding without first knowing whether it's a legal possibility in the location you've chosen, but to be on the safe side, check out the residency requirements before you get your heart set on any site in particular. The United Kingdom, for example, has recently revamped its list of requirements for the union of non-nationals, making it a much more difficult process than it has been in the past. This, in turn, has many American couples flocking to Italy, where the rules are much more relaxed.

Island-Hopping

Since many destination weddings take place in tropical locations, let's take a look at the marriage requirements for a few of the hottest spots:

* *Fiji.* You can get a marriage license upon your arrival. Marriages are not performed on Sunday. You'll need your birth certificates and, if applicable, divorce papers.
* *Aruba.* Couples must petition the Office of Civil Registry of Aruba a week or two prior to the ceremony. Copies of your birth certificates, divorce papers, passports, the names of two witnesses, and copies of *their* passports must be sent along with the petition.
* *Bahamas.* There is a one-day waiting period after you get your license. You'll need to provide your passports, driver's licenses, divorce or death certificates, and a declaration swearing that both of you are unmarried.
* *British Virgin Islands.* You can apply for a license upon your arrival; there's a three-day waiting period. You'll need your passports, divorce or death certificates, and two witnesses.
* *Jamaica.* Apply for the license when you arrive; there's a twenty-four hour waiting period. You'll need your driver's licenses, birth certificates, and divorce or death certificates.

Obviously, there are many, many more islands than those mentioned here, and not every island is so easy to work with. Bermuda, for example, has fairly stringent requirements, including publishing a notice of your intent to marry in your local paper.

❀ E~ssential

Do your research well—and think about hiring a wedding consultant to help you with the paperwork, because it would be a shame to arrive at your location and realize that you haven't met the legal requirements for marriage! ✿

Religious and Civil Ceremonies

A religious marriage ceremony is sometimes easier to plan than its civil counterpart, because many religions require specific elements. It's similar to the way a destination wedding planner narrows down your choices so that you simply check things off a list and say, "We'll do this, this, and this." If you're steadfast in your faith, a religious ceremony is a beautiful and comforting occasion. And if you aren't a particularly religious person, your ceremony can be every bit as meaningful as one held in a church.

In this section, we'll talk about how to find the readings for both types of ceremonies.

Readings for the Religious Ceremony

Most times, the readings for a religious ceremony will be provided for you by the minister, priest, or rabbi. They will come from either the Old or New Testament—or both, depending on your religious affiliation—and will focus on the joy of marriage.

E~Alert

Secular readings are generally not heard at religious weddings, although a very modern-minded priest or rabbi *might* allow this from time to time.

When you commit to a religious ceremony, you're at the mercy of the officiant and the rules of the church or synagogue (speaking in the larger sense of the entire religion, not just the specific location where your ceremony will take place). There isn't a lot of room for negotiation here, so don't expect to meet with the priest and tell him how things are going to go during your ceremony. It's pretty much going to be his way or the highway.

Keeping It Civil

Civil ceremonies allow opportunities for getting creative with your music and readings, which can be a good thing or a bad thing, depending on your ability to choose well and eliminate anything inappropriate.

Civil ceremonies aren't just for atheists and agnostics—sometimes a couple whose religious backgrounds are different will decide on a civil union to avoid choosing one church over the other for the ceremony. Or perhaps both partners are Catholic, but one has been divorced and hasn't had the first union annulled. Some couples believe in God but haven't been to church in years and don't see the point in starting now. Whatever the case, you might want your civil union to contain a *reference* to God. These are some appropriate readings for this instance:

* 1 Corinthians 13:1–13
* Song of Solomon 2:10–13
* Ruth 1:1–17

You can also put together a touching ceremony without referencing the Bible. If romantic poetry is more along the lines of what you're thinking for your ceremony readings, check out these masterpieces:

* "Wedding Prayer," Robert Louis Stevenson
* *Sonnets from the Portuguese,* Elizabeth Barrett Browning
* "An Irish Wedding Blessing" (traditional)
* "A Dedication to My Wife," T. S. Eliot
* "Sudden Light," Dante Gabriel Rossetti
* "The Passionate Shepherd to His Love," Christopher Marlowe

You can also find beautiful passages in novels, literature, song lyrics, movies—just open your mind and start reading and listening to the words of love all around you! You may also choose to use some of these writings in your vows. (For more information on writing your own vows, see Chapter 15.)

Where to Find an Officiant

Depending on where you're headed, you may be able to choose between a religious and a civil ceremony, or you may be locked in to one or the other (Bermuda permits only civil unions for nonresidents, while Bali requires that visitors declare a religion before a ceremony can take place). If you're planning a destination wedding on your own, one of your tasks is to find someone who is legally allowed to pronounce you man and wife. The following section will tell you how to do just that.

Clerics

Any house of worship has its own officiant(s) attached to it, so if you're planning to book a church or temple, you won't have to look any further for someone to preside over your vows. Some churches have more pre-marriage requirements than others, however, so be prepared to meet them. Catholics, for example, are required to complete a pre-Cana course (which focuses on the realities of marriage) and are sometimes also required to give six months' notice of their intention to become man and wife.

Questions you should ask your officiant well in advance of the ceremony include these:

* What are the requirements for marriage? (If one of you is divorced, can you still get married in the church? What other requirements will you have to meet?)
* Is the date I've chosen available?
* What is the fee for the use of the church or temple? (This is usually referred to as a *donation* and goes toward the upkeep of the property.)
* Who will perform the ceremony?
* How will the readings and music be chosen?
* Are there any restrictions on the types of decorations or flowers I can use during the ceremony?

✳ How much time will there be between my ceremony and the next service? (You don't want to be rushed out the door of the church after a three o'clock wedding because four o'clock Mass is about to start.)

You also want to know about the amount of adequate parking, whether the church or synagogue can be used for group photographs before or after the wedding, and whether you, the groom, and both sets of parents can form a receiving line after the ceremony.

Civil Officiants

There are fewer questions and requirements involved in planning a civil ceremony. Usually all a civil officiant needs from you is the marriage license and witnesses. You tell him when and where to show up, and he'll just step into place and perform the ceremony. Many couples choose a civil ceremony simply because they want to have the ceremony at their reception site, and not every religion will sanction a union outside of a house of worship. In other words, unless the ceremony takes place in the church, a religious officiant may not be allowed to preside over it.

 E~Fact

Because you aren't bound by the laws of a church or even by tradition, you can personalize a civil ceremony in countless ways. This is one more reason couples choose to go the civil route—so start your research on readings and music early! ❧

The most likely candidates for performing a civil ceremony are a justice of the peace or a judge who lives in the area where you've chosen to marry. When you apply for your marriage license, ask for advice on finding someone to pronounce you man and wife.

The Rehearsal

A night or two before the wedding, you and your wedding party will gather at the ceremony site for a walk-through of the wedding. Although this is sometimes a highly anticipated time, the true purpose of this get-together—which is essentially a dress rehearsal for the big event you've been planning for so many months—gets lost in the shuffle. Bridesmaids are giggling, ushers are talking to their girlfriends, and your ring bearer is climbing up the trellis.

It's your job to call everyone to attention so that they know what to expect during the ceremony. Play the part of mother hen with any attendant whose head seems to be lost in the clouds at this time. This is the only time you'll have everyone together at the site before the wedding. If no one is paying attention to directions, your ceremony could end up being a confused mess! In this section, we'll take a look at the major elements of the wedding ceremony so that you know what to look for and take note of at the rehearsal.

Seating Savvy

Your groomsmen are expected to seat your guests before the ceremony in a polite and timely fashion. They should be prepared to be charming to a fault. They also should know that for a Christian ceremony, the bride's friends and family traditionally are seated to the left (as one enters the site); the groom's side is to the right. The opposite is true for most Jewish weddings. Ushers should know how to seat everyone accordingly, filling the seats starting in the front and moving toward the back.

 E~ssential

You're hardly going to *force* people to sit on either side, but your guests may automatically tell the ushers, "I'm the bride's aunt," or "The groom's side, please." Your ushers should know *why* they're being given this information and how to act on it.

Parents of the bride and groom are seated in the first row of their respective sides; siblings go behind them; and grandparents sit in the third row (if there are no siblings, grandparents take the second row of seats). The last person to be seated before the ceremony starts is the mother of the bride. If one of her sons is an usher, he usually does the honor.

If your parents are divorced, your mom gets the front row at the ceremony along with the privilege of choosing who gets to sit there with her (assuming she has not remarried). If the split was friendly, your dad can sit in the row behind her; if not, separate them by a row or two. If your father is the one who raised you, though, flip-flop this arrangement.

Two by Two

Your attendants will be given instructions by the officiant or by a wedding coordinator on how to proceed down the aisle. Sometimes there is room for a little variation—such as having couples meet halfway down the aisle as opposed to lining up and walking together from the doorway—but in most instances, what's suggested by the person in charge works out just fine. Your bridesmaids go first, followed by your maid of honor, your ring bearer, and your flower girl (in that order—though child attendants sometimes walk together, and the maid of honor sometimes ends up pulling both of them toward the altar), and then you.

✿ E~Alert

Bridesmaids sometimes take note of who's lined up farthest away from the bride, especially if it's obvious that the bride has a least-favorite bridesmaid (like a pesky cousin). Sending them down the aisle according to their height—shortest to tallest, or vice versa—helps to eliminate hurt feelings. ✿

Brides often choose to have their father walk them down the aisle for the purpose of giving them away. If the bride's father has passed away, she may choose an uncle, a brother, or another male family member to perform the duty. Some brides choose to have their mother fill this role, whether their dad is alive or not, and some brides choose to have both parents escort them down the aisle (which is the norm in a Jewish wedding). Still other brides choose to walk down the aisle by themselves, figuring they are giving *themselves* to their new husband.

Put traditional etiquette aside here and figure out which arrangement makes *you* most comfortable. If you're very independent and you don't like the idea of someone else handing you off to your fiancé, then explain this to your father. On the other hand, you should also avoid having an army of parents, stepparents, grandparents, and great-grandparents walk you down the aisle. While the sentiment behind this way of thinking is lovely—the entire family is giving you away—you'll be completely lost in the shuffle.

Simply having your family at the ceremony sends essentially the same message, in a much more manageable way.

Practice for the Ceremony

During the rehearsal, you'll run through an abbreviated version of the ceremony, including where you, the groom, and your attendants will be standing and what they should be doing (the maid of honor, for example, should know to reach for your flowers once you arrive at the altar; she should also know that it's her job to make sure you look picture-perfect at all times without blocking the shot with her big head).

The officiant will have readers take their positions on the altar and will probably ask them to read an excerpt or two so that he can give them a few pointers on speaking loudly and clearly during the ceremony. The same goes for you and the groom while you're reciting your vows: Speak up! If the two of you have written your own vows and would rather save them for the ceremony, make your wishes clear. If the officiant only wants to ensure that you'll be able to speak loudly enough, he can certainly have you recite traditional vows during the rehearsal.

You'll also run through the exchange of rings and any other major elements of the ceremony, such as lighting a unity candle. Listen to your officiant's advice for taking care of your dress while you move around the altar, and make sure your maid of honor is listening, too! Although you've tried on your wedding dress several times, you haven't done anything practical (like, say, walking around a church) in it. If the officiant warns you that three brides in the past month have tripped on their dresses on their way up a set of stairs to light the unity candle, he's not trying to scare you; he's kindly trying to prevent you from becoming number four!

✿ E~ssential

If this is your first visit to the ceremony site, ask where the musicians and the videographer will most likely set up. Although you won't have much to do with that decision, it might make you feel more at ease on the day of the wedding if everything is exactly as you expect it to be. ✿

Before you know it, the rehearsal will be over and you'll be on your way out the door. The order in which the wedding party entered is reversed during the recessional: You and the groom walk out first, followed by your child attendants, honor attendants, bridesmaids and ushers, and parents.

The Rehearsal Dinner

Traditionally, the groom's parents host the rehearsal dinner. If they're befuddled by this destination wedding, help them out by providing helpful information about restaurants in the area.

If you were hosting an in-town wedding, you would be advised to invite not just members of the wedding party to the rehearsal dinner, but also any out-of-town guests. If you're having a very large destination wedding and you choose to have a formal rehearsal dinner, limit the invitations to include only the members of the wedding party and their significant others. Extending invitations to guests outside the bridal circle starts you on a slippery slope (the groom's cousins will wonder why they weren't invited if *your* cousins were) and sets up your future in-laws for footing the bill for what amounts to a pre-wedding reception.

Talk to your future in-laws. Find out what they're most comfortable doing. If they simply can't pay for a huge rehearsal dinner that includes all of your guests, then maybe you and the groom can pitch in and cover the extra expense. Or perhaps it will fall to the two of you to host the dinner on your own. Clear communication is the answer to preventing any misunderstandings about the guest list for this gathering.

❀ E~Alert

Make sure that the people you invite have been given very clear instructions on how to find the rehearsal dinner site! Some people have a terrible sense of direction, so include major landmarks along with road names and route numbers. ❧

There is very little formal etiquette written about destination weddings and rehearsal dinners, so we're left to rely on the spirit of the issues that etiquette concerns itself with most: Manners. Politeness. Doing the right thing. It's just wrong to invite half of your destination wedding guests to the rehearsal dinner and leave the other half to fend for themselves. There will be hurt feelings and resentment galore (you can almost guarantee that those not invited to the rehearsal dinner will be asking themselves why they came to your wedding only to be shunned like this). Spare your guests' feelings, and spare yourself the agony of regret. Invite everyone or invite *only* the wedding party.

Chapter 17

Eat, Drink, and Boogie: The Reception

For many people (brides, grooms, and guests included), the reception is the main event of the whole wedding. It's usually where the happy couple spends the bulk of the wedding fund, and also the area on which most of the planning is focused—and for good reason, actually. Whether you're planning a civil or religious ceremony, you're bound by certain traditions and a definite time frame, which takes some of the picking and choosing right out of your hands. The reception, on the other hand, is full of possibilities.

Planning Within a Resort

If you're thinking about having your ceremony and reception at a resort, realize that not all destination wedding sites are created equal. The vast majority will do a beautiful job of handling your reception, but certain sites are better for certain types of weddings. For example, if you're choosing a hotel on a little, out-of-the-way island in the South Pacific as your wedding site, you won't be given the option of which reception hall suits you best, because there likely will be only one. If you choose a hotel or resort near a huge metropolis, however, your planning might proceed much as it would if you were living in that town and planning a traditional wedding.

Size Matters

First things first: big wedding or small wedding? While traditional etiquette holds that certain people may be invited to the reception but not the wedding, this does not hold true for the destination wedding. If people are shelling out money to make it to the site of the wedding, they're automatically invited to both events. In other words, then, during this planning process, you shouldn't be thinking, "The ceremony will be small, but the reception's going to be much, much bigger." Find a site that will accommodate all of your guests for both parts of the wedding day.

Large resorts can usually handle weddings of just about any size, though they may have an absolute bare minimum required number of guests (twenty or so). Small resorts, on the other hand, definitely have their limits, so if the wedding coordinator at one of these tiny places tells you that they just can't handle a wedding for 100 guests, don't try to change her mind by shedding some bridal tears or offering her a bridal bribe. Be grateful that she's honest enough to be up-front with you about the site's limitations. You'll either have to cut the guest list or look elsewhere.

What's Included in a Package?

Resort wedding packages usually make an attempt to provide brides and grooms of all incomes with various options. You'll find that some places are much more expensive than others, but that usually is due to either the location or the quality of the food and drink being served.

Packages can run from a few thousand dollars into the tens of thousands, depending on the number of guests and what sorts of added "goodies" you want to throw into your reception. Some couples grab up these add-ons like crazy, reasoning that this is the kind of wedding they could only have at this particular site. Other brides and grooms prefer to keep things scaled way back, to preserve the sacredness of the occasion.

And there lies the true magnificence of destination weddings and their packaging: There's something out there that's just perfect for every bride and groom. The same resort may be able to offer the most boisterous wedding and the most sacred wedding—for two different brides, mind you, but on the same exact day.

Dig Deeper

The lesson to learn here? Do your research carefully and thoroughly. Just because you know of someone who had a teeny, tiny ceremony at a given location doesn't mean that you can't have a much larger event at that same place. These are some of the questions you should ask of a resort wedding coordinator:

* How many reception guests can this resort comfortably handle?
* What types of decorations are included at the reception, and what will cost extra?
* What types of meals are offered? (Sit-down, buffet, stations? Fish, beef, chicken?)
* What will you end up paying extra for? (In other words, what isn't included in the package?)

That last one is a biggie. Extra charges for things like glasses, linens, and plates can add up quickly. Caterers are more likely to charge these fees than resorts are, but since some resorts use caterers for their large functions, these fees could end up on your bill.

Planning the Reception on Your Own

When planning your destination reception without the help or muscle of a professional wedding resort at your disposal, you will run into the same kinds of issues that the average bride planning a wedding in her hometown would deal with—times about ten. Planning a great reception takes a lot of effort: It takes up your time, it can wear you down emotionally, and it could end up costing a fortune. The idea here is to circumnavigate the negative possibilities and try to remain calm, cool, and steady from beginning to end. (Reread this after your wedding for a good laugh.)

The Great Reception Hall Search

When you don't live in the town where you're getting married, how do you even begin to look for a reception site? Most brides and grooms have this part taken care of from the very beginning—the reason they've chosen an out-of-town spot is *because* of the site where the reception (and possibly the ceremony) will be held.

But even then, if you've chosen a historical site, or an outdoor venue, or any other place without a functioning kitchen and a chef on staff, you're going to have to find a caterer to feed your hungry wedding guests. It might be tempting—and easy—to do an Internet search to find someone (anyone) in the area who might be able to do the job for you, but don't jump the gun. Start by talking with your reception site coordinator (or whomever is handling your wedding); ask her which caterer she would recommend. If you're still in the early stages of planning, you may be surprised to learn that you have no choice in the matter, as some places are contractually obligated to use a particular caterer (for reasons that are varied and too numerous to get into here).

However, if you're left with wide-open possibilities, your site coordinator will no doubt be able to give you some advice on which caterer is best for elegant affairs, which caterer does a mean barbecue, and which caterer serves up killer appetizers. She'll also be able to tell you who's reputable in the area and who isn't.

Cutting Down the Caterer List

If you're choosing among three caterers, make things easy on yourself and first decide which type of food you want to serve at your reception. Uncle Joe's Roasters might be (locally) famous for their fried chicken and potato salad, but if you want to set up stations, it's a good bet that Joe isn't your man. It may sound as though this would be an obvious decision, but you may be overlooking one thing: Do you know what your fiancé wants to serve the guests at your reception? What he has in mind may be completely different from what you're thinking, and the two of you may need to come to a happy compromise.

 E~ssential

A big consideration when you're looking for a caterer is price. Reception costs can spiral out of control quickly, so if you're on a limited budget and the cheapest item on a caterer's menu is an $18 bowl of soup, keep on looking. 🐦

Once you find someone who meets your every need, you'll sign a contract, which will include:

* The guest count
* Food to be served
* Setup and break-down times

* Number of servers (and what they're expected to wear)
* Beverages, including the bar (something we'll discuss later)
* Rental fees: tent, chairs, tables, linens, tableware, glasses, chafing dishes, centerpieces, candlesticks, and so on.

The good news is that a well-equipped caterer can pretty much take care of everything for you, from setting up the tent to cleaning up after your guests. In the end, hiring a caterer can end up being more expensive than going with a reception site with its own kitchen, so again, if cost is your main concern, you may want to look into other options before committing to this type of reception.

What to Serve, What to Avoid

When it comes down to reception time, your guests will expect appetizers, dinner, dessert, and liquor (in that order—except for the liquor, of course). The best thing about finding a really good caterer is having the opportunity to sample his wares, so ask your caterer what his specialties are and try to include at least a couple in your choices. If you find that they're very unusual-sounding, you may want to include his specialty appetizers and go with more traditional food for dinner.

For Starters

You'll be asked if you want the appetizers laid out buffet-style or served on trays. This is a very personal choice and really depends on what your guests will be most comfortable with. Some people love having others serve them; others are so uncomfortable with the concept that they'll turn down the appetizers out of embarrassment. Also, a very elegant wedding calls for having servers making the rounds, where a less formal event just doesn't.

Appetizers are easy enough, because you really can try to please everyone and *almost* succeed at it. You can have a cheese plate, a crudités platter, a fruit plate, stuffed mushrooms, crab cakes, and a couple of the caterer's unique concoctions all sitting next to one another.

E~ssential

Setting up appetizer stations is a perfectly acceptable alternative to having waiters circulating with trays—but make sure the stations are placed throughout the reception site. As long as the appetizers are spread out enough (eliminating the possibility of a traffic jam), you shouldn't hear any complaints about the lack of trays circulating with stuffed mushrooms.

No Pushing!

Though the staunchest etiquette mavens have eschewed the buffet as being in bad taste, citing the need for guests to leave their seats and wait in line to be fed, the truth is that buffets (and stations, which basically are a buffet line spread out across the room) have come a long way. Years ago, the average wedding buffet had some chicken, some pasta, some mashed potatoes, a green veggie, and maybe—*maybe*—a fresh salad. Nowadays, you're very likely to find the best that a caterer has to offer, such as filet mignon, salmon, and roasted veggies, along with fancy mashed potatoes (herbed or smashed). This is the same food you'd choose for a sit-down meal, by the way, so you're not shortchanging your guests; you're actually giving them the opportunity to have both meat *and* fish. If you've been thinking about a buffet but you're worried about what your guests are going to think or say, take a look at your choices and decide from there. (More than one nitpicking relative has been won over by a good buffet.)

Sit-Downs

Going with a sit-down dinner is still an option, of course. Most brides give their guests the option of fish, meat, or a vegetarian meal, especially in this age of low-fat diets. (Why give the option of meat, then? Because your linebacker brother will never make it through the night on just a slab of salmon.) You can try to ascertain the caterer's serving protocol, but the truth is, you can't know how good or bad the service is unless you experience it for yourself or you find someone else who has. For this reason alone, it's worth your while to get the names of some previous brides—and call them! Ask if guests were served in a timely manner or if those at the tables way in the back were left wishing for a crust of bread while others were on the dance floor already.

Sit-down dinners are still considered the most elegant way to serve your wedding guests, so if pampering your relatives and friends is important to you, then this is the way to go.

The Bar Is Open!

When you're planning a wedding outside the confines of a resort, you'll need to answer the age-old question: open bar or cash bar?

Here's the deal: Liquor is served at almost all receptions, whether they're afternoon or evening affairs; even morning receptions usually have a champagne toast. Most of your guests will arrive expecting to have a drink or two (and some will expect to have far more). It's just wrong to invite people to a party and then ask them to pay for their own liquor.

When you're going to a friend's cocktail party, you bring something—a snack, a bottle of wine—and then you spend the night noshing and drinking on someone else's dime. Same thing when you have friends over to your house—sure, they'll bring a little something, but as the hostess, most of the financial burden is going to be yours.

So now it comes time for the biggest party of all: your wedding. Your friends have made the trip, they brought you a gift, and now you want them to pay for their own liquor? Wrong. A cash bar at a wedding reception is one of the most tactless things that you can do—so don't.

Grumble if you must about the cost of an open bar; lament the fact that you're going to pay for half-consumed glasses of wine and gin-and-tonics. Doesn't matter. This is one of those wedding expenses that just about kills you but is worth it in the end. Why? Because if you have a cash bar, you're going to hear the discontent of your guests. Some will be louder about it than others, but you can bank on the fact that no one is going to *sincerely* say, "I'm so glad I came all the way to this wedding and now I'm paying six dollars for a glass of Chardonnay!"

E~Fact

Although cocktail receptions are an option in a traditional wedding, they aren't usually seen after destination weddings. Cocktail receptions consist of appetizers, cake, and champagne and other alcoholic beverages—not very substantial fare for guests who have traveled so far to attend your wedding.

Some couples go with what they feel is a happy medium: Beer and wine are free; cocktails cost the guests. Depending on the crowd you're inviting, this could work out all right, or it could be as bad as having a cash bar if it turns out that no one drinks wine or beer—they all want vodka!

Moving and Mingling

Ask any newlywed what she remembers about her wedding, and she's likely to tell you that it passed in such a blur that she barely remembers it. One advantage to having a destination wedding is that it stretches out the event and thus slows down the time. However, you may have guests who are only able to make it for a day or two, and you'll need to touch base with every person who shows up. Do you have to wear running shoes to the reception, or might a little course in reception mingling do the trick?

The Receiving Line

Standing at attention, the bridal party meets and greets guests either after the ceremony or at the beginning of the reception—or both, if the timing happens to be one and the same. This is another one of those wedding traditions that has fallen out of favor lately. Some brides feel that it just takes too much time, it's old-fashioned, and no one wants to come through the line to say hello to the bridesmaids anyway, so why bother?

Well, it may be true enough that the bridesmaids are not the central points of interest among your guests—but you (and/or your fiancé) are. You're going to be so busy at the reception that it may be very hard to say hello to everyone. The minutes will fly by like seconds and before you know it, you'll be on your way to your honeymoon suite. Taking this block of time and dedicating it to greeting guests actually will make your day easier.

E~Question

Why do I have to have a receiving line?

Since most destination wedding guests attend both the ceremony and reception (hey, they schlepped all the way out here—you think they'd miss the ceremony?), the receiving line after the ceremony is the perfect time to say hello to everyone and then move on with the rest of the evening.

If you're worried about the size of the bridal party and the time it will take your guests to greet everyone, then cut down the line to just you, the groom, and both sets of parents. Easy as pie.

Move Around

The receiving line doesn't get you off the hook for the rest of the evening. You still need to make your best effort to mingle with as many guests as possible at the reception. Yes, you are the center of attention, and sure, people should come to you, but—you're the bride. It's your party. Be the friendly hostess and do your best to at least pretend that you're concerned about the welfare of your guests. Granted, it's not easy to balance every-thing that's going on—pictures, food, dancing—with the well-being of your individual guests, but you'll score huge points for asking people if they're having a good time or for thanking people for coming.

You say you're not interested in putting on this type of show. This is your wedding; not some popularity contest. Wrong, Sister! Your wedding *is* a popularity contest—and if people bother to show, you're winning. But you're going to lose points for acting the part of the self-important bride. Just remember that all of your guests cared enough about you to be with you on this day; show them a little love in return. It's so easy to do.

What Happens When

A decent reception has to have some order to it. You can't just expect the food, the chitchat, and the dancing to magically happen on cue if you haven't laid out a plan. To that end, you and the reception site coordinator will sit down and talk about your vision of the evening. Some traditional elements of the reception include:

* *The cocktail hour.* Lots of mingling, drinking, folks finding their seats for dinner.
* *Cutting of the cake.* Big photo op for the newlyweds, so dash into the powder room and powder your nose.
* *The introduction of the wedding party.* The emcee (either the reception coordinator or the DJ or the bandleader) will introduce the attendants, the parents of the bride and groom, and then the newlyweds just as everyone is sitting down to dinner. Cheers abound for the happy couple.
* *Toasts.* The best man is held responsible for offering the first toast to the bride and groom. If others have some sentiments they'd like to share, the traditional order of toast-makers is: best man; father of the groom; father of the bride; groom; bride; friends and relatives; maid of honor; mother of the groom; mother of the bride.

* *Dinner.* During the meal your guests will tap their silverware on their cups and expect you and the groom to stop chewing and start smooching.
* *Dancing.* The bride shares the first dance with her father; then the groom shares a dance with his mother; then the newlyweds have their first dance together. After that, the dance floor opens up to everyone else. (See Chapter 14 for information about choosing music and musicians.)
* *Tossing of the bouquet and garter.* Brides are still tossing throwaway bouquets on a regular basis, though many couples don't bother with the other part of this tradition, the garter toss. (Seems that some brides are uncomfortable having their groom literally reach up their dress in front of a large group of people.) In any event, tradition holds that the man and woman who make the lucky catches will be the next to be married—but not necessarily to each other.

In addition to these traditions, you might want to include some ethnic traditions, such as the dollar dance (Italian brides), carrying the bride and groom on chairs (Jewish weddings), or the groom wearing a hat made of fruit as a symbol of virility (Polish men).

How to Please Every Guest

You're dying to know the secret to having a reception that everyone will love, right? Why are some weddings so much fun and others so dull? If you really want to please your guests, you have to first acknowledge who they are. Your elderly relatives are not going to enjoy an extremely loud, bass-booming sound system. Your bratty teenage cousins are going to be bored to death if you choose a five-piece band to play oldies.

When it comes to pleasing everyone, you have to realize that you may not be able to, especially if you're having a large wedding and especially if you've got some friends or relatives who can be real sticks in the proverbial mud. Contrary to what you may believe, reception choices are more about the guests than they are about the bride and groom—you're deciding what you're going to feed your guests, whether you're going to pay for their drinks, what type of music will bring everyone onto the dance floor. Keep your guests happy, and your reception will be a hit. That's rock-solid advice.

How do you keep them happy? By taking into consideration what *most* people will enjoy—or at least tolerate. We know that your older relatives (which, for the sake of this discussion, includes anyone in their fifties or older) will hate loud technotronic music at the reception; that's a given. But will *your* friends really mind dancing to milder tunes? (Honestly, does *anyone* object to big-band music?) Probably not. Where one group of people is likely to be so unhappy or bothered by the music that they may get up and leave, the other group may accept the mellowness of the music and go with it. Your DJ or band should be able to mix things up enough so that everyone has a great time.

It's not easy to please diverse tastes and/or age groups. The name of the game here is mitigating negative reactions and giving everyone food, drink, and entertainment that they won't hate. And when you look at it from that standpoint, it's not so hard to do, after all.

Chapter 18
The Week Before the Wedding

The bride who plans her wedding in her hometown might spend the days leading up to the ceremony catching up on last-minute errands: purchasing gifts for the bridesmaids, picking up her dress, planning a lunch date with attendants and/or her mother, and packing for her honeymoon. The destination bride, on the other hand, has to know how to plan ahead and delegate responsibilities to others so that when she hits the road for her wedding trip, she doesn't leave something behind—and take a whole lot of stress along for the ride!

En Route

Remember: Organization is your saving grace when you're planning a wedding. Never is this more true than when you're leaving for a destination wedding. You need to have a checklist for everything you should take along. You need another checklist for everything that you have to accomplish (meeting with the wedding coordinator, attending the rehearsal, presenting the attendants' gifts) once you arrive. You need still another list for things that you'd like to do while you're away (scuba diving, hiking, chatting poolside with the girls, and so on).

Make a List

The most important list to assemble is the one that includes everything you need to pack. You do not want to arrive at your destination only to realize that you've forgotten the marriage license or—gasp!—the vows that took you so long to compose. Here are some other things that you won't want to overlook when packing:

* *The rings.* If they're in your possession now, make sure you take them. If you're flying, pack the rings in your carry-on luggage!
* *Your reservation information.* Confirmation numbers, credit card receipts, e-mail correspondence—anything that will help clear up any confusion upon checking in to your hotel or picking up your rental car.
* *Your bridal folder or notebook.* Be sure this includes contact information for all of the vendors you've been working with. (Obviously, this applies to brides who are working with several vendors.) Keep phone numbers and contract information at your fingertips. You'll need to be in contact with these people in the days leading up to the wedding.
* *Wedding gear.* The dress, the groom's suit, your undergarments. Make a separate list for your many accessories (shoes, handbag, earrings, and so on), and check them off as you pack them.

✳ *Vacation gear.* If you're off for a wedding *and* a honeymoon, make sure you pack accordingly. Take extra sunscreen, appropriate footwear, and enough formal and casual wear to see you through whatever you have planned. If you're driving, make sure you have a map leading you to your destination and a map of the area to use once you arrive.

If you're flying, also remember to take your plane tickets for the return flight home (yes, you really do have to come back—sorry). You'll need a valid form of ID in order to get on the plane, so make sure to book those tickets in your maiden name!

Bag It or Buy It?

You know, you can look at a list of things you'd pack to take on vacation and say to yourself, "I can buy that when I get there." And thankfully, you're right. If you forget to pack sunscreen, you could certainly pick that up anywhere. But if money is any sort of concern, plan ahead and purchase it at home!

❁ **E~Fact**

Pack soaps, shampoos, or anything that could spill in your suitcase in plastic bags—either the kind with a "zipper" top, or the kind that you can suck all of the air out of. If you're flying, make sure those bags are clear plastic in case your bags are selected for inspection by hand. 🕊

Think about this: When you run out of toothpaste at home, you have the option to stop by the convenience store and pick up a tube or drive two miles down the road and purchase it at the drugstore. Many people choose to drive down to the drugstore, even in this age of skyrocketing fuel prices, because the toothpaste in the convenience store will cost you roughly double the normal price. Shops in tourist towns are the same. If you've forgotten to pack just one or two necessities, you won't exactly go broke purchasing them out of town. But it's just not wise to plan to buy everything once you get there just so you don't have to pack it. That's just throwing your money away.

Particulars

Every bride has her own individual list of needs, so make sure you add those to your list, too. (Medications, reading material, contact lens solution, and anything else you can't do without.) And start the list nice and early—at least two weeks prior to taking off for your destination wedding. Even if you become completely overwhelmed by last-minute planning, you'll have a solid list to rely on to ensure that the essentials aren't left behind. If you've already started a detailed packing list, you'll stay one step ahead of any panic that sets in as you get closer to your date of departure.

Where's the Red Carpet?

Once you arrive at your destination, you should expect the entire resort or town to shut down and welcome you with open arms, right?

That largely depends on the site you've chosen. Some resorts are very good at making brides feel as though they are the first—and will be the last—woman to take her vows there; others have a decidedly more casual feel to the entire event. Yes, you're special, but there's so much going on in or around the site that it's sort of expected that you're enamored of the place (so how can you expect anyone to be enamored of you)? This is especially true in a town like Las Vegas, which welcomes flocks of brides who are looking for fun, out-of-the ordinary ceremonies.

Try not to have exceedingly high expectations of the hotel staff rushing to greet you upon your arrival. If you're spending time waiting for a tiara to arrive on a pillow, you'll lose focus of the things that need to be done, such as meeting with your wedding coordinator and reuniting with your wedding dress!

✿ E~ssential
Don't worry if you're not greeted like royalty when you arrive at your wedding site. Keep in mind that the resort hosts weddings all the time, and although the staff will work to do the best job for you they can, this is just another "job" for them. Keep in mind that you'll certainly be the center of attention on your wedding day, and your guests have come a long way just to honor you on this wonderful occasion! ✿

Meeting the Coordinator

If you've booked your wedding at a site that has a wedding coordinator, you've probably already made provisions to meet with her when you arrive; if you haven't done this, it's in your best interest to call the site as soon as possible to ensure that the coordinator has time to sit down and speak with you. At this meeting, she should walk you through the ceremony and reception sites (especially if you've planned this wedding sight unseen) and answer any questions you may have.

Take Note

If you're feeling nervous, excited, and just a little out of your mind when you first meet with the coordinator (so many thoughts swirling in your brain!), you may forget to ask her something that's quite important to you. You don't want to lose a moment's sleep in your luxurious suite worrying over something you just have to have the answer to, so make sure that you cover the major bases with her, including:

＊ *The rehearsal.* Many of your questions about the ceremony will be answered during the rehearsal, including where you will enter, where the vows will take place, where the musicians will be seated, and so on. You need to know the time and date of the rehearsal and how long it will last.

* *The ceremony.* Who will perform the marriage? Who needs to see the marriage license and when?
* *The reception.* Where will the band set up? Where is the dance floor? Where is the cake placed? Can you change any of these things if you aren't 100 percent pleased?
* *The vendors.* Has everyone been contacted this week? Any last-minute changes or substitutions?
* *Hair, makeup, nails.* If your coordinator made reservations for you with the resort's beautician, you should plan on meeting with this woman before your wedding day.

Bring a notebook with you to this meeting. Chances are, your coordinator won't forget to cover all the details, but you might forget what she's said! Take notes as the two of you are speaking, and don't be afraid to ask her to slow down or to repeat something she's said. You only get to do this wedding thing once—make sure you know *what* you're supposed to be doing and *when*!

Beautifying the Dress

Whether your dress was shipped to the site ahead of you or it made the trip in the back seat of your car, chances are it will need a steaming. Your wedding coordinator should be able to either take care of this for you or find a steamer on site that you can use yourself.

 **E~Alert**

If your groom is renting a tux, he needs to hightail it down to the tuxedo shop as soon as possible after your arrival. Even if he sent his measurements ahead, there's a lot of room for error. Be sure he actually tries it on.

Again, this list is a jumping-off point for your final list. If you've planned for some really spectacular events during the course of your wedding and/or reception (you'll be arriving on the back of a camel, for example, or you're having hula dancers at the reception), you need to remember to ask your coordinator about the details surrounding those plans, as well.

Checking In with Your Guests

When you've invited scores of people to your destination wedding, they become part and parcel of your plans during your wedding week. In other words, you can't invite every friend and family member you can think of to attend your cruise ship wedding and then announce upon their arrival that you really need your privacy in these days before the ceremony. That's just not going to fly. Instead, remember that they're here to share your joy with you—and you and your new hubby will have lots of alone time to look forward to later.

Group Outings

In the interest of exploring the area together, charter a bus and coordinate a tour of the area for anyone who's interested. If you're in Hawaii, for example, wouldn't it be cool to check out a volcano with a slew of wedding well-wishers? Or if you're off to New England, your guests might want to go on a whale-watching tour.

Obviously, these things are easier to plan if your wedding is on the smaller side (fewer than a hundred people), but if you know that only fifty family members are going to be with you for the entire week, it's not so difficult to plan some interesting activities.

A place like Las Vegas or Disney World or a cruise ship already has enough activities to keep everyone amused without your having to plan an extra outing. In this case, you're off the hook as far as chartering a bus or a boat goes. Still, you should provide your guests with enough information about the area so that they can choose the best options for themselves. Even though your cousin has made the trip to Las Vegas for your wedding, she may not be much of a gambler. Does she realize that there's more to Vegas than shooting craps? She might be surprised to learn that she can catch a Broadway-caliber show and do some Fifth Avenue–style shopping in Nevada. Or maybe she'd be more interested in hopping on a four-wheeler and checking out the desert. Either way, she can't do these things if she isn't aware that they're viable options.

✿ E~Question

How can I make sure everyone will be amused once they arrive at our wedding site?

Do your research thoroughly and include a list of interesting activities (or better yet, a small local travel book) when you send your save-the-date cards. Your guests then can do further research into activities that interest them before they arrive at your wedding site. ✧

If you're a born planner, take your laptop along and make up a daily itinerary for yourself; hand out copies to whomever is interested in spending time with you and your groom. It doesn't have to be anything fancy. If you're a laid-back girl, your itinerary might look something like this:

* 9 A.M. to 10 A.M. Breakfast in the Mirror Lounge.
* 10 A.M. to 12 P.M. Poolside.
* 2 P.M. to 3 P.M. Volleyball on the beach.
* 4 P.M. to 6 P.M. Scuba diving. Must make reservations before 2 P.M. if interested. Equipment rental is $50 per person.
* 8 P.M. Dinner at the Tiki Torch. Entrees range in price from $17.50 to $39.
* 10 P.M. to ? Dancing and drinks at the Diamond Head Club.

Notice that you have not accounted for every single minute of your day on this sample itinerary. From noon to two o'clock, for example, you might be off taking a nap or meeting with a vendor or the wedding coordinator. Your guests don't have to be with you every single second, but make sure that you give them plenty of opportunity to see you and to have some kicks with you.

Make sure to preface any itinerary with a line or two that lets the guests know that this is where you will be at any given time, and they are welcome—but not obligated—to join you. Also, include ticket or meal prices (in ranges, if appropriate) so that your guests know that you will not be picking up the tab for everyone.

Alternatively, you can divvy up activities between yourself and the groom. If you hate sitting next to the pool, for example, maybe you can hit the town to do some shopping while he catches some rays.

Get into the Mix

One big reason that brides plan destination weddings is so they can spend lots of time with their guests, and one big reason guests love destination weddings is because of their one big happy family / weeklong party atmosphere. So plan to indulge your guests in this way. They want to see you, and they want to have some laughs with you.

❀ E~Alert

Don't play the part of the shrinking violet (or worse, the pampered princess). Get in the pool with your family. Play volleyball on the beach with your friends. Hit the casinos with your grandma. Have fun during your wedding week, and any stress you're feeling will dissipate! ❧

Any bride who has had a destination wedding will tell you that spending fun, quality, laid-back time with guests is the biggest perk of planning a wedding out of town. Brides who plan in-town weddings are often running around like madwomen the week before their ceremonies, feeling rushed and out of sorts. Many women don't take vacation time the entire week before their nuptials if they're getting married in their hometown. It just feels like too much of a luxury, especially because she's heading out of town for her honeymoon the following week.

Here's where you, as a destination bride, have an edge: You have to take time off before the wedding. It's not a luxury; it's a necessity. You can't pop into town and expect your wedding to fall magically into place twenty-four hours later. Even with the best wedding coordinator on the planet, that would be stretching the limits of probability.

✿ E~ssential

You can't plan every deep conversation, every joke, every hearty laugh, every hysterical anecdote—but you can open the door for them merely by planning the destination wedding and making time to connect with your guests. ✿

The time that destination wedding couples are able to spend with family and friends in the days leading up to the ceremony is something that couples who marry in-town really miss out on. So enjoy it and make the most of it!

Keeping Your Cool

Maybe you looked at the sample itinerary in this chapter and thought, "Oh, that would never do. We have so many things to accomplish. We'll be on the go, go, go the entire week!" And then you proceeded to fill up six single-spaced pages on your computer with activities you're planning to squeeze into one week.

If you over-plan the week leading up to your wedding, there's a good chance you're going to drive yourself a tad bit nuts. By the time the ceremony rolls around, you might feel worn out and eager to just get it over with so you can take off for your honeymoon and sleep. On the one hand, that's not such a bad thing—it means that you really packed a lot into your week with your guests. On the other hand, though, if you've lost sight of the reason for this trip in the first place (which would be the ceremony), then there's just too much going on.

E~Fact

The best way to find a balance between being busy having fun and getting things done is to *plan ahead* (organization saves the day again!) and have an itinerary for meeting with your vendors. Put yourself on a schedule, and the fun will fall into place.

You'll probably be on the go most of the week no matter how little you do in the way of actually planning activities. Earlier in this chapter, you read about meeting with the wedding coordinator to work out the last-minute details. If there is no wedding coordinator in the picture, you'll make those final calls yourself, recounting the terms of the contracts and solidifying arrival and delivery times. Lest this sound like an impossible task, relax—it's not. Brides who plan in-town weddings often confirm dates and times by themselves, usually without a single hitch.

However, brides who are planning weddings in their hometowns are either in their own element or are relying on someone else (such as mom) to pick up some of the slack, as would be the case for a bride who is returning to her hometown from the Big City in order to recite her marriage vows. When you hit the road and have no one but yourself to see you through to your own wedding day, at least in the way of planning, it's important not to overload yourself with too many unfamiliar things at once.

Packing an outrageous amount of sightseeing into a day when you're also supposed to touch base with the minister, the baker, the caterer, and the photographer will backfire on you in a big way, especially if something goes awry with one of your vendors.

Put the Wedding Party to Work!

Back in Chapter 7, you read about choosing attendants for the bridal party. Much of the focus there was on choosing well, because your attendants have actual, real-live duties to perform, and you and your fiancé should be able to call on any one of these people for assistance without a moment's hesitation. When you arrive at your destination and realize that there's a lot to be done in the coming week, you'll be relieved if you've surrounded yourself with dependable attendants.

Same Titles, Big Differences

A bride who has planned a one-day wedding in her hometown may not need a whole lot of help, really, beyond the basics: She'll want her maid of honor to help her choose a dress for herself and the bridal party; she'll ask the bridesmaids to help address envelopes; the female attendants will also be responsible for hosting a bridal shower. On the day of the wedding, the bride may send an attendant or two on a last-minute errand, and the maid of honor is expected to step up and help the bride at any moment, whether that means straightening the bride's veil, fixing her train during the ceremony, holding her flowers at crucial moments (like the ring exchange) or holding on to a secret stash of tissues for the bride to wipe her tears of joy.

E~ssential

While attendants for a destination wedding will perform the same tasks as their counterparts at an in-town wedding, they should be up to doing *more*. Why? There are just more opportunities for attendants to be of real assistance in the week before a destination wedding.

The very act of taking a wedding on the road opens up potential areas of difficulty. For example, if the groom's tux doesn't fit, how will you track down appropriate formalwear for him on a small island—when you're booked solid with activities with your guests? Enter the best man! Send him along with the groom to track down some decent formalwear.

What if—heaven forbid—you shipped your wedding dress, but it doesn't arrive at your destination? Who's going to hold your hand, tell you everything is going to be all right, and help narrow down your dress-shopping options for you? One of your bridesmaids, of course!

Social Directors

Your attendants should also be able to step in and be incredibly sociable with your guests. If you're running late to the barbecue that you've invited everyone to, send your maid of honor ahead as your stand-in. When you're feeling worn out from a week's worth of fun, make your apologies early one evening and leave your attendants to entertain the guests. This is why you chose these particular people to be in your wedding party, so let them show you what they're capable of. They want to help; *trust them* with the things you need help with.

 E~Alert

During the week before your wedding, let go of any tendencies you may have to be in control of everything *all the time*. Handing over duties to your attendants will make them feel that they're playing a bigger role in the wedding, and will alleviate your stress, too. ✿

Destination weddings are so different from in-town weddings because the guests really get to know each other fairly well over the course of the week. You might be surprised to realize that you're becoming part of the wedding crowd—that your guests would just as soon spend time with your maid of honor as with you. Don't feel badly, as though you've somehow not been charming enough. You want this kind of bonding to happen!

When your guests are as comfortable with your attendants as they are with you, then you don't have to feel bad for not spending every single second with the people you've invited to share the week with you. The bridal party becomes an extension of you, and everyone starts to feel as though they're family.

Chapter 19
The Honeymoon

Now's the time you've been waiting for—alone time with your new hubby. Whether you choose to honeymoon immediately following the ceremony or months after the fact, you want to make sure you've planned a fun, safe trip, and that you know what to do with yourselves once you arrive there! This chapter will offer advice not only for planning the honeymoon, but for making sure that you come home with good memories—and not a single regret!

Honeymoon Packages

A lot of destination wedding sites offer terrific deals on their wedding and honeymoon packages. Some offer a free ceremony if you book the honeymoon, for example, while others flip the deal around and offer several nights of free lodging after you book the ceremony. These deals tend to even out among themselves, so try not to be pulled into one destination because it's offering you a free night's stay. Another location—maybe one you'd like better—probably has a deal that comes pretty darn close.

E~ssential

You should base your destination on where you'd most like to be, not on which resort is going to give you an extra night of free lodging. By the time you've spent all that money, one free night isn't that much of an incentive.

Some resort packages also include free activities for the bride and groom (such as snorkeling and scuba diving), so if you didn't have time to visit the man-made reef during your first week on the island, your honeymoon might be the perfect time to try on those flippers!

Delayed Honeymoons

You might figure that you've already spent a week before the wedding having the time of your life: soaking up the sun, checking out the sights, and hanging out with your friends. Maybe you feel as though you don't need another week to do more of the same. Some couples choose to delay their honeymoons, and they do so for several reasons.

Distinct Vacations

Your destination wedding can definitely take on the feeling of a big family vacation, which is fine—if you didn't want all of your loved ones with you, you wouldn't have invited them—but it may not be the ideal setup for the honeymoon of your dreams. A honeymoon planned for several months after the wedding (and in a different location altogether) has its own feel. It will be just the two of you from start to finish, and you can concentrate on the vacation itself without throwing a wedding into the mix. A lot of couples also don't like the idea of using most of their yearly vacation time in one fell swoop. Delaying the honeymoon for several months—or even a year—allows you to have two shorter vacations instead of one.

No Time Like the Future

Some couples are just not able to take two solid weeks off from work, even if it is for the best possible reason. And even if they're able to take the time off, they just may not be born vacationers. You know the type: After a week away from the office or from their business, they start to get nervous. The phone calls to the office start. Pretty soon, they're searching high and low for Internet access so that they can check their e-mail.

We're not going to get into a discussion of whether this is right or wrong; this is just the way some people are, and there's little anyone can do to change them. Obviously, these men and women make great businesspeople and are usually wonderful providers for their families; however, they can be tough to vacation with. You know whether you're marrying a man who fits this description; you also know whether this description sounds a lot like someone else you know very well (that would be *you*). If a later, separate, shorter honeymoon is going to make both of you happy in the long run, then *don't* try to force in an extra week of fun now.

Regrouping the Finances

Finances are another reason some couples end up delaying the honeymoon. It can be awfully expensive to pay for a wedding; rather than go into immediate newlywed debt, these couples would rather go home, recharge their savings account, and plan a honeymoon that they know they can comfortably afford.

Vacationing while worrying about debt isn't fun. If you know that spending two solid weeks somewhere will only elicit thoughts such as, "We shouldn't eat much today. We've spent way too much money already," then you might be a prime candidate for scheduling a separate honeymoon with its own expense account.

Dream Registries

These days, you can register for just about anything—lawn mowers, furniture, appliances—and yes, even your honeymoon. Honeymoon registries allow your friends and family to contribute to your dream vacation. *When* you take that trip is up to you.

Registering for a honeymoon is an excellent idea for the couple who has already established a home and therefore doesn't need anything in the way of housewares or wedding gifts. Find a good travel agent to help you plan your ideal honeymoon; he or she can set up an online account so that your friends and family can donate to your fund easily.

Planning Your Own Honeymoon

If you aren't booking your honeymoon through a destination wedding resort and you also aren't using a travel agent, there are some things you should know about trip planning before you start shelling out deposits. A little foresight can go a long way toward making your honeymoon memorable for the right reasons, not because you ended up sleeping on the streets after you forgot to confirm your hotel reservations.

Direct Dealings

In certain sectors of the travel industry, there's a sort of backlash against customers who use travel Web sites to book their vacations; it's as though the businesses feel that their customers are ripping them off by looking for the lowest rate. (Mr. and Mrs. America know that this is a ridiculous notion, and if a business doesn't want to sell a hotel room for $150 a night, they shouldn't post it on a travel site in the first place—but that's a whole other book in and of itself.)

E~Fact
When you use a travel Web site, *you* end up in the middle between a hotel, for example, whose room you paid bottom dollar for, and a Web site that probably isn't going to go to bat for you if something goes wrong—or at least not right away.

If you check into the hotel room that you've booked through a travel site and are met with a major problem—let's say the room isn't the honeymoon suite you thought you reserved, but more like a dirty shoebox next to the vending machines—good luck getting the front-desk manager to fix the problem. You see, because you paid the travel site for the room, you'll be referred back to the site to fix the problem. (Yes, this has happened to real, live people who've paid good money for their vacations.)

Calling the Web site may not yield immediate results. You may eventually (weeks or months down the line) receive some sort of financial restitution, but if your honeymoon was ruined—not just by the lousy room but by the lousy attitudes of the businesspeople you've been forced to deal with—you may feel as though no amount of money is enough to remedy what you've been through.

Do yourself a huge favor: If you won't use a travel agent, book your honeymoon arrangements directly. Call the hotel yourself. Tell whomever you're speaking to that you're booking your honeymoon trip. Note the person's name, along with any sort of deal she presents to you. Write down the particulars of the type of room you've reserved and get the name of the person you've spoken with. Call the airline. Call the car rental company. Again, make copious notes about the details of your reservations. Organize it neatly, put it into a honeymoon folder, and bring it along on your trip. This may not ensure that absolutely nothing will go wrong, but you'll have far more leverage with any company if you can present names, dates, times, prices, and confirmation numbers at a moment's notice.

Safety First!

Educating yourself about the area to which you're headed can go a long, long way toward preventing or at least minimizing problems while you're there. If you're headed to a country where you don't know the language, take the time to learn a few important phrases (such as "Help!" and "Where is food?"). Learn about the local customs so that you aren't walking around offending people by giving them the thumbs-up sign for "okay" (which, in some countries, is the equivalent of flipping the bird) or making direct eye contact (which is a definite no-no in many Eastern cultures).

E~Alert

Even the nicest cities have a few rotten apples wandering around. Tourist spots are popular with criminals because out-of-towners are easily distracted and usually have some sort of currency on them.

Don't set yourself up as a target, no matter where you're going. Tourists are easy marks for nefarious characters, so don't wear your stars-and-stripes T-shirt while visiting the pyramids. (This is not a slam against patriots. If you want to make your country proud, don't act like a silly tourist.) Likewise, if you're in Manhattan, avoid doing anything to announce to professional pickpockets that you're just visiting.

Here are some safety tips for travel:

* *Try to blend in with locals as much as possible.* If you aren't Asian, you're going to be somewhat noticeable in Tokyo—but if you do your best to act like one of the crowd, you will give the impression that you might be a businessperson who lives there and knows your way around, and therefore are not someone to mess with.
* *Don't carry lots of cash.* If it gets stolen, it won't be coming back. Credit cards and even traveler's checks are much more secure forms of currency.
* *Use your carry-on wisely.* Pack documents, medicines, and valuables in a bag that stays with you throughout your travels!
* *Invest in a money belt.* Let your new hubby keep any cash that you have right where he can protect it. Your credit cards and traveler's checks can also slide right in.
* *Always keep your bags in front of you.* Con artists are always thinking up new ways to separate you from your possessions. A disoriented, exhausted tourist is not going to be much of a match for a professional thief.
* *Don't carry a purse.* Straps can easily be grabbed or even cut to make stealing it as easy as 1-2-3.
* *Know the way out.* When you check in at your hotel, take note of how many doors are between you and the stairway. In the event of a fire, you can feel your way to the correct doorway.
* *Don't wear or pack a lot of flashy jewelry.* Ever visit a pawn shop? Some of those things came from unfortunate tourists.

* *Know where you're going.* Look at the map before you leave your hotel room. No one is an easier target than a lost tourist standing on the sidewalk studying a map.
* *A "Make Up This Room" sign on your hotel room means you're not there.* Let the maid in during her morning rounds so you don't have to announce your absence to thieves.

Use your common sense to protect yourself. Also, try to think like a criminal would. If you were living a hand-to-mouth existence and you saw a couple flashing big bills, what would you do?

Goodbye, Guests!

If you're staying put for your honeymoon, you have an advantage over brides who spend a day at the ceremony and reception and then have to catch an early-bird flight out of town the following day. By the time these girls arrive at their honeymoon spot, all they want to do is snooze. However, because you aren't disappearing after the reception, you may have to face a problem of your own: How can you tactfully tell your guests to scram (aside from leaving the word *scram* out of the conversation)?

Most guests have the good sense to realize that newlyweds want to have some time to themselves in the days after the wedding. You can prevent most miscommunications between yourselves and guests who might not get the hint by making an announcement at the end of the reception, such as, "Phil and I will be retiring to our own bungalow for the rest of our time here. We wanted to thank everyone for coming to our wedding; it meant the world to both of us." Short, sweet, and to the point.

E~ssential

Many couples plan brunch or a get-together on the day after the wedding, when most guests head home. One last hurrah with the whole group is a nice way to touch base with everyone before you part ways.

If you and your groom have no desire to end the wedding party after the ceremony, don't feel bound by some larger rule of etiquette to do so. It's usually a rare occasion when most of your friends and family are able to gather together in one spot, so enjoy it while you can!

Save the Best for Last

Although the week leading up to the wedding is going to be filled with lots of fun and activity, try to reserve a special outing or two (or three or four) for just yourselves so that you will have some memories that belong only to the two of you. Obviously, you'll have plenty of alone time during that second week, but even couples who love to do nothing but snuggle need to leave the room and do *something* at some point. If you've saved a few fun activities for after the ceremony, you know that your second week will be as interesting as the first.

Know the Area

Planning. Organization. As you've already learned, those are the keywords of planning any wedding, and especially the destination wedding. If you don't know anything about the area you're in, then you don't know what kinds of possibilities are available for your honeymoon!

E~Fact

Your concierge can secure you tickets for shows, games, and other events. Call ahead and ask for his assistance *before* you arrive—and don't forget to tip him for his services ($5 to $10 per event he scores tickets for)!

If you book a trip through a resort, you'll be given plenty of information about activities at the site and in the surrounding area. But what if you've chosen a site that's less popular? Do your research! Get on the

Internet and look into local sights, sounds, and scenes. Focus on what appeals to you most, but don't overlook a potentially interesting outing just because it doesn't sound like your cup of tea. If every Web site you visit says that you just have to climb to the top of Mount Julius, find out *why*—even if you normally roll your eyes at the thought of a long trek up a mountain. Maybe there's an ancient ritual performed up there and you'd kick yourself later for missing out on this bit of culture.

❈ E~ssential

When you're in any vacation spot, don't be limited by the fears and annoyances that rule your everyday life (assuming there are a couple of them). Try new things. Go forward with an open mind! ॐ

Two Can Play That Game!

If you spent the week before the wedding playing volleyball on the beach with your guests, maybe you'd like to spend the week after the wedding in a kayak built for two. Or on a moped zooming down the local roads. Your honeymoon is a time for the two of you to reconnect after the hectic months and weeks that led up to the wedding, so make sure you're putting yourselves in the right setting to do so: Two lounges by the side of the pool might work well for handholding and frequent murmurs of "I love you"; hanging out in a nightclub might not—although maybe the opposite is true for the two of you. Activities that encourage that feeling of intimacy are unique to every couple. If sitting by the pool is going to bore the two of you to tears, don't do it. Do what feels most natural, and your honeymoon will be a blast!

Play Fair

Make sure that the activities you're planning for your honeymoon week appeal to both of you. This is where you're going to learn the fine art of give and take. You can't plan a week of shopping and expect your sports-loving, boutique-hating new husband to keep his mouth shut for too long. Sure, he's a great guy and he wants you to be happy—but this is his honeymoon too.

Ideally, you should try to find a location that has plenty to offer both of you, no matter how diverse your tastes are. To that end, if a quiet honeymoon filled with relaxation sounds like a week of pure boredom to you, don't book a honeymoon on a remote island where there's little to do except soak in the isolation. If your husband-to-be hates crowds, don't drag him to New York City. If neither of you enjoy extensive amounts of traveling, don't book a whirlwind tour of Europe for your honeymoon.

 E~ssential

Not sure if a particular spot is right for your honeymoon? Contact the area's office of tourism or visit its chamber of commerce Web site for more details on what the region has to offer.

The world is a great big place, so if you're having a hard time coming up with ideas for enjoyable honeymoon locations, talk to a travel agent or get on the Internet and do some research. Although this book has advised against booking your honeymoon with a travel Web site, there's nothing wrong with clicking around on one of these sites to get some ideas about places you might be interested in visiting.

Knowledge Is Power

Saving money is great, and looking for bargains is smart—as long as you're not setting yourself up for trouble. Wondering why you're getting such a great deal on a car rental near a big city? Maybe it's because you don't need one. If you're headed to a city that offers excellent public transportation, renting a car is not only unnecessary, it's also going to end up costing you an arm and a leg to park it in a safe location.

You can save a lot of money by booking off-season travel. Just make sure you know what you're in for once you arrive. Not every area has the threat of major natural disaster looming over its head during the off-peak tourist season, but some do, so check this out for yourself very carefully. Heading down to Cancun in August may seem like a great idea until you turn on the news in late July and watch as a hurricane barrels toward the hotel where you've booked your honeymoon suite.

The All-Important Passport

Unfortunately, passports are not nearly as intriguing as they sound, and obtaining one does not qualify you for membership in some elite society; it merely proves that you are who you say you are, that you are not a threat to national security, and that you can pass through certain borders and enjoy your vacation.

If you know you're going to need a passport, start the process as soon as possible. Although most applications take only a matter of weeks to process, a few people do run into snags or delays. You wouldn't want to be counting down the last few days until your honeymoon only to learn that you need to resubmit some piece of information.

Download the application for your passport online at *www.state .gov/travel*. If you are applying for a passport for the first time, you'll have to take the application to a passport acceptance facility. These facilities vary in their locations, but can often be found in post offices, county offices, or large public libraries.

Along with the application, you'll need:

* Your birth certificate or naturalization papers
* Your social security number
* A photo ID (such as a driver's license)
* Money

* Two passport photos (any one-hour photo shop can provide these for you; make sure you tell them that these are passport pictures, as they need to be a specific size)

The total fee for processing the application for an adult is $97. You can expect to receive your passport in about six weeks, although you can pay for expedited service (which cuts down your waiting time to about two weeks).

Don't Forget to Tip!

Tipping is about the most confusing—and for some, infuriating—part of traveling. It can start to seem that handing out tips left and right will be the thing that breaks your bank account, so before you start *over*tipping, you should know who gets tipped, who doesn't, and how much is enough.

First, though, let's talk about tipping as a general practice. You aren't imagining things—more and more people out there in the service industries expect to be rewarded for doing jobs that don't seem to require a whole lot of service beyond what they're being paid to do (say, handing you the $5 cup of coffee that you ordered).

This book will advise you to definitely dole out the tips, but to do so wisely. The bellboy who hauled your eight heavy suitcases into your hotel room with a smile on his face has earned a tip; the girl in the ice cream parlor who scooped up your cone without ever making eye contact with you probably hasn't.

If you're the most generous person on the face of the earth, feel free to tip everyone. If you're like the rest of us, you have to draw the line somewhere. Save your tipping for the people who are actually working hard to serve you, such as:

* *Hotel maids:* Leave a couple of dollars out for your maid each day (because you may not have the same one twice) and put it on a

piece of paper marked, "For the maid." Maids are instructed not to take cash that isn't clearly marked as theirs.

* *Waiters/waitresses:* For a job well done, tip 20 percent of your final bill.

* *Bellboys:* $2 per bag and for each hospitable gesture he performs (turning on the TV; flicking on the stereo, and so on).

* *Valets:* Give the guy $2–$3 (more if he had to run a mile in the snow to get your car).

* *Doormen:* They don't get a tip every time they open the door for you. (Phew!) If he hails you a cab, give him a few bucks ($2–$3 is plenty). If he helps you with some of your heavy suitcases or packages, give him $1 per bag; add a little more if he carries them to your room.

* *Concierge:* If he helps you make reservations or secures tickets for a show for you, $5–$10.

* *Cab drivers:* 15 percent of the total fare.

* *Skycaps:* $1–$2 a bag.

Be aware that if you order room service, a 15 percent gratuity is often automatically added to the bill; the same is true of restaurants in many foreign countries, so always read the fine print on the bottom of the bill!

Chapter 20
Coming in for a Landing

Home Sweet Home is never sweeter than when you return to it as husband and wife—but are you ready? Whether your ceremony consisted of you spending a week at a resort with your friends and family or two weeks in blissful solitude, sooner or later you have to come back to reality—literally. You may be expected at an in-town reception, for one thing, and you'll have some thank-you notes to get started on. You'll also have to notify businesses if you changed your name, and generally settle into married life.

20

Receptions after the Fact

If you weren't able to invite many people to your destination wedding, or if many of those invited were unable to attend, you may be giving thought to a hometown reception in the weeks or months after you return home. What is the point of these after-the-fact affairs, and are they socially acceptable, or not?

The Hosts

First of all, you shouldn't host a reception for yourself. Even though it would be perfectly acceptable for you to pay for your own ceremony and reception on the day of your wedding, this is a different situation. You're asking people who possibly weren't invited to the wedding to come out and wish you well, and that's going to go over a whole lot better if it comes from your parents rather than from you.

❀ E~ssential

If you are not comfortable with the idea of having a delayed reception, then decline your hosts' offer in the nicest way possible. This is an event honoring you and your new husband; you shouldn't be there under duress. ✿

This is a celebration of your union, and though receptions given on the day of the ceremony are technically supposed to serve the same purpose—they're just different. The people who will come to your post-wedding reception most likely didn't get to witness your vows, for various reasons. This is a more subdued get-together without the bouquet toss and the wedding dress. It's a *party*, and traditional etiquette states that one never hosts a formal party in one's own honor. It's just in bad taste. (Yes, this book has dispensed with traditional etiquette on some issues, but this is a good rule to stick with, even in the twenty-first century.)

Surprise—We Got Married!

Here's the reason that post-wedding receptions are sometimes interpreted as being in bad taste altogether, regardless of who's hosting: If the people on the guest list for the reception were not on the guest list for the wedding, they're going to wonder why.

If you didn't invite the people on your reception guest list to the wedding—why not? If you wanted a very private ceremony, then why bother to invite them to a celebration of the marriage? If you couldn't afford a large reception at the time of your wedding, why have things suddenly changed? If you just didn't want to deal with planning a big wedding, then why the big reception?

These are the questions that are going to be bandied about the reception hall, so be prepared to handle them. It's a fairly safe bet that no one is going to come out and ask you why she wasn't invited to your ceremony, but you might want to have a blanket statement at the ready throughout the night: "You know, we just got married so quickly that there wasn't time to plan a big wedding. That's why we wanted to invite everyone to this reception, so that we could thank everyone for being so supportive." With this statement, you've done three things:

* You've taken the heat off yourself. Apparently, hardly anyone was invited to the wedding itself.
* You've given a decent reason for the lack of invitations to the wedding. No time? What could you do? You were in love!

* You're thanking people for being supportive, possibly before they've had the chance to be—which will make them *want* to be.

Of course, if you actually had a large wedding and didn't invite the people you've now invited to your reception, that's a different situation, and not one that portrays you in the most flattering light. (More on that in the following section.) Whatever the case, it's fine to show some appreciation for your guests, but don't attempt a blatant lie, especially in matters that concern family and friends. These people talk to each other, and you can count on getting busted.

The B List

Brides often have what they refer to as a *B list* for their receptions. As regrets come in from the A-listers (their first-choice guests), brides will send out invitations to B-list friends and relatives. It's a risky practice even when you're inviting people to a ceremony and reception in your hometown. Again, people talk—and people also can figure things out for themselves. If your friends from work don't receive their wedding invitations until three weeks before the wedding, for example, they'll know there's a good chance that they were not on your list of first-choice guests.

When you have a fair-sized destination wedding, then, and later invite a bunch of people who weren't included in the ceremony to an in-town, after-the-fact reception, you may be playing with fire. It's far more likely that these invitees are going to view this invitation as a request for a gift, and you're going to come off looking like a selfish bride. And again, you have to ask yourself the question: If you didn't invite them to the wedding (especially when you invited so many others), why invite them now?

Formal or Casual?

Your hosts will have a large say in what type of reception this turns out to be. There aren't set-in-stone rules about these delayed receptions, but many of them turn into brunches or early evening events. However, if your family loves its formal events and your parents are willing to shell out big bucks for a band, a sit-down dinner, and an open bar, your guests are probably not going to mind one bit.

To Give or Not to Give

Should you expect guests to bring gifts to a reception given weeks after the wedding? Well, let's back up and cover the rules of traditional etiquette here. You should never *expect* a gift from anyone. On the other hand, guests shouldn't show up to a party empty-handed. Since most people would never dream of showing up to a reception without a gift in hand, let's talk about what you should expect.

I Want That!

You cannot request a particular gift. Don't try to do it unless someone specifically asks if you need or want something. For example, it's in the worst taste to announce that you are only accepting money for your wedding, no matter how desperately you don't need anything except cash.

 E~Fact

You can ask your mother or grandmother to spread the word that you'd really appreciate monetary gifts, but they have to be able to do so with some subtlety. In other words, having your mother tell the relatives to break out their checkbooks is not acceptable. ✿

You also can't slip those little registry cards into reception invitations (a practice that etiquette mavens have always found to be in poor taste anyway, even when they're placed inside the shower invitations). The whole idea behind gift-giving is that it's supposed to be as much fun for the giver as for the recipient, but this assumes that the giver is an avid shopper who loves to browse stores for the perfect wedding gift. This isn't always the case, and many times, it's just easier for people to give money or for them to look up your registry. Again, have your mother and other close relatives spread the word about your registry.

Don't Be Greedy

The problem with after-the-fact receptions is that they are sometimes seen as an opportunity for the bride and groom to cull gifts from people they didn't want at their wedding in the first place. You can put these suspicions to rest by acting the part of the gracious newlywed couple during the reception. Make sure to speak with *everyone* who shows up; thank them for coming; look happy to see them. The brides who find themselves accused of being greedy gift-seekers break all of these rules. They speak only to their close friends and/or seem to be put out by having to mix with the other guests. Invitees to the reception feel shunned all over again—and may wonder how they can sneak their gifts back out the door without anyone noticing.

The Big Thank-You

Inevitably, whether you have a big wedding or a small wedding, and whether you have a reception afterward or not, you'll receive some wedding gifts. Being married is one sign that you have moved into responsible adulthood—and knowing how to write a good thank-you note is another. Each gift that you receive has to be acknowledged—in a timely manner!

Do It Soon

You have one month from the time you receive a gift to write a thank-you note for it. That's it. Not three months; not six months; definitely not a year. *One month*. "One month?" you're thinking. "I can't write 200 thank-you notes in one month!" Oh, sure you can. You're not writing 200 distinct dissertations on why destination weddings are preferable to traditional ceremonies; you're thanking people for giving you nice gifts. And since these people went to the trouble to make sure *you* received the gift in time for your wedding, the very least you could do is make sure *they* receive a written acknowledgment of their gift—and soon.

❀ E~Question

Can I purchase thank-you notes for wedding gifts in just any old store?

Sure, as long as they're of good quality, which may be hard to come by in the average shop. Many couples order thank-you notes from a stationer when they order their wedding invitations. ❧

Once that first month passes, the novelty of being surrounded by all of your new stuff wears off, and your wedding money is either spent or tucked safely away in a savings account. You're more likely to forget what you've been given or how much you genuinely appreciated receiving it at the time you unwrapped it. Writing the thank-you notes as soon as possible allows your gratitude to shine through in the most genuine way.

What to Say

Writing thank-you notes may be time-consuming if you actually do have 200 of them to complete. Each individual note, though, is a piece of cake. Just make sure that when you open your gifts, you record who gave you what. Writing the notes is this easy:

Dear Aunt Kate and Uncle Drew,
Thank you so much for the beautiful antique lamp. Marty and
I just love it, and it goes perfectly with our living room décor. We

were so happy the two of you could make it to the wedding; we really enjoyed spending time with both of you!

Hope to see you soon!

Love,

Maggie and Marty

That note would take you less than five minutes to write by hand, which, you may be disappointed to learn, is the only acceptable way to write your thank-yous. Typing them on your computer is just too cold and businesslike for such a personal communiqué.

Let's focus on the major elements of the satisfactory thank-you note:

* It's handwritten.
* It specifically names the gift.
* It mentions how much you love the gift.
* It tells how you're using the gift.
* It thanks the addressee for attending the wedding, reception, or both (if applicable).

If the person you're writing to didn't come to the wedding or reception, you could simply say:

Dear Aunt Meg,

Thank you so much for the candlesticks. We just love them and have set them out on our dining room table.

We were so sorry that you were unable to make it to the wedding, but we understand that Jamaica is a long trip to make from California. It was very thoughtful of you to send us such a lovely gift.

Love,

Maggie and Marty

See how easy it is? Once you get going you'll get the hang of it, and you'll have all of those cards done in almost no time at all!

Many Thanks for the Moola

When you're writing a thank-you note to someone who sent you money, *never* mention the amount! Rather, tell the giver what you intend to do with the money so that he or she knows you're not spending it on lipstick and glossy magazines. For example:

> *Dear Mr. and Mrs. Keller,*
> *Thank you so much for the very generous wedding gift. Bob and I will use it toward the purchase of a new couch, as our old one is in dire need of replacement!*

. . . and then proceed with thanking them for coming, or telling them how sorry you were that they were unable to make it, sign your names, and you're done.

Who Sent This?

If you have no idea what Mr. and Mrs. Keller gave you—but you know that they handed you an envelope at the reception—or you really can't recall what Aunt Kate and Uncle Drew sent, it's better to fake your way through a thank-you note than not send one at all. This should be the exception to the rule, however! A good, general thank-you note goes something like this:

> *Dear Aunt Kate and Uncle Drew,*
> *Thank you so much for the wedding gift. We were thrilled that you could join us on our wedding day. Having you at our ceremony meant the world to both of us, and we hope to see you again soon.*
> *Love,*
> *Maggie and Marty*

See what you've done here? You've thanked them for the gift, and then you've focused on how happy you were to see them. Having them at your wedding was gift enough, you're telling them. With any luck, they won't even notice that you didn't mention the silver platter they gave you.

Turn Off That Printer!

Under no circumstances is it acceptable to send out a computer-generated thank-you note for which you only have to fill in the giver's name and sign your name to 200 identical letters. It is *not* all right to send out something like this:

> *Dear _____,*
> *Thank you for coming to our wedding! We were so happy to see you and appreciate your gift! See you soon!*
> *Love,*
> *Maggie and Marty*

This is wrong on so many levels. It's incredibly impersonal and sends the message that if your guests think that you have time to write separate thank-you notes for everyone, well, they have another think coming. Show the people who sent you gifts that you are really, truly grateful—grateful enough to write them their own individual card of thanks.

E~ssential

You don't have to write every thank-you card by yourself. Hand your new husband a pen and instruct him on how to write a good thank-you note. You'll be finished twice as quickly!

It's just as wrong to let a three-page newsletter serve as a thank-you note. While it may be natural to want to share the entire story of your wedding—especially with people who weren't able to attend—you still have to send separate, individualized thank-you notes.

Getting Back to Normal

Returning home after any wedding—destination or no—is sometimes a bit of a letdown. You may have spent a year or more planning the perfect wedding. You also may have spent your entire childhood, teen years, college days, and adulthood to this point dreaming of the day you would become the bride of the perfect man. All of that is behind you now. It's natural for you to feel as though something major has been left behind, because it has. It's important, though, for you to be able to focus on the future instead of living in the past.

What About Me?

Here's one thing that a lot of brides have trouble dealing with after the wedding: Life goes on. Someone else is engaged now, and it's her time to be in the spotlight. And even if none of your friends or family members are in the midst of planning their own weddings, you only get to have excessive amounts of attention focused on you for so long. This ends shortly after you return, when you're supposed to settle into life as a happy newlywed—a life in which the only attention you need is from your husband.

E~Alert

Accept this natural progression from bride to married woman. Trying to fight it and keep everyone's attention on yourself is something that others will most likely start to find irritating—sooner rather than later.

Other people are very forgiving when it comes to the bride who's planning a wedding. They're quick to say, "Well, she's self-absorbed these days, but that will end after the ceremony." When that kind of "Me! Me! Me!" attitude continues for months after the day you've said "I do," you can be fairly sure that someone is going to call you out on it. Or, worse, they'll just stop calling you at all.

Moving On

Letting go of the bride persona can be tough, but it has to be done if you're to move on with your life and not dwell on the fact that once upon a time, you planned the world's greatest wedding. If you suspect that you're going to have some trouble in this area, start looking beyond the end of your own nose. A lot has gone on since the day you got the engagement ring and left the real world behind. Take a friend to lunch and make an effort to talk about her life, or take the initiative and call your mom just to see how she's doing.

As easy as it is to get wrapped up in other people catering to you, it's just as easy to find your way back to normal life once again.

Name That Bride!

Back in your grandmother's day, brides rarely kept their maiden names after the wedding. It was seen as a radical gesture and disrespectful to the groom if his wife clung to her old surname. Of course, these days, it's hardly surprising to hear that a woman is keeping her name in one form or another: by keeping it exactly as it's always been, using her maiden name as her middle name in all business transactions, or hyphenating both surnames and creating one larger name from the two.

A woman might choose to keep her name for all sorts of reasons. Most often, the reason is that she's worked long and hard to earn a place in her field of expertise, and she's not about to go messing with her identity now. (And since her husband is hardly expected to forge ahead in his line of work with a brand-new name, you can hardly argue with this logic.) Other women simply like their maiden names and want to keep them.

Is Change Good?

Whatever you decide about your name, make sure you're doing it for the right reasons: It's what you want and it's what's best for you. In other words, don't give in to pressure from your mother, your mother-in-law, or your friends on the name issue. More than at any other time in history, this particular issue has become a highly personal topic that each bride needs to work out for herself.

Keep in mind, though, that you really should let your husband (or fiancé) in on this discussion because it may affect him, too. If you decide to keep your maiden name, for example, and the two of you plan to have kids eventually, he may be wondering what *their* surnames will be.

E~Fact

When a woman keeps her own name in a marriage, the issue of which name to give to the children may come up eventually. Many couples choose to give the kids either a hyphenated surname or the father's surname.

If you're choosing to go with a hyphenated version of both names immediately after the wedding, do you also expect your new husband to adopt this new name? If his family isn't keen on you keeping your own name, why not?

Knowing the answer to these questions may not change your mind, but it may help you to dispel any misconceptions concerning the reasons you've chosen to keep your own name.

Go for It

If you have decided to take any surname that is different from your maiden name (this includes hyphenated combinations of your maiden name and your husband's surname), you need to notify the government—and the sooner the better. Sure, it seems like it's unnecessary to rush right out and change a name that you've been attached to for the past few decades, but it's really in your best interest to do so. When it comes time to file a joint tax return, your boss and your accountant will have some *very* unfriendly words for you if you've been receiving a paycheck under your maiden name and you've decided to sign your tax return in your married name. (Suffice it to say this will cause a lot of complications for everyone involved.)

So, when you start changing your name, start with the Social Security Administration (SSA) first. You can download a new application online at *www.socialsecurity.gov/online/ss-5.html*, which may save you time once you arrive at the SSA office. You need to complete the application and take it to a local SSA office—you can find the address of the location closest to you online (*www.ssa.gov*)—along with your marriage license, a valid photo ID, and your birth certificate. Other than possibly sitting for a long period of time in the waiting area (this is a government office, after all), this is a painless, easy process. You'll get your new Social Security card in the mail within a few weeks, and your new name will be official.

You needn't wait for this new card to notify other agencies and businesses of your name change. Here's who you'll need to contact:

* Credit card companies
* Utility companies
* Department of motor vehicles
* Doctors' offices
* Banks
* Anyone else you do business with

Getting the name change done and out of the way while you're still excited about it is wise. Again, this isn't a difficult task, but it may be time-consuming. The longer you put it off, the less you'll feel like making all of those calls, and the better the chance that your credit cards will still be in your maiden name ten years from today. You're just messing with and possibly complicating matters for yourself (especially when it comes time for tax returns and credit checks in the future), so be sure to get it done!

You've Changed—or Have You?

If you've decided against taking your husband's surname, then you obviously won't have to notify any companies of this. However, you'll probably be faced with someone calling you by the wrong name, because people still assume that every bride takes her husband's name. The best way to handle this is simply to be very nonchalant in saying, "Oh, no, I'm not Mrs. Smith. I kept my maiden name; it's Ms. Hill." If you don't make a big deal out of someone else's goof, it's not a big deal. On the other hand, if you act offended by this natural mistake, you're just behaving badly, and there's no reason for it. Correct the person and move on with the conversation.

Moving In

Because so many couples live together before the ceremony, there's a good chance that you've already adjusted to life under the same roof. If you're moving in together for the first time after the ceremony, though, or if the two of you are pulling up stakes and moving to a new home, there's bound to be a bit of tension.

✿ E~ssential

Moving just tends to bring out the worst in everyone; in fact, along with the first year of marriage, moving is one of the most stressful experiences that people go through in their lives. ✿

Consider this: Moving usually means that you're shelling out some big bucks for the move itself, if not for housing, also. You're entering into a new environment where you're not comfortable yet (even if you're only moving two miles down the road). You're going to need new furnishings, window coverings, and other housewares, so you have no idea where your finances are going to settle when all is said and done. You can't find anything because all of your possessions are either in boxes or in a storage shed. And to top it all off, you're supposed to be blissfully happy because you're newlyweds!

Give yourself a break when you're setting up house together: Don't expect perfection. Having an unrealistic view of how life *should* be can only set you up for disappointment. It takes time for newly married couples to find a rhythm to their life together, even if they were living together before the wedding! Be kind to one another, look for joy in the simple things in life, and remember the reasons that you wanted to be together in the first place. The rest will fall into place—and you've got the rest of your lives to carve out your own perfect little corner of the world.

Appendix A

Destination Wedding and Travel Sites

If you're heading out of town for your wedding, you might need some ideas for planning or ideas about where to go. This appendix lists some destination wedding and travel sites to make your planning a cake walk!

Popular Destinations and Web Sites

Aruba
*www.aruba.com
*www.arubaweddingsforyou.com

The Bahamas
*www.bahamas.com
*www.bahamacruiseweddings.com

Bermuda
*www.bermudatourism.com
*www.bermuda.com/weddings

The Dominican Republic
*www.dominican-wedding.com
*www.dr1.com/travel

Florida
*www.floridaweddings.com
*www.flwedding.com

France
*www.weddingsinfrance.com

Greece
*www.blueaegean.com/weddings.htm
*www.greeceathens.com

Hawaii
*www.gohawaii.com/weddings
*www.hawaiiweddingguide.com
*www.paradisemaui.com/weddings

Ireland
*www.wedding-ireland.com

Italy
*www.bestitalianweddings.com
*www.weddingitaly.com
*www.weddingsitaly.com

Jamaica
~www.visitjamaica.com
~www.weddingsinjamaica.com
~www.tropicalweddingsjamaica.com

Las Vegas
~www.lasvegasweddingsdirectory.com
~www.lvwedding.com

Mexico
~www.cancunmexicoweddings.com
~www.cozumelwedding.com
~www.puerto-vallarta-wedding.com

Portugal
~www.weddingsinportugal.com

Scotland
~www.scotlandweddings.net

Spain
~www.weddingsinspain.com
~www.weddingsinspain.net

The U.S. Virgin Islands
~www.usvi.net
~www.viweddingservices.com

Other Helpful Web Sites

Destination Wedding Travel (DWT)
This site calls itself the "only true full-service destination wedding expert on the Web." Indeed, the links are plentiful and worth checking out.

~www.destinationweddings.com

Disney Weddings
Weddings in the Magic Kingdom are anything but "Mickey Mouse"! You may be surprised to learn that you can plan a very formal wedding at Disney, complete with trumpeters heralding the bride's arrival.

~www.disneyweddings.com

Royal Caribbean International
Looking to sail off into happily ever after? Royal Caribbean's Web site has loads of information to help you say "Ahoy! And I do!" Go to the "All About Cruising" menu and click on "Weddings."

~www.royalcaribbean.com

Sandals

Research the popular couples-only resort and learn about its various sites, wedding packages, add-ons, and complimentary bonuses.

✍ *www.sandals.com*

World Weddings

Hopping the pond, are you? This site gives you a really great idea of the wedding possibilities that await you in Europe.

✍ *www.world-weddings.com*

Wyndham Hotels and Resorts

Wyndham has hotels and resorts in the Caribbean; the southern, western, and southwestern United States; and in Mexico. The company also recently teamed up with WeddingChannel.com to make your planning a snap!

✍ *www.destinationweddingsbywyndham.com*

Appendix B .
Dos and Don'ts for Your Destination Wedding

Destination weddings are such a new phenomenon, it's easy for a bride to get confused, carried away, or overwhelmed by the things she feels she should or shouldn't do. Without traditional wedding etiquette and/or planning books to fall back on, what's a bride to do? Just as important, what are the things a bride shouldn't do? Here are some dos and don'ts to guide you to destination wedding success!

Dos

Do send out save-the-date cards about six months before the wedding, especially if it's planned around a holiday weekend. Give everyone time to make their travel arrangements.

Do let your attendants know upfront what they'll be expected to pay for. Traditional wedding etiquette holds the bride and groom responsible for attendants' lodging expenses, but in reality, many bridesmaids and groomsmen end up paying their own way.

Do plan on spending time with all of your guests. That's why you invited them to this weeklong wedding party, after all.

Do take the time to talk with your onsite wedding coordinator and/or wedding vendors before you book them. Ask all the questions you can think of, and get (and check!) referrals.

Do view your week away as a vacation, but *don't* overlook the fact that you're getting married! It's not just another getaway, after all. Take some time to connect with your fiancé and appreciate the magnitude of the event after you've unpacked your bags.

Don'ts

Don't announce your wedding and/or talk excessively about it to those who aren't invited. The one exception is if you're having a teeny, tiny wedding with immediate family members only.

Don't get in way over your head financially. Yes, you only get to do this once, but honestly, lots of couples plan beautiful, relatively inexpensive weddings. It just takes time and research.

Don't plan on paying for all of your guests' expenses unless your last name happens to be Moneybags.

Don't drink too much the night before the wedding. Sure, all you have to do is put on your dress and walk down to the beach in the morning, but you don't want to look green, tired, or puffy-eyed in your wedding pictures.

Index

THE EVERYTHING SERIES!

BUSINESS & PERSONAL FINANCE

Everything® Accounting Book
Everything® Budgeting Book
Everything® Business Planning Book
Everything® Coaching and Mentoring Book
Everything® Fundraising Book
Everything® Get Out of Debt Book
Everything® Grant Writing Book
Everything® Home-Based Business Book, 2nd Ed.
Everything® Homebuying Book, 2nd Ed.
Everything® Homeselling Book, 2nd Ed.
Everything® Investing Book, 2nd Ed.
Everything® Landlording Book
Everything® Leadership Book
Everything® Managing People Book, 2nd Ed.
Everything® Negotiating Book
Everything® Online Auctions Book
Everything® Online Business Book
Everything® Personal Finance Book
Everything® Personal Finance in Your 20s and 30s Book
Everything® Project Management Book
Everything® Real Estate Investing Book
Everything® Robert's Rules Book, $7.95
Everything® Selling Book
Everything® Start Your Own Business Book, 2nd Ed.
Everything® Wills & Estate Planning Book

COOKING

Everything® Barbecue Cookbook
Everything® Bartender's Book, $9.95
Everything® Chinese Cookbook
Everything® Classic Recipes Book
Everything® Cocktail Parties and Drinks Book
Everything® College Cookbook
Everything® Cooking for Baby and Toddler Book
Everything® Cooking for Two Cookbook
Everything® Diabetes Cookbook
Everything® Easy Gourmet Cookbook
Everything® Fondue Cookbook
Everything® Fondue Party Book
Everything® Gluten-Free Cookbook
Everything® Glycemic Index Cookbook
Everything® Grilling Cookbook

Everything® Healthy Meals in Minutes Cookbook
Everything® Holiday Cookbook
Everything® Indian Cookbook
Everything® Italian Cookbook
Everything® Low-Carb Cookbook
Everything® Low-Fat High-Flavor Cookbook
Everything® Low-Salt Cookbook
Everything® Meals for a Month Cookbook
Everything® Mediterranean Cookbook
Everything® Mexican Cookbook
Everything® One-Pot Cookbook
Everything® Quick and Easy 30-Minute, 5-Ingredient Cookbook
Everything® Quick Meals Cookbook
Everything® Slow Cooker Cookbook
Everything® Slow Cooking for a Crowd Cookbook
Everything® Soup Cookbook
Everything® Tex-Mex Cookbook
Everything® Thai Cookbook
Everything® Vegetarian Cookbook
Everything® Wild Game Cookbook
Everything® Wine Book, 2nd Ed.

GAMES

Everything® 15-Minute Sudoku Book, $9.95
Everything® 30-Minute Sudoku Book, $9.95
Everything® Blackjack Strategy Book
Everything® Brain Strain Book, $9.95
Everything® Bridge Book
Everything® Card Games Book
Everything® Card Tricks Book, $9.95
Everything® Casino Gambling Book, 2nd Ed.
Everything® Chess Basics Book
Everything® Craps Strategy Book
Everything® Crossword and Puzzle Book
Everything® Crossword Challenge Book
Everything® Cryptograms Book, $9.95
Everything® Easy Crosswords Book
Everything® Easy Kakuro Book, $9.95
Everything® Games Book, 2nd Ed.
Everything® Giant Sudoku Book, $9.95
Everything® Kakuro Challenge Book, $9.95
Everything® Large-Print Crossword Challenge Book
Everything® Large-Print Crosswords Book
Everything® Lateral Thinking Puzzles Book, $9.95
Everything® Mazes Book

Everything® Pencil Puzzles Book, $9.95
Everything® Poker Strategy Book
Everything® Pool & Billiards Book
Everything® Test Your IQ Book, $9.95
Everything® Texas Hold 'Em Book, $9.95
Everything® Travel Crosswords Book, $9.95
Everything® Word Games Challenge Book
Everything® Word Search Book

HEALTH

Everything® Alzheimer's Book
Everything® Diabetes Book
Everything® Health Guide to Adult Bipolar Disorder
Everything® Health Guide to Controlling Anxiety
Everything® Health Guide to Fibromyalgia
Everything® Health Guide to Thyroid Disease
Everything® Hypnosis Book
Everything® Low Cholesterol Book
Everything® Massage Book
Everything® Menopause Book
Everything® Nutrition Book
Everything® Reflexology Book
Everything® Stress Management Book

HISTORY

Everything® American Government Book
Everything® American History Book
Everything® Civil War Book
Everything® Freemasons Book
Everything® Irish History & Heritage Book
Everything® Middle East Book

HOBBIES

Everything® Candlemaking Book
Everything® Cartooning Book
Everything® Coin Collecting Book
Everything® Drawing Book
Everything® Family Tree Book, 2nd Ed.
Everything® Knitting Book
Everything® Knots Book
Everything® Photography Book
Everything® Quilting Book
Everything® Scrapbooking Book
Everything® Sewing Book
Everything® Woodworking Book

Bolded titles are new additions to the series.
All Everything® books are priced at $12.95 or $14.95, unless otherwise stated. Prices subject to change without notice.

HOME IMPROVEMENT

Everything® Feng Shui Book
Everything® Feng Shui Decluttering Book, $9.95
Everything® Fix-It Book
Everything® Home Decorating Book
Everything® Home Storage Solutions Book
Everything® Homebuilding Book
Everything® Lawn Care Book
Everything® Organize Your Home Book

KIDS' BOOKS

All titles are $7.95

Everything® Kids' Animal Puzzle & Activity Book
Everything® Kids' Baseball Book, 4th Ed.
Everything® Kids' Bible Trivia Book
Everything® Kids' Bugs Book
**Everything® Kids' Cars and Trucks Puzzle
& Activity Book**
Everything® Kids' Christmas Puzzle
& Activity Book
Everything® Kids' Cookbook
Everything® Kids' Crazy Puzzles Book
Everything® Kids' Dinosaurs Book
**Everything® Kids' First Spanish Puzzle and
Activity Book**
Everything® Kids' Gross Hidden Pictures Book
Everything® Kids' Gross Jokes Book
Everything® Kids' Gross Mazes Book
Everything® Kids' Gross Puzzle and
Activity Book
Everything® Kids' Halloween Puzzle
& Activity Book
Everything® Kids' Hidden Pictures Book
Everything® Kids' Horses Book
Everything® Kids' Joke Book
Everything® Kids' Knock Knock Book
Everything® Kids' Learning Spanish Book
Everything® Kids' Math Puzzles Book
Everything® Kids' Mazes Book
Everything® Kids' Money Book
Everything® Kids' Nature Book
Everything® Kids' Pirates Puzzle and Activity
Book
**Everything® Kids' Princess Puzzle and
Activity Book**
Everything® Kids' Puzzle Book
Everything® Kids' Riddles & Brain Teasers Book
Everything® Kids' Science Experiments Book
Everything® Kids' Sharks Book
Everything® Kids' Soccer Book
Everything® Kids' Travel Activity Book

KIDS' STORY BOOKS

Everything® Fairy Tales Book

LANGUAGE

**Everything® Conversational Chinese Book
with CD, $19.95**
Everything® Conversational Japanese Book
with CD, $19.95
Everything® French Grammar Book
Everything® French Phrase Book, $9.95
Everything® French Verb Book, $9.95
Everything® German Practice Book with CD,
$19.95
Everything® Inglés Book
Everything® Learning French Book
Everything® Learning German Book
Everything® Learning Italian Book
Everything® Learning Latin Book
Everything® Learning Spanish Book
**Everything® Russian Practice Book with CD,
$19.95**
Everything® Sign Language Book
Everything® Spanish Grammar Book
Everything® Spanish Phrase Book, $9.95
Everything® Spanish Practice Book
with CD, $19.95
Everything® Spanish Verb Book, $9.95

MUSIC

Everything® Drums Book with CD, $19.95
Everything® Guitar Book
Everything® Guitar Chords Book with CD,
$19.95
Everything® Home Recording Book
**Everything® Music Theory Book with CD,
$19.95**
Everything® Reading Music Book with CD,
$19.95
Everything® Rock & Blues Guitar Book
(with CD), $19.95
Everything® Songwriting Book

NEW AGE

Everything® Astrology Book, 2nd Ed.
Everything® Birthday Personology Book
Everything® Dreams Book, 2nd Ed.
Everything® Love Signs Book, $9.95
Everything® Numerology Book
Everything® Paganism Book
Everything® Palmistry Book
Everything® Psychic Book
Everything® Reiki Book
Everything® Sex Signs Book, $9.95
Everything® Tarot Book, 2nd Ed.
Everything® Wicca and Witchcraft Book

PARENTING

Everything® Baby Names Book, 2nd Ed.
Everything® Baby Shower Book
Everything® Baby's First Food Book
Everything® Baby's First Year Book
Everything® Birthing Book
Everything® Breastfeeding Book
Everything® Father-to-Be Book
Everything® Father's First Year Book
Everything® Get Ready for Baby Book
Everything® Get Your Baby to Sleep Book, $9.95
Everything® Getting Pregnant Book
**Everything® Guide to Raising a
One-Year-Old**
**Everything® Guide to Raising a
Two-Year-Old**
Everything® Homeschooling Book
Everything® Mother's First Year Book
Everything® Parent's Guide to Children
and Divorce
Everything® Parent's Guide to Children
with ADD/ADHD
Everything® Parent's Guide to Children
with Asperger's Syndrome
Everything® Parent's Guide to Children
with Autism
Everything® Parent's Guide to Children with
Bipolar Disorder
Everything® Parent's Guide to Children
with Dyslexia
Everything® Parent's Guide to Positive Discipline
Everything® Parent's Guide to Raising a
Successful Child
Everything® Parent's Guide to Raising Boys
Everything® Parent's Guide to Raising Siblings
**Everything® Parent's Guide to Sensory
Integration Disorder**
Everything® Parent's Guide to Tantrums
Everything® Parent's Guide to the Overweight
Child
Everything® Parent's Guide to the Strong-Willed
Child
Everything® Parenting a Teenager Book
Everything® Potty Training Book, $9.95
Everything® Pregnancy Book, 2nd Ed.
Everything® Pregnancy Fitness Book
Everything® Pregnancy Nutrition Book
**Everything® Pregnancy Organizer, 2nd Ed.,
$16.95**
Everything® Toddler Activities Book
Everything® Toddler Book
Everything® Tween Book
Everything® Twins, Triplets, and More Book

PETS

Everything® Aquarium Book
Everything® Boxer Book
Everything® Cat Book, 2nd Ed.
Everything® Chihuahua Book
Everything® Dachshund Book
Everything® Dog Book
Everything® Dog Health Book
Everything® Dog Owner's Organizer,
    $16.95
Everything® Dog Training and Tricks Book
Everything® German Shepherd Book
Everything® Golden Retriever Book
Everything® Horse Book
Everything® Horse Care Book
Everything® Horseback Riding Book
Everything® Labrador Retriever Book
Everything® Poodle Book
Everything® Pug Book
Everything® Puppy Book
Everything® Rottweiler Book
Everything® Small Dogs Book
Everything® Tropical Fish Book
Everything® Yorkshire Terrier Book

REFERENCE

Everything® Blogging Book
Everything® Build Your Vocabulary Book
Everything® Car Care Book
Everything® Classical Mythology Book
Everything® Da Vinci Book
Everything® Divorce Book
Everything® Einstein Book
Everything® Etiquette Book, 2nd Ed.
Everything® Inventions and Patents Book
Everything® Mafia Book
Everything® Philosophy Book
Everything® Psychology Book
Everything® Shakespeare Book

RELIGION

Everything® Angels Book
Everything® Bible Book
Everything® Buddhism Book
Everything® Catholicism Book
Everything® Christianity Book
Everything® History of the Bible Book
Everything® Jesus Book
Everything® Jewish History & Heritage Book
Everything® Judaism Book
Everything® Kabbalah Book
Everything® Koran Book
Everything® Mary Book

Everything® Mary Magdalene Book
Everything® Prayer Book
Everything® Saints Book
Everything® Torah Book
Everything® Understanding Islam Book
Everything® World's Religions Book
Everything® Zen Book

SCHOOL & CAREERS

Everything® Alternative Careers Book
Everything® Career Tests Book
Everything® College Major Test Book
Everything® College Survival Book, 2nd Ed.
Everything® Cover Letter Book, 2nd Ed.
Everything® Filmmaking Book
Everything® Get-a-Job Book
Everything® Guide to Being a Paralegal
Everything® Guide to Being a Real Estate
    Agent
Everything® Guide to Being a Sales Rep
Everything® Guide to Careers in Health
    Care
Everything® Guide to Careers in Law
    Enforcement
Everything® Guide to Government Jobs
Everything® Guide to Starting and Running
    a Restaurant
Everything® Job Interview Book
Everything® New Nurse Book
Everything® New Teacher Book
Everything® Paying for College Book
Everything® Practice Interview Book
Everything® Resume Book, 2nd Ed.
Everything® Study Book

SELF-HELP

Everything® Dating Book, 2nd Ed.
Everything® Great Sex Book
Everything® Kama Sutra Book
Everything® Self-Esteem Book

SPORTS & FITNESS

Everything® Easy Fitness Book
Everything® Fishing Book
Everything® Golf Instruction Book
Everything® Pilates Book
Everything® Running Book
Everything® Weight Training Book
Everything® Yoga Book

TRAVEL

Everything® Family Guide to Cruise Vacations
Everything® Family Guide to Hawaii

Everything® Family Guide to Las Vegas,
    2nd Ed.
Everything® Family Guide to Mexico
Everything® Family Guide to New York City,
    2nd Ed.
Everything® Family Guide to RV Travel &
    Campgrounds
Everything® Family Guide to the Caribbean
Everything® Family Guide to the Walt Disney
    World Resort®, Universal Studios®,
    and Greater Orlando, 4th Ed.
Everything® Family Guide to Timeshares
Everything® Family Guide to Washington
    D.C., 2nd Ed.
Everything® Guide to New England

WEDDINGS

Everything® Bachelorette Party Book, $9.95
Everything® Bridesmaid Book, $9.95
Everything® Destination Wedding Book
Everything® Elopement Book, $9.95
Everything® Father of the Bride Book, $9.95
Everything® Groom Book, $9.95
Everything® Mother of the Bride Book, $9.95
Everything® Outdoor Wedding Book
Everything® Wedding Book, 3rd Ed.
Everything® Wedding Checklist, $9.95
Everything® Wedding Etiquette Book, $9.95
Everything® Wedding Organizer, 2nd Ed.,
    $16.95
Everything® Wedding Shower Book, $9.95
Everything® Wedding Vows Book, $9.95
Everything® Wedding Workout Book
Everything® Weddings on a Budget Book,
    $9.95

WRITING

Everything® Creative Writing Book
Everything® Get Published Book, 2nd Ed.
Everything® Grammar and Style Book
Everything® Guide to Writing a Book
    Proposal
Everything® Guide to Writing a Novel
Everything® Guide to Writing Children's
    Books
Everything® Guide to Writing Research
    Papers
Everything® Screenwriting Book
Everything® Writing Poetry Book
Everything® Writing Well Book

Available wherever books are sold!
To order, call 800-258-0929, or visit us at *www.everything.com*
Everything® and everything.com® are registered trademarks of F+W Publications, Inc.